A History of Youth

Michael Mitterauer

TRANSLATED BY
Graeme Dunphy

BLACKWELL
Oxford UK & Cambridge USA

Copyright © Suhrkamp Verlag, Frankfurt am Main 1986

English translation copyright © Basil Blackwell Ltd 1992

First published in Germany in 1986 as *Sozialgeschichte der Jugend*

English translation first published 1992
First published in USA 1993

Blackwell Publishers
108 Cowley Road
Oxford OX4 1JF
UK

238 Main Street
Suite 501
Cambridge
Massachusetts 02142
USA

British Library Cataloguing in Publication Data

A CIP catalogue record for this book is available from
the British Library.

Library of Congress Cataloging-in-Publication Data

Mitterauer, Michael.
[Sozialgeschichte der Jugend. English]
A history of youth / Michael Mitterauer; translated by Graeme Dunphy.
p.   cm. – (Family, sexuality, and social relations in past times)
Translation of: Sozialgeschichte der Jugend.
Includes bibliographical references and index.
ISBN 0–631–17983–6 (hbk.: alk. paper). – ISBN 0–631–17984–4 (pbk.: alk. paper)
1. Youth – Germany – Social conditions.   2. Youth – Central Europe –
Social conditions.   3. Youth – Germany – Attitudes – History.
4. Youth – Central Europe – Attitudes – History.   I. Title.
II. Series.
HQ789.G5M5713   1992
305.23'5'0943 – dc20   92–15432   CIP

Typeset in 11 on 13 pt Garamond
by Graphicraft Typesetters Ltd, Hong Kong
Printed in Great Britain by T.J. Press Ltd, Padstow, Cornwall

This book is printed on acid-free paper

Contents

Preface

The historical study of youth is a relatively new discipline. It is certainly still too soon for a balanced survey. None the less, it may be useful to attempt a chronologically and geographically comprehensive overview. While there is a great deal which must remain sketchy or hypothetical, it will be possible to clarify what insights emerge from the historical work which has already been done, where interdisciplinary co-operation seems to be necessary, and in which areas research needs to be intensified in order that present problems may be understood in terms of their historical dimension.

The breadth of the field makes it necessary to single out areas for special attention. In the context of a social history of youth it is, in my opinion, particularly important to examine the immediate world in which young people lived in the past: the family; the workplace; the school; and, above all, the youth group. The history of youth groups is dealt with in an extensive chapter, because the specific characteristics of youth can best be seen in this social form. This emphasis on the social groupings which represent the immediate environment of young people pushes other areas of research into the background. The history of political youth organizations is not a major theme in this book, nor is the political conduct or political protest of young people. Neither are we concerned with the character of the younger generation of any one particular period. The problem of identifiable generations in history is only pursued in so far as it is necessary to explain the assumptions about social structure which make it possible to speak of general and uniform characteristics of the members of a cohort.

Historical accounts of youth frequently place the history of students in the foreground. This approach is encouraged by the traditional source material. A special interest in youth movements can also lead to this kind of emphasis. Likewise, if we concentrate on political history or the history of education, we are immediately confronted by this group. Yet until fairly recent years, students have always represented an insignificant minority among young people. From a social-historical perspective it seems to me to be important to look in much greater depth at the living conditions of young people from other milieux. An important theme is therefore the rural situation, first, because for many centuries this was where the vast majority of young people lived, and secondly, because the traditional rural milieu presents a particularly striking contrast to the urban industrial world of the present day.

A historical-anthropological approach to the theme of youth could prove particularly fruitful for the shaping of political awareness in the present day. It is hoped here to provide some starting points. These require a comparative methodology on several levels. It seems to me to be of the greatest importance to pursue gender-specific factors in the lives of young people in earlier times. However, the necessary prerequisites for such an analysis are for the most part missing. The history of youth has so far been mainly the history of male youth. In spite of all efforts to distinguish between the sexes, it has not been possible to make up for this deficiency here. Likewise, the attempt to make comparisons of different social milieux is not exactly helped by the available literature. Geographically, a comparative approach with a historical-anthropological thrust would certainly have to extend beyond the European continent. In the meantime, this remains wishful thinking. Considering the current state of research, it may indeed be a widening of horizons if in some respects differences between the various parts of Europe and their structural backgrounds are explored. Finally, in order to grasp the general trends of development, diachronic comparisons are important. Correspondingly, a number of aspects of medieval social conditions have been included without, however, making any claim to be able to maintain the same historical depth for all the themes which are touched upon.

The comparative approach makes it impossible to offer a chronological account. The chosen method of examining, so to speak, a longitudinal section of history is not without its problems. It forces us to make great leaps through time. Often it is impossible to describe sequences of developments in all their complexity. Contrasting parallels must, of necessity, provide a simplified picture. If, in the process, such generalizing terms as 'traditional society' or 'old European society' are used, these may appear unsatisfactory, but in a general survey they can hardly be avoided.

Another consequence of the comparative approach, aiming as it does at structural perspectives, is the abstract nature of the account. Youth in history is certainly a theme on which one could paint lively pictures. When we are concerned with structural contexts, however, the colourful details fade. The social history of youth faces the same difficulty as the sociology of youth: the vitality and dynamism of young people are not easily put into categories.

To write a social history of youth while one's own children are in this phase of life is to endow the theme with a special importance. Things past have a greater relevance to things present. Scholarly work comes in closer contact with personal life. The conversations which I have had with my sons during this time have been very important for me, and I hope, also a little for them.

M. Mitterauer

Translator's Acknowledgements

I am grateful to Professor Mitterauer for clarifying numerous points, and to Lilias Dunphy and Rhona Dunphy for their careful readings of the text.

I am indebted to Professor G. E. Rickman, Miss Ann Kettle, Dr Andrew Pettegree and Dr Christine McGladdery of St Andrews University for providing correct translations of certain technical terms.

G. Dunphy

To my dear sons,
Lukas, Matthias, Thomas and Florian

1

Puberty – Adolescence – Youth

The idea of treating youth as a theme in social history requires to be clarified by a number of basic questions. How can this academic discipline contribute to our treatment of the topic? Is youth a legitimate theme in historical studies in any case? Social history is concerned with the processes of social change. At first sight, however, youth appears to be an anthropological constant. In all human societies there is a transitional phase between childhood and adulthood. All humans undergo a process of physical growth and sexual maturing. Sexual development is a physiological experience which, though it affects boys and girls in different ways, is common to all. It would appear to belong in the field of human biology, not of history.

However, it needs to be stressed that, while we shall certainly be concerned with processes of physical development, the theme of youth is also deeply linked to social phenomena. We can see this clearly in the concept of 'adulthood', the ultimate goal of the process of youth. Originally, the word 'adult' comes from a Latin term meaning 'grown up', having completed the process of growth. Today, however, this definition, with its focus on external physical features, is no longer prominent. Far more important is the sense in which the word highlights personality. The concept 'adult' refers to the completion of emotional and social development. At the same time, it signals a role in society which differs from that of the adolescent. So youth, as a phase in the cycle of life which leads into the role of adulthood, embraces physical, emotional and social processes which are causally related to each other. For the sociologist, and therefore also for the historian, those aspects which can be connected with social conditions will stand in the foreground of any analysis.

It is of the greatest importance to see youth not only in its biological determinants, but also as socially conditioned and his-torically changeable. In this respect, youth bears a similarity to other themes with biological components, such as male and female roles, sexuality, and family: if a study deals only with natu-ral forces and data, the impression is given that the theme is static and unchanging. Such supposedly 'anthropological constants' are dangerous, for they hide the possibility of variation. A historical-sociological approach, on the other hand, admits the concept of change. What appeared to be the natural order turns out to be socially shaped. In this respect, social history may be able to con-tribute to the development of our understanding of youth in the present day.

If we pursue the question of how nature relates to socially conditioned aspects of youth, we find that social factors play a considerable part even in what appear to be purely biological phenomena, such as the age of attaining sexual maturity, the period and extent of bodily growth, the development of physical strength, or the age at which the voice breaks. In all these respects, striking variations frequently emerge between different periods of history or different parts of Europe, between urban and rural, and most of all between different social classes. These variations cannot be satisfactorily explained by the facts of the natural environment, such as climate. The causes must be sought in the social con-ditions prevailing.[1]

The effect of social differences on the course of puberty was observed by scholarship long ago. As early as 1620 a doctor named Guarinonius established that peasant girls in the Tyrol reached sexual maturity significantly later than the daughters of bourgeois and noble families. In 1798 Buffon pointed out differences in age at the start of menstruation between the French urban and rural populations. A survey taken in 1857 found unmistakable class-related differences within the population of Vienna. At that time, the average age for the beginning of menstruation was 15.7 among the middle bourgeois, 16.2 among manual workers and domestic servants and 16.8 among day labourers. In Berlin, a study made in

[1] J. M. Tanner, *Wachstum und Reifung des Menschen* (Stuttgart, 1962); A. Schumacher, 'Die sexuelle Reifung', in G. W. Müller (ed.), *Geschlechtsreife und Legitimation zur Zeugung* (Freiburg, 1985), pp. 17ff.; H. Ch. Ehalt, 'Über den Wandel des Termins der Geschlechtsreife in Europa und dessen Ursachen', in *Saeculum*, 36 (1985), pp. 226ff.

the 1860s calculated an average age of 15.2 for 'women of higher standing' and 16.1 for 'women of lower standing'. Countless other nineteenth-century investigations into menarche rates confirm this class-related distinction.[2]

The data obtained in the nineteenth century for the sexual maturity of girls makes wider comparisons possible. We can illustrate the rate of change by comparing some of the early averages for menarche with equivalents for the present or recent past:[3]

Germany	1808:	16.8	1981:	12.5[4]
France	1830:	15.3	1979:	13.0
England	1832:	15.7	1973:	13.0
Denmark	1850:	17.3	1968:	13.2
Sweden	1844:	16.2	1976:	13.1
Finland	1883:	16.6	1971:	13.2
Netherlands	1873:	16.1	1976:	13.4
Norway	1839:	17.0	1973:	13.2

These data show that in some parts of Europe female maturity has been brought forward by more than four years since the first half of the nineteenth century. Furthermore, the rate at which these figures are falling has shown a marked acceleration during the twentieth century.

The more recent results show smaller variations between the different countries of Europe than do those from the nineteenth century. Even in class-related comparisons, a levelling-out of the data can be established. This suggests that the conditions which determine the rate of sexual development among children and juveniles have become more uniform, both within and between the industrial nations of Europe.

The general drop in the average age of physical maturity in the last couple of centuries raises the question whether we should assume a high average age in the old European societies, or whether the decline in recent times was preceded by a rise in previous centuries. This question has the greatest importance for any conclusions about the factors involved. In Roman law girls came of age at 12 (boys at 14), and some writers have linked this with

[2] Cf. the tables in Ehalt, 'Über den Wandel des Termins', pp. 260ff.
[3] Thus ibid., pp. 273ff.
[4] Thus *Jugend '81* (Opladen, 1982), p. 180.

sexual maturity. It must, however, be remembered that this age was a minimum, not an average, since the law had to take account of the earliest possible advent of sexual maturity. The distribution of ages of first menstruation was extremely wide in the populations of the past: it not infrequently preceded 12, yet it occasionally exceeded 20.

The acceleration of male youth in recent times is less well documented than that of females. The available data relates more to height than to genital development. Measurements taken by the military provide a starting point for comparisons over longer periods of time. Norway provides sources stretching back to 1741. These show that adults in 1830 were only slightly taller than in the mid-eighteenth century. Between 1830 and 1875 average height increased by 1.5 cm (0.3 cm per decade), between 1875 and 1935 by about 4 cm (0.6 cm per decade).[5] What seems particularly important is that until the early twentieth century men continued growing until their mid-twenties. Between the ages of 20 and 26 they grew by 3.5 cm in Norway in 1813, by 2 cm in Great Britain in 1880, and by 1 cm in Sweden in 1900.[6] By contrast, young men in the better-off populations of Western Europe today are fully, grown by the age of about 18. Nowadays we are 'grown up' in the biological sense many years earlier than in centuries past. Complete development of muscular strength does not run quite parallel to growth in height. Generally it comes about one year later.[7] A French encyclopedia of the mid-sixteenth century actually places this at the 28th year of life.[8] The relatively late development of muscle power in old European societies is of the greatest importance since it has definite social consequences. Work, particularly in an agricultural setting, requires physical strength. Generally, it would only be possible to become a farmer when one was strong enough. Where the norms of an agrarian society linked marriage to the holding of a proper farm job, this in turn meant that men would be married at a relatively late age.

Information regarding height and muscular strength provide important clues about the period of growth in young men, which was much longer than it is today. We can chart the changing age

[5] Tanner, *Wachstum und Reifung*, p. 161.
[6] Ibid., p. 163.
[7] Ibid., p. 218.
[8] P. Ariès, *Geschichte der Kindheit*, (Munich, 1975), p. 76.

of puberty from the albeit sporadic information available about the breaking of the voice. We know the ages at which the great composers had to leave boys' choirs. In the case of Haydn it was 18, Schubert 16, Bruckner 15, but in the twentieth century it is often as early as 14 or 13.[9] These figures display clearly the acceleration of male development in the last 200 years.

What were the reasons for such a wide variation in the time-scale of sexual maturity and of the somatic phenomena which accompany it? It is a problem which has certainly not been exhaustively researched. However, there are two socially conditioned factors which undoubtedly provide an important starting point: nutrition and work-load. As far as food is concerned, we are thinking less of the quantity or the calorie count than of the composition. The consumption of meat, fat, sugar, fruit and vegetables seems to be particularly significant for the acceleration of physical growth.[10] Meat consumption has always been far higher in the cities than among the rural population, and much more prevalent among the upper classes than among the lower ones. Throughout Europe it has increased sharply since the first half of the nineteenth century. Likewise, sugar is historically a typically urban commodity which has become more important since the nineteenth century. However, the changing nutritional situation does not form a linear process. In particular, the two world wars represent serious interruptions. As a consequence, obvious delays in the pubic development of young people can be observed in each case.[11] The retarding effect of heavy physical labour was acknowledged last century.[12] It helps especially to explain the differences in physical processes between upper and lower classes, and to some extent also between city and country. This can clearly be seen in the stunted development of the children of mountain peasants, who were given a particularly strenuous work-load. The accelerated development since the nineteenth century could no doubt be seen as a result of the technological revolution, against the background of the abolition of child labour and the decline

[9] M. Rassem, 'Entdeckung und Formierung der Jugend in der Neuzeit', in *Jugend in der Gesellschaft* (Munich, 1975), p. 98.
[10] Ehalt, 'Über den Wandel des Termins', p. 241.
[11] Tanner, *Wachstum und Reifung*, pp. 136ff.
[12] Friedrich Engels, for example, established this in England. Cf. H. Kreutz, *Soziologie der Jugend* (Munich, 1974), p. 135.

of heavy labour generally. The development of schooling in the twentieth century has, after all, led to the majority of young people being unavailable for work. In these ways, fundamental processes of social change have exerted a profound influence on physical development in the last two centuries. In view of such thorough going changes, it is clearly not possible to regard the processes of physical maturity as anthropological constants. The phenomenon of youth is by no means a one-sided interaction of the somatic and the social in which the former is the constant and the latter the variable.[13] Obviously, there are also influences in the opposite direction. In this sense, the development of the human body is indeed a subject for historical study.

The way in which the biological and the social interact becomes even clearer if we attempt to approach youth from the psychological angle. It is usual to refer to psychological development in youth by the term adolescence, as opposed to puberty, which represents the physical processes.[14] The same question which we asked about puberty must now be asked about adolescence: to what extent is it endogenous and to what extent exogenous? The answer is to some degree predetermined if we define adolescence as 'a psychological coming to terms with sexual development', or 'a child's personality adjusting to puberty'.[15] The psychological mastering of other problems of youth, particularly those which arise from the sociological framework and its historical flux, are thus pushed into the background. In this concentration of interest on the physical aspect there is a danger that adolescence, too, might be interpreted as an anthropological constant.

Non-historical, static conceptions of adolescence have their roots principally in two fields of scholarship: developmental psychology and psychoanalysis. Of particular importance in developmental psychology was the book by Eduard Spranger, *Psychologie des Jugendalters*, published in 1924. Its influence on ideas about the psychological character of youth went far beyond its own field. In hindsight, it is easy to see how far this image of young people,

[13] The assumption that 'growing up is a universal, clearly defined biological event, and therefore a constant' is to be found in T. Brocher and D. Eckensberger, 'Zur psychoanalytischen Theorie des Jugendalters', in F. Neidhart et al., *Jugend im Spektrum der Wissenschaften* (Munich, 1970), pp. 121ff.

[14] P. Blos, *Adoleszenz. Eine psychoanalytische Interpretation* (Stuttgart, 1973), p. 13.

[15] Brocher and Eckensberger, 'Zur psychoanalytischen Theorie', pp. 121ff.

with its pretensions to universal validity, is in fact based on the upper-class high-school pupils of the author's own acquaintance.[16] Likewise, the influence of the *Jugendbewegung*, the German Free Youth Movement of the 1920s, is unmistakable, for example, when the awakening of a feeling for nature is seen as typical of the beginning of adolescence, or especially when it is postulated that a 'sharp distinction between erotic and sexual experience' is a characteristic of the early years, whereby eroticism is defined as an 'aesthetic form of love, which devotes itself without desire — with inner satisfaction — to the beauty of human body and soul.'[17] The Free Youth Movement was by and large responsible for the view commonly held throughout the German-speaking world that certain attitudes and behaviour, which actually belonged to a particular period and class, were to be regarded as the universal, unchanging pattern of youth. The large number of educationalists who emerged from the Movement and the influence they have exerted on educational theory have contributed to the spread of this idea. By contrast, thinking which links adolescent development with social conditions has wielded less influence. Such thinking was indeed to be found among Spranger's contemporaries. Siegfried Bernfeld pointed to the class-related factors in the moulding of young people's emotional development. Charlotte Bühler demonstrated, by a study of girls' diaries through three generations, how the psychological processes are subject to historical change.[18] In his study *Flegeljahre*, the theorist Hans Heinrich Muchow was clearly critical of the 'anthropological constant' strand of developmental psychology when he later summed up the problem:

We may therefore hypothesize that in conditions not complicated by civilization, neither emotional puberty nor the so-called *Flegeljahre* (rebellious years) would be recognized or recognizable. Consequently, these do not appear to spring from rules of psychological development which would apply then too. Nor do they seem, as was in the past assumed, to be caused by physiological changes. Rather, they appear to represent symptoms and expressions of the particular historical-cultural setting of a young person. If this hypothesis is correct, it must be possible to demonstrate that

[16] See B. Schäfers, *Soziologie des Jugendalters* (Opladen, 1982), pp. 74ff.

[17] E. Spranger, *Psychologie des Jugendalters* (Heidelberg, 1924; 1963 edn), p. 85.

[18] C. Bühler, *Drei Generationen im Jugendtagebuch* (Jena, 1934).

in so-called primitive societies, youth may run its course without emotional puberty or teenage rebelliousness.[19]

A more thorough treatment of these 'historical-cultural settings', which would explain specific forms of emotional development in the lives of young people, has, however, only recently been begun.[20]

However, despite the fact that the static non-historical concepts of classical developmental psychology can no longer be maintained, their underlying mode of thinking continues. This becomes clear if we look at an example. Among the 'endogenous developmental mechanisms' which are regarded by psychology as bases for youthful behaviour, several authors mention juvenile wanderlust.[21] Without referring to these authors, but obviously with unquestioning faith in the validity of such generally accepted assumptions, one medievalist sees behind the migrations of the journeymen a 'factor which in popular thinking might be classed as a "thirst for adventure", or an "interest in tourism"'. He writes: 'This reveals a feature of youth in the Middle Ages which remains to be satisfactorily researched. Between childhood and full integration into the adult world, they went on journeys.'[22] Such statements throw up a plethora of questions. If we are dealing with 'a feature of youth', why was it that so many young men, but so few young women, went on journeys? Why did the lads who had learned a trade wander vast distances, while farm lads travelled only short distances, if at all? Why did sons who stood to inherit nothing take to the road, while those who could hope for an inheritance stayed at home? Was it really pleasure which drove them forth? One might think of the Swiss boys in early modern times who served as mercenaries, of whom it was said that their most common complaint was home-sickness. Can the migrations of young tradesmen really be classed as 'travel' in the same sense that twentieth-

[19] H. H. Muchow, *Flegeljahre: Beiträge zur Psychologie und Pädagogik der 'Vorpubertät'*, 2nd edn (Ravensburg, 1953), pp. 11ff.
[20] Cf. U. Herrmann, 'Probleme und Aspekte historischer Ansätze in der Sozialisationsforschung', in K. Hurrelmann and D. Ulrich (eds), *Handbuch der Sozialisationsforschung* (Weinheim, 1980), pp. 227ff.; U. Herrmann, 'Was heißt "Jugend"?: Jugendkonzeptionen der deutschen Sozialgeschichte', in H. G. Wehling (ed.), *Jugend – Jugendprobleme – Jugendprotest* (Stuttgart, 1982), pp. 11ff.
[21] R. Bergius, 'In Richtung auf eine psychologische Theorie des Jugendalters', in Neidhardt et al., *Jugend im Spektrum*, p. 62.
[22] W. Reininghaus, *Zur Entstehung der Gesellengilden im Spätmittelalter* (Münster, 1980), p. 164.

century developmental psychology speaks of, 'wanderlust' as an 'endogenous developmental mechanism'? Certainly, the social historian will wish to state that in European history youth has always been a particularly mobile time of life. But this statement will then have to be linked with specific social considerations: with working conditions, such as farm and domestic service; with family structures, such as neolocal residential patterns; with educational opportunities; and also with moral concepts, such as the way in which various ideas about virginity restricted the freedom of girls to leave home. The elucidation of social factors of this kind should do more to explain the historical facts of the mobility of young people than recourse to the endogenous forces of a supposedly universal psychology of youth.

Similar observations identified a vast number of other attitudes and patterns of behaviour which were, and continue to be, regarded as 'typically youthful' by scholarly writers. We might point here to such stereotypes as the tendency towards idealism, a strong value-system, a strong sense of justice, revolutionary attitudes, the rejection of parents, the quest for alternative role-models, enthusiasm, introspection, the need for solitude, a tendency to brood, a tendency to philosophize, and so on.[23] With all of these typically teenaged characteristics, we must ask how far they can be conceived as constants in the light of comparisons between different social classes, different cultures, and most of all, different epochs. For the majority of the phenomena which developmental psychology has regarded as endogenous, a comparison with the traditional rural situation is enough to show that they cannot be generalized. For the most part they are abstractions drawn from the experience of the urban middle class. Endogenous explanations connected with pubic development are therefore far less plausible than socio-historical explanations. Yet it has to be said that social historians have also been guilty, with very few exceptions, of making too little effort to find sociological explanations for the psycho-structure of youth.

What is true of inappropriate generalizations and one-sided endogenous models in developmental psychology applies also to

---

[23] The attempt by developmental psychology to apply such categories to all times and to all social classes can be found, for example, in H. Bertlein, *Jugendleben und soziales Bildungsschicksal. Reifungsstil und Bildungserfahrung werktätiger Jugendlicher 1860–1910* (Hanover, 1966).

certain assumptions in the theories of psychoanalysis. Wolfgang A. Gestrich has shown, with respect to the identity theory of Erik Erikson, to what extent generalized assertions by psychoanalysts about the course of adolescence can prove to be relative when they are confronted with the facts of youth in a historical rural community.[24] In a chapter on 'Youth and crisis' in his study of the young people of the Württemberg village of Ohmenhausen between 1800 and 1913, he analyses Erikson's thesis about the necessarily crisis-ridden course of adolescence. He insists: 'Major crises of adolescence as strategies of emancipation from mental and social fetters in the battlefields of trust, self-confidence and future perspectives did not occur among the young people of Ohmenhausen until the time immediately before the First World War.'[25] And further:

> From this enumeration of types of conflict and crisis situations it becomes clear that Erikson sees the formation of a sense of identity in adolescence principally from the perspective of the successful or unsuccessful development of individuality, that is, that emotional process by which an increasingly independent ego integrates childhood experiences with the possibilities of a future in adult society to make a self-confident, responsible adult personality; or else, foundering under the burden of this onerous task, regresses in various ways, and does not match up to society's requirements of an adult . . . The autonomy problem has become the epicentre of crisis for today's adolescents, and it is this which has produced a large proportion of the crises which provide the clinical 'material' behind Erikson's theory. However, if we look at the young people of Ohmenhausen, we have to tackle the problem of why no crises erupted here, why there were no adolescents here who 'struggled for their lives like wild animals' when the unfolding of their individuality was threatened, why there was never an emancipation from the family and its traditions and values. Autonomy in the sense of a wide-ranging independence of the individual from the life, values and judgements of the social environment of childhood was not an indispensable component in the formation of personal

---

[24] W. A. Gestrich, 'Jugend in Ohmenhausen, 1800–1918. Eine sozialgeschichtliche Studie zum Wandel des Jugendlebens in einem württembergischen Dorf unter dem Einfluß der Industrialisierung', Dissertation, Tübingen, 1983; published as 'Traditionelle Jugendkultur und Industrialisierung', in *Kritische Studien zur Geschichtswissenschaft* (Göttingen, 1986).

[25] Ibid., p. 310.

identity in Ohmenhausen. Crises caused in this way were therefore rare.[26]

Underlying Erikson's identity theory, then, is a process in the history of European social development which is related to a particular time and a particular milieu. Gestrich sums up: 'The crises in the adolescent phase are not an anthropological constant in the sense that they appear at all times and in all cultures in the same or even parallel forms.'[27] Erikson, on the other hand, states that in puberty 'all identification and all security on which one was previously able to rely are again placed in question on account of the rapid physical growth which only compares with that of early childhood, and which is now compounded by the completely new element of physical sexual growth.'[28] The decisive causes are therefore seen to be somatic. As a rule, the assumptions which Erikson, following Freud, has made about the origins of personality are based on the idea that the development of identity is closely related to sexual maturity. In this strand of psychoanalysis, endogenous accounts of the course of adolescence come to the fore.

Social conditions to explain the adolescent crises which the psychoanalysts have observed are not only to be derived from historically orientated comparisons, as Gestrich attempted with his example of a traditional peasant community. They are also, in a similar way, to be found in cross-cultural comparisons with conditions outside Europe. While the process of individualization taking place in Europe may prove to be a source of crisis, there are tension-creating factors which have a far wider effect, which may also have been present in Old-European agrarian societies. Ruth Benedict states in her study on 'Continuities and discontinuities in cultural conditioning':

From a comparative point of view our culture goes to great extremes in emphasizing contrasts between the child and the adult. The child is sexless, the adult estimates his virility by his sexual activities; the child must be protected from the ugly facts of life, the adult must meet them without psychic catastrophe; the child must obey, the

[26] Ibid., pp. 312ff.
[27] Ibid., p. 299.
[28] E. Erikson, *Identität und Lebenszyklus* (Frankfurt, 1977), p. 106.

adult must command this obedience. These are all dogmas of our culture, dogmas which in spite of the facts of nature, other cultures commonly do not share. In spite of the physiological contrasts between child and adult these are cultural accretions.[29]

These tension-creating factors vary in their age and distribution in European history. The concept of childhood as an age of protection, which causes a crisis when the protection is removed in adolescence, is relatively new, and limited to certain milieux. The same is probably true of the unsexing of the child. However, the discontinuity between subordination and authority, which Benedict sees as the most obvious example of this category of behaviour, is very old and wide-spread. It is significant that this tension between the father-role and the son-role is particularly sharp in the development of European society – a circumstance which is surely of importance in explaining the differences in adolescent experiences between boys and girls. It seems to be a basic problem that we teach our children something which we later expect them to un-learn. 'Against [the] background of social arrangements in other cultures the adolescent period of *Sturm und Drang* with which we are so familiar becomes intelligible in terms of our discontinuous cultural institutions and dogmas rather than in terms of physiological necessity.'[30]

Like the physical processes of puberty, adolescent emotional development is a legitimate theme in social history on account of its sociological determinants and the effects which result as these alter in the course of social change. Researchers involved with the history of youth are here confronted with a number of important tasks. However, the decisive emphases of a socio-historical treatment of the theme of youth will go far beyond puberty and adolescence. They will deal with the social conventions by which the transition from child to adult is regulated in various historical societies, the social relationships which exist at any one time between adult and adolescent, the groupings in which young people congregate, and the forms of cultural expression which they evolve. Youth, in this sense, presupposes somatic and emotional development, but it is far from being a biological commodity.

---

[29] R. Benedict, 'Continuities and discontinuities in cultural conditioning', *Psychiatry*, 1 (1938), p. 161.

[30] Ibid., p. 167.

If we conceive of youth as a social phenomenon, going beyond the physical processes, the question arises whether there has in the past ever been a society in which this phenomenon was not known. Youth, as it has been shaped by society in history, need not be universal. To put it bluntly, can we as historians speak of puberty without youth? It is a topical question, being explored both by historians and by sociologists. According to Robert R. Bell: 'There are societies without a socially defined period of youth. In these societies a child is treated as a child until it qualifies for adult status; it undergoes the "rites of puberty" of that society, and from that point on is regarded as an adult.'[31] Leopold Rosenmayr puts it more cautiously: 'Research which has been done on initiation rites shows that in primitive societies there is no such thing as youth as an age of life, in the sense familiar in the higher cultures. The transition from minority to majority occurs abruptly by means of a test or a ceremony.'[32] In European history, initiation rites in a strict sense do not figure largely, but even here, particularly in ages past, a sudden progression in status is not unknown. For the historian, the theory of the child as a 'little adult', developed by Ariès in his history of childhood, is of particular importance in this context. With reference to the period of youth, Ariès states:

> I have claimed that it [ancient society] had only a poorly developed concept of childhood, and this is even more true of adolescence. The period of childhood was limited to the tenderest ages of infancy, to the period when the little creature could not have survived without the help of others; as soon as a child was physically able to cope on its own it was treated as an adult, sharing both the work and the games of adulthood, without any intermediate period. While still a small child it became a young adult, without first going through the stages of youth which possibly had currency before the Middle Ages, and have become a significant part of the highly developed society of the present day.[33]

And with respect to the absence of a specific vocabulary for the phases of childhood and youth prior to the seventeenth century,

[31] R. R. Bell, 'Die Teilkultur der Jugendlichen', in L. von Friedeburg (ed.), *Jugend in der modernen Gesellschaft* (Cologne, 1971), p. 83.

[32] L. Rosenmayr, 'Jugend', in R. König (ed.), *Handbuch der empirischen Sozialforschung*, 2nd edn, vol. 6 (Stuttgart, 1976), p. 50.

[33] Ariès, *Geschichte der Kindheit*, pp. 45ff.

he writes: 'Although terminology for early childhood had emerged and become widespread, the boundary between "childhood" and "adolescence" or "youth" was blurred. There was no concept of that which we call adolescence, and it would be a long time before one appeared.'[34] This thesis, 'that people in Europe had no idea of what we call adolescence', was adopted by a number of leading scholars in the field of social history.[35] Jos van Ussel put it particularly clearly: 'From the fifteenth century onwards, two age-groups began to evolve, first the child (fifteenth to eighteenth centuries) and then the juvenile (eighteenth century).'[36] With this kind of assumption in mind, there is then talk of the 'discovery' or 'invention' of youth in the eighteenth century.[37] As with Ariès, much of the argumentation is concerned with the history of concepts. The appearance of such terms as 'juvenile' and 'teens' is seen to signal the emergence of a new social type.[38] On the basis of these notions, it seems natural to begin a history of youth in the eighteenth century, as John Gillis does in his definitive work.[39]

The arguments which are offered for restricting the social phenomenon of youth to the modern advanced civilizations and hence mitigating against the existence of youth in earlier European history are to be found on various different levels. The first of these has already been mentioned with reference to initiation as a sudden transition to adulthood. It is not possible at this point to discuss in detail whether the existence of a rite of initiation in non-European cultures excludes the possibility that youth may be a feature of society. As far as European history is concerned, however, it must be said that simply reaching the legal age of majority, which in early times was frequently bound up with sexual maturity, was not enough to effect a complete transition to adult roles. This was linked to other factors, particularly marriage and becoming master

[34] Ibid., pp. 86ff.
[35] Summarized by R. Thompson, 'Adolescent culture in colonial Massachusetts', *Journal of Family History*, 9 (1984), p. 127.
[36] J. van Ussel, *Sexualunterdrückung. Geschichte der Sozialfeindschaft*, 2nd edn (Gießen, 1977), p. 105.
[37] Herrmann, 'Was heißt "Jugend"?', p. 15. 'The Invention of the Adolescent' has been taken as a chapter heading by both F. Musgrove (*Youth and the Social Order*, 2nd edn (London, 1968) and J. Kett (*Rites of Passage: adolescence in America, 1790 to the present* (New York, 1977). Lutz Roth entitled a book *Die Erfindung des Jugendlichen* (Munich, 1983).
[38] In particular, see Roth, *Die Erfindung*.
[39] J. Gillis, *Geschichte der Jugend* (Weinheim, 1980).

or mistress of a house. Meanwhile, adolescents had their own groupings, with specific ways of life and a specific group culture. Likewise in the workplace, coming of age had nothing to do with full adult roles. Here, young people assumed roles which corresponded to their physical abilities. Being recognized by society as an adult, which takes a ritual form in initiation ceremonies, does not necessarily imply a simultaneous assumption of full adult roles. It is fairly irrelevant whether the intervening period is described as youth or early adulthood. The important thing is whether such a transitional period, with specific social tasks such as courting, preparation for marriage and setting up home, rehearsing for adult work-patterns and so on, actually occurs. For early Europe, the answer is a decided: yes!

The second level, represented by Ariès's thesis, relates to the extent of the differences between children and adults before the beginning of the modern era, and hence on the question of the existence and nature of an intervening phase in earlier ages. This great French scholar certainly made a lasting contribution when he recognized that the gap between childhood and adulthood was smaller before the seventeenth century than it has been since. Similarity of clothing, sharing in work, identical games, only minor differences in the way they are depicted in art – all of these are important clues to the fundamental socio-historical processes which have operated since then. They are of central importance for the study of youth, because they point to the fact that even in European history the discontinuity of social integration in Benedict's sense was once less than it is today. Under these conditions, the transition was certainly less difficult. To conclude, however, that young people in those days did not have to pass through the stage of youth is certainly going too far.[40] This argument ignores substantial aspects of the social situation of youngsters in the past, particularly those of authority and dependence. It makes a very significant difference whether one is subject to the power of the head of the household or wields this power oneself.

The third level on which it has been attempted to argue against the existence of youth as a social phenomenon in early times is a

---

[40] For a critique of the Ariès theory, cf. esp. N. Z. Davis, 'The reasons of misrule', in *Society and Culture in Early Modern France* (London, 1975), p. 108. Cf. also M. Mitterauer, 'Gesindedienst und Jugendphase im europäischen Vergleich', *Geschichte und Gesellschaft*, 11 (1985), pp. 180ff.

terminological one. The use of nomenclature is certainly an indicator of social awareness. In this sense, it would probably be advantageous to research the theme of youth on the basis of a comparative analysis of the history of words and phrases in the various European languages. A temporary haziness in the use of the different terms for children and teenagers in the French language is, however, not satisfactory evidence that traditional European society prior to the seventeenth and eighteenth centuries had no clear concept of adolescence. Arguments which rely in this way on the history of language must surely have a wider basis. There are European languages which differentiate very precisely between the different stages of youth. We might point, for example, to Swedish,[41] Estonian[42] or Romanian.[43] And even if a lack of differentiation in the terminology of childhood and youth could be demonstrated, it would be rash to assume that there was therefore no clear conception of these phases in the cycle of life. The great importance which was attached in early European agricultural society to the development of physical strength makes it most unlikely that people were not acutely aware of the various stages of youth, in which this changes so rapidly. Conclusions based on the history of vocabulary are stretched too far when the development of new words for youth are directly linked with new concepts of youth, or even with new social forms.[44] Further questions would ask who, in each case, is supposed to have conceived the new idea, and whether such conceptions correspond to anything in social reality. It is this last point which a social history of youth is actually concerned with.

Despite the necessity of seeing youth, a topic in social history, as something which has itself been shaped historically, the question none the less remains whether we might find a terminology capable of sustaining a discussion of much longer periods of history. Here, the definitions offered by sociology provide a starting point. In the sociology of youth, the definition of August Hollingshead is beyond dispute:

[41] K. R. Wikman, *Die Einleitung der Ehe* (Åbo, 1937), pp. 32ff.

[42] J. Kahk and H. Uibu, 'Familiengeschichtliche Aspekte der Entwicklung des Bauernhofes und der Dorfgemeinde in Estland in der ersten Hälfte des 19. Jahrhunderts', in J. Ehmer and M. Mitterauer (eds), *Familienstruktur und Arbeitsorganisation in ländlichen Gesellschaften* (Vienna, 1986).

[43] O. Buhociu, *Die rumänische Volkskultur und ihre Mythologie* (Wiesbaden, 1974), p. 80.

[44] Cf. Roth, *Die Erfindung*, in respect of the terms *Jüngling* and *Jugendlicher*.

Sociologically, adolescence is the period in the life of a person when the society in which he functions ceases to regard him (male or female) as a child and does not accord to him full adult status, roles, and functions. In terms of behaviour, it is defined by the roles the person is expected to play, is allowed to play, is forced to play, or is prohibited from playing by virtue of his status in society. It is not marked by a specific point in time such as puberty, since its form, content, duration, and period in the life cycle are differently determined by various cultures and societies.[45]

This definition is obviously sufficiently flexible that it may equally well be applied to societies of the past. It is of course very formal, in that it defines youth as a phase between childhood and adulthood without entering into a discussion of content, of what it is to be a child or an adult. Where that is attempted, problems of generalization usually arise. We shall look at two such attempts, chosen because they open up interesting perspectives when they are applied to history.

As opposed to children and adults [states Friedhelm Neidhardt] youths may be defined as those who with puberty have reached biological sexual maturity, without having gained possession, through marriage and employment, of the general rights and privileges which allow or require responsible participation in the significant fundamental processes of society.[46]

On the choice of puberty as a cut-off point he explains: 'The event of puberty becomes important for the characteristics peculiar to youth only in the context of certain social norms.' This social interpretation of sexual maturity is easily put into operation in history. For girls, it is often going to a dance which is the social event marking off the beginning of youth. For boys, joining the activities of a youth group often plays a similar role, for here they begin to have contact with girls in a controlled environment. Neidhardt's upper limit, 'marriage and employment', also seems to be reasonable in history. It presents more problems when applied to the society of the present day, since, generally speaking, marriage and

[45] A. B. Hollingshead, *Elmtown's Youth* (New York, 1949) pp. 6ff. On the widespread acceptance of this definition, see K. R. Allerbeck and L. Rosenmayr, *Einführung in die Jugendsoziologie* (Heidelberg, 1976), p. 19.
[46] F. Neidhardt, 'Eine soziologische Theorie der Jugend', in Neidhardt et al., *Jugend im Spektrum*, p. 14.

the beginning of working life no longer coincide. Neidhardt attempts to solve this problem by using the term 'young adult' to apply to unmarried people in employment and married people without employment – two completely separate groups.[47] For the historian, this problem does not arise to the same extent, since marriage and occupational independence often came together in the past. In the context of a family economy, marriage was not possible until financial independence had been achieved. A few exceptions will be discussed later. In a system where labour was rewarded on an individual basis, the older standards still held good. So what Neidhardt has identified as the two main aspects of present-day adult roles were linked together in their historical origins. The processes involved in the parting and separate development of what were originally single complexes of roles will bear a more general examination when the meaning of adulthood is considered from a historical perspective.

Theodore Scharmann places a different emphasis from that of Neidhardt when he includes adult roles in his definition of youth:

> The general meaning and purpose of this period of transition and radical change is the same in all cultures; it is the step from the under-age, dependent child to the mature, responsible person, adjusted to reality, whose income and ability to support others is so far developed that he or she can go on to take the second great life-decision, the choice of a partner, and can consider or achieve the founding of a family.[48]

Marriage and the economic basis of starting a family also play a part in Scharmann's concept, but for him these presuppose a 'mature, responsible' personality, which is 'adjusted to reality'. This is the actual goal of the development which takes place in youth. Neidhardt also uses the word 'responsible', but for him, marriage and employment are prerequisites for 'participation in the significant fundamental processes of society'. Seen from a historical perspective, both emphases can be justified. Scharmann's definition is directed more at the autonomous individual, while in Neidhardt's it is the independent householder and citizen. When applied to

---

[47] Ibid., p. 15. W. Hornstein, *Unsere Jugend* (Weinheim, 1982), p. 264, speaks in this context of 'after-youth' and 'post-adolescence'.

[48] T. Scharmann, *Jugend in Arbeit und Beruf* (Munich, 1965), p. 186.

the past, however, a problem emerges with both: when they are historicized, they show an exclusive orientation towards the masculine. In the one case, it is finding employment, in the other, achieving financial stability, which tend more to accentuate adult male roles as the ultimate aim of youth. We shall encounter this phenomenon time and again: our understanding of youth is, in its historical roots, generally conceived in strongly masculine terms.

The unity of marriage and economic independence (better than 'entering employment' when the reference is to the past) as a basis for adopting adult roles seems to be widespread in European history, but it is certainly not the universally dominant form. It belongs to a particular pattern of household formation which in turn corresponds to the so-called 'European marriage pattern'.[49] This European marriage pattern is characterized by a relatively high age at marriage, both for husband and wife, this being dictated by the fact that marriage is only possible when the man has taken his place as master or leader of the home. The home is frequently founded neolocally, that is, in a new place. If the young couple settles patrilocally, the father must either have died or have surrendered his position as head of the house. In the agricultural sphere, this happens when the parents move out of the farmhouse into another part of the small-holding which has been reserved for them. The typical forms of family life in this system are, very much simplified, the nuclear family comprising only parents and children, and the three-generation family with authority resting in the middle generation. Unmarried assistants often live with the family. Male and female servants are a typical but non-essential element in this concept of family. This in turn contributes significantly to the raising of the marriage age and the frequency of neo-local families.

[49] J. Hajnal, 'European marriage patterns in perspective', in D. V. Glass and D. E. C. Eversley (eds), *Population in History* (London, 1965), pp. 101ff.; 'Two kinds of pre-industrial household formation systems', in R. Wall et al. (eds), *Family Forms in Historic Europe* (Cambridge, 1983), pp. 65ff.; P. Laslett, 'Characteristics of the western family considered over time', in *Family Life and Illicit Love in Earlier Generations* (Cambridge, 1977), pp. 12ff.; 'Family and household as work group and kin group: areas of traditional Europe compared', in Wall et al., *Family Forms*, pp. 513ff.; M. Mitterauer, 'Komplexe Familienformen', *Ethnologia Europaea*, 11 (1980), pp. 158ff.: M. Mitterauer and A. Kagan, 'Russian and Central European family structures: a comparative view', *Journal of Family History*, 7 (1982), pp. 103ff.; M. Mitterauer, *Ledige Mütter. Zur Geschichte unehelicher Geburten in Europa* (Munich, 1983), esp. pp. 41ff.

The system of forming families connected with the so-called European marriage pattern is typical of the conditions prevailing in Western, Central and Northern Europe, and also occurs around the Mediterranean. It has not yet been definitely established how far back in time it goes. However, it can certainly be traced in rural populations as far back as the early Middle Ages. It seems to have spread into the Eastern parts of Central Europe along with Western agrarian structures as part of the colonization of the East. Eastern and South-eastern Europe, on the other hand, are characterized by a different manner of founding a household. Here marriage is not necessarily connected with the establishment of an independent home. The young couple generally settle not neo-locally but patrilocally. A son, or several sons, may marry while their father is still alive without any need for the role of head of the household to be transferred. This produces complex family structures, families comprising three generations with the authority position in the oldest generation, or 'joint families' which, on the parents' death, can develop into the shared households of several married brothers. Where these family structures are common, domestic service is unusual. Since there is no automatic link between marriage and the leadership of the family, the average age for marriage is generally considerably lower than in areas where the European marriage pattern prevails.

The relatively high age of couples entering marriage in the European marriage pattern proves in an inter-cultural comparison to be unique.[50] The traditional practice of Eastern and South-eastern Europe on the other hand has parallels in societies outside Europe. This has significant consequences for the evaluation of the phenomenon of youth from a historical perspective. Along with marriage customs and their corresponding pattern of home-building, youth must also be characterized by local peculiarities in the history of Western, Central and Northern Europe. A number of aspects may be given particular emphasis here.

In the first place, later marriages mean that youth lasts longer. In the age-group 25–9, more than half to two-thirds of the men and almost a half of the women were still single where the European marriage pattern held sway, as opposed to about a quarter of the men and barely one-tenth of the women in Eastern and

---

[50] Hajnal, 'European marriage patterns', pp. 101ff.

South-eastern Europe. In West, Central and Northern Europe, then, one belonged to the category 'youth' for longer, and this category made up a very large proportion of the total population, the number of 'older youths' among them being high. Consequently, as we shall see, autonomous youth organizations had great importance in these areas. The length of the adolescent phase had many ramifications. Only one of these will be mentioned here: Nowhere else in history was such a large proportion of the population excluded for so long from legitimate sexual activity. The particular rigidity of the sexual norms in European history must be seen in this social context. This surely is one of the reasons for the heightened tension involved with being young in Europe.

A second aspect of the effects of the European marriage pattern and the associated family structure on the course of adolescence relates to discontinuity. If, on getting married, one also becomes master or mistress of a home, marriage represents an especially sharp turning point. The change from dependence to independence, from subordination to authority, is abrupt in this system. In the more complex family structures known in Eastern and South-eastern Europe, and in many cultures beyond Europe, this discontinuity does not seem to arise. The young husband and, most of all, the young wife remain subject to a patriarchal authority. The discontinuity in the transition to adult roles, which Benedict identified in the European cultural tradition is no doubt partly a result of this feature of the European marriage pattern.

Various elements of youth have taken on a distinctive form under the influence of the European marriage pattern. The years between sexual maturity and marriage, especially the last part of this period, are generally the years of selecting a partner. The conspicuously long span of youth has led to the development of a specific culture of courting, kept alive in young bachelor circles. Although, even in these societies, the family continued to exert an influence on the choice of a partner, later marriages and the role of the youth group as a balance to the family did make possible a more individual and personal choice. As the age of courting, youth has developed differently for males and females, according to their different traditional stereotypes.

Youth, in general, is a time when the individual separates him or herself from parents and siblings, and builds a pair-relationship. But this process differs according to the family system in force. In patrilineal complex family forms, such as those which used to be common in Southern and South-eastern Europe, the young men remained in their family of origin. The new pair-relationship meant for them merely a reorientation within this unit. For the young brides, on the other hand, marriage marked a more abrupt change. At a very young age they had to form new relationships not only with their partner but also with his family. Under the European marriage pattern things were quite different. Even when the young couple settled patrilocally, as often happened in peasant communities, a radical restructuring of family relationships was necessary as control of the farm was passed on and the older couple moved into subsidiary accommodation. Marriage, the conclusion of youth, was partner-centred rather than family-centred. In the case of the neolocal pattern, both partners left their family of origin. Here, however, the process of breaking away from the family did not begin with marriage but was prepared for in small steps during an extended adolescence. Two institutions were especially important here: the youth group and domestic service. Both are, as has already been mentioned, typical phenomena under the European marriage pattern. Sons and daughters left their parents to go into domestic service long before they were old enough to marry: at any rate, at the beginning of adolescence, sometimes even in childhood. This significantly slackened the bonds with the family. For those who remained at home, contact with other young people played an important part in the emancipation process, for sons far more than for daughters. All in all, the breaking of family ties must have led to a far greater degree of individualization during the years of youth under the European marriage pattern than in more complex family systems.

The neolocal pattern gave youth a distinctive significance as the period of preparation for setting up home. The necessary financial means had to be saved over a long period of time. Saving was a characteristic of youth, not only among labourers but also among tradesmen and in agriculture. Training was also of central importance, being a prerequisite for proper employment. In contrast to saving, which was important for both prospective marriage partners, professional training was in traditional European society a characteristic of male youth.

Finally, we must take account of a specific consequence of domestic service which is associated with the European marriage pattern. Service in the home of a stranger means a change of the family circle in which one lives; it means a change of locality, often a change of milieu. In a special sense, youth became a time of mobility. Especially for young men, this was a time for travel over long distances, institutionalized as part of professional training. To travel was to learn, not only to acquire professional skills, but also to broaden one's horizons generally. One picked up foreign customs, learned new ways to understand oneself, was forced to reassess one's own world view. The high mobility of young people in old European society certainly contributed to a sense of individuality and independence which developed in the course of their youth.

The development of an autonomous personality is the second element of youth as a span of life between childhood and adulthood, which we met in the sociological definitions. An important feature of adulthood in our modern understanding is certainly the ability to question assumptions which were received and accepted in childhood. Socio-cultural independence only comes with such reflexion. It is a central task of youth.

This concept of youth as a time of building an independent and individual personality is the product of a historical development. Both as a demand and also in its realization, it presupposes certain social conditions. How it contrasts with autonomous personality in older European social history can be illustrated by means of a comparison which has been made by Jürgen Habermas.[51] Habermas begins with the assumption that personal identity emerges in a series of stages, from the 'natural identity' of the infant, through the 'group or role identity' of the child, to the 'self identity' of the adult. In this step-by-step construction, he sees a parallel between ontogenesis and phylogenesis. According to this idea, the development of a 'self identity', which we today see as the aim of personality formation, would have been preceded in history by a phase when 'group or role identity' was characteristic also for adults. Habermas links this 'group or role identity' with the limiting internalization of parental authority, which allows the individual to act according to the norms and role expectations of society. On the level of 'group or role identity' it is the immediate awareness

[51] J. Habermas, 'Moralentwicklung und Ich-Identität', in *Zur Rekonstruktion des Historischen Materialismus* (Frankfurt, 1976) pp. 63ff.; 'Können komplexe Gesellschaften eine vernünftige Identität ausbilden?', in ibid., pp. 144ff.

of role expectations in the interaction process which is dominant; building on this, 'self identity', is characterized by a conscious detachment from the standards of behaviour which have been internalized, and their reflexive application.

In a study of the 'Requirements for the formation of identity in socio-historical perspective', Hannelore Orth-Peine has combined this three-stage concept of Habermas with aspects of Krappmann's identity theory, refined in an analysis of historical autobiographies.[52] According to this, on the level of 'group or role identity', traditional society lacks a reflective analysis of its own development.[53] The quest is to conform to symbolic generalities. There is a tendency towards superstition and prejudice. Children remain conditioned by their parents' hopes and ideals throughout their lives. These characteristics are summed up as a lack of 'role detachment'. In contrast to 'self identity', the previous stage of development also lacks 'tolerance of ambiguity'; life is conceived as a single harmonic entity, there is no room for ambivalence, the individual strives for complete satisfaction of all needs, as rank and sex entitle. A 'lack of empathy' explains a tendency to act according to the rules of conventional morality, an inability to relate to the special problems and wishes of others or to childish thinking and behaviour. Finally, a 'lack of self image' is seen in the fact that, out of a sense of duty or a voluntary subordination to a leader, an individual behaves in accordance with the roles expected of him; in the fact that he cannot admit mistakes or misfortunes either to himself or to anyone else; and in the fact that such people do not experience identity crises.

Whatever view one may take of the application to history of categories which originate in sociological identity theory, or of the possibility of confirming these from historical source material, significant features of the changing role of adults – and therefore of the objectives of youth – in recent history seem to be implied. These agree in many respects with what Ariès has said about the narrower gap from childhood to adulthood in ancient times, and what Elias in his 'socio-genetic and psycho-genetic explorations' *Über den Prozeß der Zivilisation* has expressed: 'The gulf

[52] H. Orth-Peine, 'Bedingungen der Identitätsbildung in sozialgeschichtlicher Perspektive', Dissertation, Bielefeld, 1984, MS; L. Krappmann, *Soziologische Dimensionen der Identität* (Stuttgart, 1971).
[53] Orth-Peine, 'Bedingungen der Identitätsbildung', esp. pp. 97ff.

between the behaviour and the whole psychological make-up of children on the one hand and adults on the other has widened in the course of the process of civilization.'[54] The antithesis of 'group or role identity' and 'self identity' corresponds to some extent with the contrast between a personality which takes its orientation from tradition and one which is rooted within itself. Likewise, the process of formation of a 'super-ego' in the psychoanalytical sense may be connected with this tendency.

The cultivation of an autonomous personality with a 'self identity' during adolescence is a highly complex process, both in conception and as a social reality. It is not easily dated. Attempts at a chronological classification normally place it in the seventeenth or especially the eighteenth century. With reference to the end of the eighteenth century, Kreutz writes:

Youth is conceived as a separate phase of life in which the individual finds his individuality, his identity. In this phase, the adult personality is recreated, the starting point of adult life lies in this 'second birth', and not in the family of origin. The person with an 'inner orientation' who has internalized the demands of society emerges in this phase.[55]

The idea of the 'second birth' through which a person becomes an adult can be found in Rousseau, who is regarded as the 'master builder of youth'.[56] This idea is certainly not new. It appears, for example, in Pietism as the requirement of 'rebirth'. Pietism gives great importance to the concept of youth as a period of spiritual and moral renewal.[57] In the religious sphere, the roots can be traced back further. They reach back to the end of the Middle Ages, although this can only be mentioned in passing here.

The idea of adult conversion, religious awakening, the personal decision of faith, was strongly proclaimed by the penetential brotherhoods, the *confraternitates penitentiae*. They attempted to infuse the laity with elements of monastic life. The idea of adult baptism no doubt follows on from the monastic vows as a kind of 'monks' baptism'. The fact that the Anabaptist movement later met

---

[54] N. Elias, *Über den Prozeß der Zivilisation*, vol. I (Frankfurt, 1976), p. lxxiv.
[55] Kreutz, *Soziologie der Jugend*, p. 52.
[56] Musgrove, *Youth and the Social Order*, p. 33.
[57] Gillis, *Geschichte der Jugend*, p. 92.

with such wide approval among the population can perhaps be explained by this impressing of monastic elements on the laity.[58] A personal internalization, and therefore a growing religious and ethical independence of the laity from the spiritual leadership of the priests was in the fourteenth and fifteenth centuries a major objective of the *devotio moderna*. A 'basic problem of the time, the problem of Christian maturity' (Lortz) was taken up in this movement for religious renewal.[59] It appears as the precursor of the reforming traditions. In the Reformation, the idea of religious autonomy in general was encouraged. Of the various reforming confessions, the idea of adulthood as the precondition for responsible action was most strongly developed among the Anabaptists. Following their lead, the independent churches made it a basic tenet that membership of a community of faith must result from a personal decision – in contrast to the national Churches, to which one belonged from birth.[60] The importance of Calvinism for the individualization of religion lies in the rejection of Catholic and Lutheran sacramental teaching and in the emphasis on personal responsibility for the renewal of the soul. Conversion became the central event in the process of spiritual growth, shaping the religious life of young people.[61] The importance of the experience of awakening for a new conception of youth is generally to be found in schools of thought influenced by Calvinism. On the Protestant side it was Pietism which now took the matter further, while within the Catholic Church, Jansenism took up Calvinist ideas. Puritanism, Pietism and Jansenism saw themselves, each in its own way, as protest movements within the Church, emphasizing personal responsibility in spiritual things, as opposed to the authoritarianism of the established churches.[62] Having a subjective orientation, they encouraged individualistic tendencies. They also shared a common quest for better education of the young,

[58] Kind suggestion of Prof. P. Isnard Frank OP.

[59] Quoted from F. W. Kantzenbach, *Christentum in der Gesellschaft: Grundlinien der Kirchengeschichte*, vol. I (Hamburg, 1975), p. 294.

[60] On the importance of the independent Churches, see esp. E. Troeltsch, *Die Bedeutung der Freikirchen für die Entstehung der modernen Welt*, 5th edn (Tübingen, 1911), pp. 28ff.

[61] Cf. the chapter 'Youth and religious conversion', in Kett, *Rites of Passage*, pp. 62ff.

[62] R. van Dülmen, *Entstehung des neuzeitlichen Europa, 1550–1648* (Frankfurt, 1982), p. 279.

with the aim of achieving personal religious autonomy. This educational zeal, aimed at the formation of an independent personality, was taken up in a secularized form in the educational theory of the Enlightenment.

Clear indications that the process of individualization in youth has its origins in religion are to be found in two literary forms which arose at the end of the Middle Ages and the beginning of the Modern Era. The diary and the autobiography both typify that 'reflective analysis of one's own development' which is a central aspect of the developing 'self identity'. Both are 'ego-documents', with a high degree of internalization.[63] The diary has its roots in religious self-observation, and it came into its own with the careful and apprehensive heart-searching of the Pietists. Likewise, the autobiography arose out of the need for religious self-examination.[64] Pietism very much encouraged it as a form of self-depiction of the individual. A significant feature of almost all the early autobiographies is that they end with the sense of identity which was achieved in adolescence. Childhood and youth are seen as the dynamic age of life. The adult, on the other hand, is the individual who has found himself in society.[65]

Through the centuries, the diary has remained a popular outlet for youthful self-reflection.[66] It would appear, then, to be a suitable source for a study of the development of the individualization process in adolescence. This was attempted by Charlotte Bühler in her comparison of girls' diaries through three generations. In particular, in the generation born around 1900 she observed a surge of individualization beyond that of their mothers' generation: 'In this generation, individualism is carried to the point of indifference to the community in which one lives. Feelings are stirred to a hatred of the mistakes of family members, a hatred of the demands and norms of the family which inhibit the unfolding of the young personality.'[67]

As an outlet for youthful self-reflection, the diary also provides

[63] van Ussel, *Sexualunterdrückung*, p. 40.
[64] L. Stone, *The Family, Sex and Marriage in England, 1500–1800* (London, 1977), p. 226.
[65] E. Dittrich and J. Dittrich-Jacobi, 'Die Autobiographie als Quelle zur Sozialgeschichte der Erziehung', in D. Baacke and T. Schulze (eds), *Aus Geschichten lernen* (Munich, 1979), p. 100.
[66] Discussed in detail in *Jugend '81*, pp. 434ff.
[67] Bühler, *Drei Generationen*, p. 22.

an indication of which population groups are subject to the process of individualization and personal autonomy. The material used by Bühler from the nineteenth and early twentieth centuries stems almost exclusively from the educated and property-owning middle class. The fathers of the young writers were mainly teachers, ministers, artists, civil servants, lawyers, authors or merchants, and they lived predominantly in the large cities.[68] The elevated bourgeoisie, and with them also the nobility, stand out in history as the leading exponents of this literary form. Even as late as the nineteenth century, diaries from the agricultural milieu or from the circles of the urban lower classes are extremely rare. This social division reflects the extent of the individualization process. The demand for personal autonomy, the growing awareness of self and the desire for a stable personality are all phenomena which emerged primarily among the educated bourgeoisie, and throughout the middle and upper classes generally. And it is here in the first instance that we see being realized the concept of youth as a means to socio-cultural independence.

Youth as a period of maturing towards an autonomous personality presupposes social factors which have not been constant in all social milieus in history. For a peasant lad in a remote mountain valley who was never able to leave his home community, there was sometimes no opportunity to develop a 'self-identity' in Habermas's sense, even in the twentieth century. Individualization requires exposure to alternative modes of thinking and acting. Personal independence can only emerge where there is the opportunity to make choices and decisions. The process of individualization is therefore dependent to a significant extent on the existing structures of communication. Broadly speaking, alternatives were always far more readily available in the cities, with their many and multifarious perspectives, than in the country. In the course of modernization in recent times, the range has increased enormously. At the same time, the relationship of urban to rural youth has drastically altered – a factor which must be borne in mind in any assessment of the opportunities of individualization for today's young people. Furthermore the opportunity to confront new ideas, and with them alternative methods of orientation, is a question of mobility. The greater the mobility in adolescence,

[68] Ibid., p. 2.

the greater the likelihood of an independent personality developing. Mobility is another factor which, in European history, favoured the urban populations over the rural ones, in particular the urban upper and middle classes. Here again there were differences between males and females. For reasons of morality, girls always had far less scope.

Alongside forms of personal contact, account must also be taken of transmitted forms, most importantly of reading, as a means of gaining alternative perspectives. The reading of books and of other printed material has been of extraordinary importance in European social history as a basis for the development of personal autonomy. This goes a long way towards explaining why the educated classes were so far ahead. But also, with respect to the major European denominational groupings, there are considerable differences in the importance attached to the reading of books. In the Protestant confessions which grew up from the Reformation, reading played a far greater role than in Catholicism, particularly in the schools which emphasized subjective religious experience. To this day there are continuing educational differences which can be traced back to this distinction. The reformed emphasis on the personal decision of faith not only created the ideal conditions for the development of the concept of the unfolding of the individual personality, it also provided important social prerequisites for putting the concept into practice.

The fact that youth has, in European history, become a period of development of independent personality, has certain consequences which are important for our present-day understanding of youth. If adolescence is regarded by psychoanalysis as a time of crises, this refers to the early forms of the development of 'self identity' in the religious sphere. Kett has referred to the obvious analogies between the course of religious conversion among young people of different Protestant denominations and Erikson's identity theory[69] – a clue, incidentally, that these adolescent crises are not to be thought of as endogenous. The road to 'awakening', 'rebirth' and personal 'decision', be it in the Calvinist tradition or in Pietism, is generally agonized and crisis-ridden. Religious influences help considerably in explaining why brooding, introspection and critical self-appraisal have become characteristics of youth.

[69] Kett, *Rites of Passage*, p. 80.

When more than one denomination was present, the personal decision could involve a rejection of the religion of the home. The rejection of denominational ties generally is a logical next step. The phenomenon that an adolescent re-examination of childhood beliefs can lead to an abandoning of faith altogether has become more and more significant in the last 200 years for an understanding of youth.

From a time of religious reorientation, youth next becomes a time for rethinking one's whole world-view. The right of the young person to decide against the denomination of the parents provides the basis for a freedom to ideological self-determination. With the emergence of political-ideological pluralism, this facet of the young person's development of autonomous personality has become more and more significant. Two factors are of particular importance for this development. First, the increase in the rate of social change has lead to a corresponding acceleration in the change of values, making it more common for children to think differently from their parents. Secondly, the opportunities for children to take a different stance from that of their parents have increased tremendously with the growth of the mass media. Consequently, ideological conflict with parents has made youth a more volatile phase of life.

With the advent of a pluralism of thought and value, adolescence has become a time for making important personal decisions. This is true not only of political or ideological matters but of the whole business of planning out one's life. In old European society, the general shape of a person's life was, in all respects which really mattered, predetermined by sex and social standing. By contrast, the dissolution of the old order brought a widening variety of alternatives. For a start, we may mention decisions about education and career, along with greater freedom in the choice of a partner. Sexual stereotypes have also declined in importance in the more recent past. This means that girls in particular have an increasingly difficult choice between traditional and modern models and conceptions.[70] The opportunity to choose from a multitude of possible life-styles has certainly made adolescence more complicated than in ages past. The relatively new competence of young people to make decisions of life-changing importance

---

[70] *Jugend '81*, p. 130.

independently stands in tension to their prolonged subordination to parents and teachers.[71] The idea that young people are to be protected by their dependence on others is therefore directly contradicted by the requirement that they show more and more responsibility as they set a course for adult life.[72]

The view that adolescence is a time of developing an independent personality presupposes that when adolescence comes to an end the major decisions have been made, life planned out, an ideology adopted, a 'self identity' achieved, a personality fully developed. Behind this lies a static view of adult life, against which the dynamic adolescent years stand in contrast. The adult is 'finished'; he is not permitted to change.[73] This begs the question whether such a static concept of adulthood can be permanently sustained. The question does not so much relate to the role of adults in family and professional life. The problem lies with the idea that, in an age in which social change is accelerating as never before, the development of personality ceases at a particular point in life. If we set against this the necessity of a life-long process of socialization in the course of which ideas, values and behaviour patterns which had previously been adopted must constantly be revised, important elements of the traditional concept of youth are placed in doubt. If the formation of personality continues in all stages of life, the boundary which had been drawn between adolescence and adulthood blurs appreciably.

The two main aspects of the conventional concept of youth which have been described – youth as a time of gaining independence through marriage, and youth as a time of forming an autonomous personality – are two stages of a historical development. We can see this in the changing concept of majority. The old European concept of coming of age (German: *mündig*), being released from the authority (Old English: *mund*) of the father or master of the house, relates to particular positions in the household community which, under the European marriage pattern, are left when a person marries. It did not imply the individual passing through various stages towards emotional and intellectual maturity. This concept changed when, in the eighteenth century, the

[71] G. Wurzbacher, *Gesellungsformen der Jugend* (Munich, 1965), p. 116.
[72] Ibid., p. 121.
[73] M. Pieper, *Erwachsenenalter und Lebenslauf. Zur Soziologie der Altersstufen* (Munich, 1978), p. 117.

place of parental authority in the psychological and cognitive gap between children and adolescents on the one hand, and adults on the other, was reassessed. Authority was no longer to be exercised until the child married, but was instead a right held for a limited period of time, depending on the development of the adolescent.[74] In law, the idea that *patria potestas* invariably ends when the son reaches an age of majority was accepted only slowly. In the German-speaking world, the Austrian *Allgemeines bürgerliches Gesetzbuch* gave this its first clear expression.[75]

Of these two main aspects of the concept of youth – a stage of life leading to marriage and a period of development of an autonomous personality – the former is clearly the older. Nevertheless, it has some validity even in the present day, as the sociological definitions based on it have shown. The juxtapositioning of two separate sets of parameters for the same concept can, however, lead to complications in a historical analysis. Is, for example, a 40-year-old unmarried farm labourer in the eighteenth century to be included in a study of youth? Certainly not according to our usual understanding of youth, although there are modern sociological definitions, such as Neidhardt's, which apply to him. Our everyday understanding, influenced by the newer concept with its focus on development of personality, is tied firmly to age and not to family status. By the age of 40, by modern reckoning, a person must long since have become an adult in terms of the psycho-social aspects. To apply this concept to eras and milieux which did not know it, however, would be anachronistic. In the social reality of the rural population in the eighteenth century, domestic status took precedence over actual age in the defining of age-groups. Correspondingly, a 20-year-old peasant-farmer was an adult in those days, not a youth. One could of course say, out of justice to our modern concept of youth, that in such situations, other terms should be chosen, such as 'single person' rather than 'young person'. A similar reasoning is invoked when, with an eye on our modern concept of family as a group of related people living together, groupings including unrelated persons such as servants

[74] R. Wimmer, *Zur Soziogenese von Erziehung* (Vienna, 1982), MS, p. 43.

[75] R. Buchda, 'Kinder und Jugendliche im deutschen Recht (Mittelalter und neuere Zeit)', in *L'Enfant,* vol. II (Brussels, 1976), p. 389. W. Ogris, 'Das Erlöschen der natürlichen Gewalt nach deutschen Rechten des Mittelalters und der Neuzeit', in ibid., p. 449.

are classed as 'domestic groups'. Nevertheless, just as research into the history of families cannot avoid including 'domestic groups' with unrelated adherents in its analysis of family, it does seem to be necessary to deal with older unmarried persons in past ages in the framework of a social history of youth. The continuity of the material forces this upon us. Just as modern families are part of the same developmental continuum as historical 'domestic groups', so a relationship can be established between modern youth groups and the groupings of single people in the past. Consequently, maintaining a terminological distinction between 'young people' and 'single people' would do little to ease understanding.

The example of the 20-year-old peasant-farmer and the 40-year-old farm labourer shows to what extent the respective status of adult and young person in the old European social order was linked to the shape of the authority structure. Youth meant domestic dependence. Under the European marriage pattern one became an adult by achieving domestic independence through marriage. In old European society this relationship of power between the adult and the not-yet-adult was not simply a question of the authority involved in the passing on of knowledge and experience from one generation to another, as structural functionalist theorists postulate.[76] The duration of dependency was not dictated by the duration of learning, but rather the other way around. Of course, a journeyman would be learning throughout the time of his travels, but his independence came primarily from the opportunity of finding a position as a master, perhaps by marrying a master's widow. In the rural milieu, the duration of domestic dependence had even less to do with gathering empirical knowledge. Inheriting, being handed down a farm, marrying into a situation, purchasing a house, these were the most important ways in which a young man could achieve independence. And certainly, the duration of youth among young women in old European society cannot be explained by such supposedly functional necessities.

In the areas influenced by the European marriage pattern, young people's subordination to parental authority generally lasted a relatively long time. With the growth of domestic service, a specific special form of household authority developed. If we are

[76] For a critique of the theses of S. N. Eisenstadt, see Kreutz, *Soziologie der Jugend*, p. 81.

right in assuming that the European marriage pattern and the related family system were originally connected with particular rules of manorial order,[77] it would be possible to explain special forms of adolescent dependence in European social history in terms of wider authority structures.

The fact that youth and domestic dependence are no longer equated in this manner which was so characteristically Old European surely has to do with the way in which authority structures have changed. Whereas, when society was ordered by inherited status, even mature offspring were subordinate to paternal control as long as they lived in their family of origin, since the eighteenth century the legal maxim has been accepted that they are emancipated from *patria potestas* on reaching an age of majority. This corresponds to a general tendency in the evolution of modern statehood to eliminate intermediary powers, and to assert the equality of adult citizens. Domestic authority was also affected by this trend. What remained were parents' rights with respect to children still in their minority. As the thresholds of majority came to be established by law, the duration of adolescent dependence began to be fixed according to age.

[77] See note 49.

2

Milestones in Youth

Attempts to define youth have frequently led to a desire to draw clear lines of demarcation with childhood and adulthood, upper and lower thresholds marking the beginning and end of adolescence. A typical feature of this is the debate on the question of whether historical development has seen a lengthening or a shortening of the duration of youth. Many sociologists hold that in recent times a noticeable lengthening has taken place.[1] Their principle argument for this is the increasing length of time spent in education. Against this, however, John Modell, Frank F. Furstenberg and Theodore Hershberg attempt, through an exact analysis of data, to prove that the duration of youth in the last century has receded.[2] The sources for their calculations are census results from 1880 for Philadelphia, and from 1970 for the whole of the USA. They come to the conclusion that in this period the duration of youth for men decreased from 21.7 years to 14.4 years, in other words by about one-third. In 1880 it ran from the ages of 12.6 to 34.3, in 1970 it began at 14.2 and ended at 28.6.[3] The starting point for these calculations was an analysis of five transitions in status, namely leaving school, finding employment, leaving home, setting up home, and marriage. These seem well-suited to a discussion of the problems of a historical concept which sees youth as a span of time between fixed beginning and end points. We shall begin by looking briefly at each of them.

[1] König (*Jugendlichkeit*, 126) for example speaks of 'significant lengthening of actual youth'; F. Tenbruck ('Moderne Jugend als soziale Gruppe', in L. von Friedeburg (ed.), *Jugend in der modernen Gesellschaft* (Cologne, 1971), p. 87) of an 'enormous lengthening of the span of youth'. American representatives of this view are listed in J. Modell et al., 'Sozialer Wandel und Übergänge ins Erwachsenenalter in historischer Perspektive', in M. Kohli (ed.), *Soziologie des Lebenslaufs* (Darmstadt, 1978), p. 226.
[2] Modell et al., 'Sozialer Wandel', pp. 225ff.
[3] Ibid., p. 240.

With the spread of compulsory primary education, the end of compulsory schooling became for more and more people an abrupt turning-point. So long as leaving school meant a transition to working life, this threshold involved a radical change in life-style; it was the end of childhood, the lower threshold of youth. In the nineteenth century, this seems to have been the case for a large proportion of the population. In the course of time, however, this boundary became less significant as more and more people went on to the upper school and to higher education. But leaving these schools was in no sense comparable to leaving school at the end of primary education. No one who stays on in secondary education continues to have the status of a child. Even if one does not accept the thesis that the duration of youth was extended by the lengthening of education, leaving higher education certainly has more to do with the end of youth than with the beginning of it. So, to place the age of leaving school in 1880 and in 1970 beside one another is to compare two quite different types of threshold. Going back further in history, it becomes harder to argue for leaving school as the standard point of transition from childhood to youth, since school-going was less common, and school-leaving was significant for only a small part of the population.

Taking the first day at work as the starting point of youth also poses problems for wider chronological comparisons. Only in a society of individual wage-earners is it possible to establish this with any degree of accuracy. Even here there is doubt about whether practical professional training counts as employment. Those sociologists who link starting work with the end of youth think not. Historically speaking, this question is of particular relevance, since for long periods of time proper apprenticeships were only available for male occupations, not for female ones. The movement of vocational training away from the workplace and into colleges raises further problems. Entry into employment is pushed further back and can certainly no longer be equated with the beginning of youth. When labour is organized as a family concern, as was usual in old European society and is not uncommon even today, it is simply not possible to state an age for starting work. Children grow gradually into working life. Far from beginning in youth, it was quite typical for small children to be found helping their parents. The work of the housewife is to be seen as a continuation of these 'family economy' forms of work. In the biography of girls who never sought paid employment outside the home, the only working threshold was when as children they began to assist their mothers. Boundaries relating to the world of work seem as a rule to be ill-suited for the delineation of female youth in history, as they take their orientation from the patterns of male careers.

Moving out of the parental home also proves historically to be a very important threshold, but in the past it had quite a different meaning and distribution. In present-day society, shaped by the principle of neolocality, almost all young people leave home sooner or later. Young farmers are the only real exception. In the past, however, patrilocality was much frequent. In all inheritable family concerns, at least one child would remain in the parental home. Today, moving away from parents usually involves the founding of an independent household. It is, therefore, a decisive transition between dependence and autonomy. Historically, this was certainly not always the case. In centuries past, it was common to leave home with a view to entering service. This meant that one was just as much under domestic authority as before. Whereas today leaving home belongs more to the set of changes which mark off the end of youth, some historians see entering service as the great threshold marking its beginning.[4] However, this misses the mark since, depending on family circumstances, it was possible to enter service in a strange house at any time from childhood through to a fairly late stage of youth.[5] Nevertheless, entering service does tend more towards the beginning than the end of youth. Historically, leaving home only marked an end of youth for those children (mostly daughters) who remained in their family of origin, changing home only when they married.

Setting up home, which under the European marriage pattern was bound inextricably with marriage, was historically a clear mark of the end of youth. Today this is not necessarily the case. Many young people set up a home long before they enter any permanent relationship. In the way they live, the groups they form, the things they buy, the way they spend their free time, in fact in all the most important socio-cultural details, unmarried people living

[4] E.g., R. Thompson, 'Adolescent culture in colonial Massachusetts', *Journal of Family History*, 9 (1984), p. 127.
[5] See pp. 90ff.

alone are no different from other young people. With respect to participation in the group culture of youth, the same is to a great extent true of young couples without children. The birth of the first child is now an important point of transition for the social behaviour of young people. Whatever we make of the problem of classifying childless couples, the historically relatively new category of unmarried people living together in independent households certainly demands the classification 'youth'.

For an examination of the duration of youth over longer historical periods, the most reliable of all five of the indicators of transition of status which have been mentioned is still marriage. Throughout history, especially in traditional agrarian societies, this was generally the decisive upper threshold, bringing youth to an end. We shall later be discussing the external symbols which display the importance of this transition.[6] An exception was perhaps the long-term relationship without social recognition which was already not uncommon in the cities of the nineteenth century.[7] In the developments of the last decades, however, it is possible to speak of a more general de-institutionalization of marriage. For fairly wide population groups, the wedding has lost its traditional character as the decisive rite of passage in the cycle of life. In view of this development, a clear demarcation of youth of the sort known in earlier times no longer seems to exist.

If we wish to obtain data on the duration of youth and how this has changed in the course of history, it seems to make sense to take one's bearings from the age at which people marry. Imhof has made calculations on the life-span of women in the Schwalm area of Hessen between sexual maturity and marriage, running from 1680 to the present day. Here, of course, it must be remembered that for the duration of youth it is not sexual maturity itself which is decisive but the ways in which it was acknowledged socially. As a general standard, this kind of calculation is more useful than those carried out by John Modell and his colleagues. Imhof shows that in the rural area under examination the length of youth has indeed become shorter since the nineteenth century, both in terms of its absolute duration and also, just as important from a social-historical point of view, as a proportion of total life

[6] See p. 79.
[7] Cf. M. Mitterauer, *Ledige Mütter. Zur Geschichte unehelicher Geburten in Europa* (Munich, 1983), esp. pp. 15ff., 106ff.

expectancy.[8] However, such results, based as they are on calculations of average values, are less than satisfactory since the mean
variation in ages for marriage in the nineteenth century was so
wide. Consequently it is not possible to speak of a normal biography in old European society in which youth forms a chronologically fixed phase of life.

These few examples are sufficient to show that the classical
thresholds of youth can change their values in the course of historical development; they can split in two; they can be shunted
out of order; they can change from being upper or lower thresholds to become interruptions somewhere in between. Such
variations also say a great deal about changes in the nature of
youth and of its social context. These turning points therefore
need to be examined separately in greater detail. The important
thing which emerges is that youth cannot be seen as a period
of time between clearly defined starting and finishing point, but
rather as a phase of many partial transitions. The way in which the
meaning of individual turning points has changed is seen especially
graphically if we first attempt an analysis of present-day thresholds
and examine their historical roots, and then look at the thresholds
accepted in earlier times and see what has become of them.

I. Modern Milestones

An appropriate starting-point for consideration of the major events
of a present-day biography of youth would be a compilation put
together in West Germany in 1981 as part of a major sociological
investigation of youth.[9] An average age was offered for each of the
following highlights:

	Years
• falling in love for the first time	15.4
• making own decisions about one's appearance	15.5
• first sexual experience	16.2
• ability to conduct oneself socially	16.8
• allowed to come and go as one will	17.1

[8] A. Imhof, 'Von der unsicheren zur sicheren Lebenszeit', *Vierteljahrschrift für Sozial – und Wirtschaftsgeschichte*, 71 (1984), pp. 181ff.
[9] *Jugend '81* (Opladen, 1982), p. 274.

- beginning to think about one's own future   17.1
- first holiday without parents   17.2
- making a larger purchase on own initiative   17.7
- addressed by most people as *Sie*   17.9
- able to present one's point of view to superiors   18.3
- owning one's own car   19.3
- completion of professional training   20.2
- moving out of the parental home   20.6
- earning enough to be able to support oneself   20.7

Among these highlights of the 'normal biography' of the modern young person, it is possible to make a fairly crude distinction between those which are traditional highlights of youth and those which arise out of the social changes of the recent past. Among the latter, the most important is certainly the very early sexual experience. Historical demographic investigations of births outside marriage and of pre-nuptial conceptions show that in European history there has always been sexual activity before marriage, but never before was it so wide-spread at such an early age.[10] The radically changed sexual behaviour of young people reflected in this survey is the result of a process in the 1960s and 1970s which is rightly called a 'sexual revolution'.[11] According to a study done in 1973, the proportions of students born in 1945 and 1946 who had had sexual relations before their seventeenth birthday were only 3 per cent and 6 per cent respectively; of those secondary school pupils born in 1953 and 1954, however, the figures were 26 per cent and 38 per cent. Among young workers, the increase in these years was not as dramatic but was nevertheless significant.[12] This development was obviously given a major boost by the availability of safe contraceptives, but it certainly cannot be explained by this cause alone. Equally important was the change in values and ideas on sexuality and the human body which ran parallel, or perhaps a little ahead.[13] The decline of traditional ecclesiastical norms in a widely secularized society also contributed.

[10] For an overview of this, see Mitterauer, *Ledige Mütter*.
[11] For a historical view of this, E. Shorter, *Die Geburt der modernen Familie* (Reinbek, 1975), pp. 130ff.
[12] V. Sigusch and G. Schmidt, *Jugendsexualität* (Stuttgart, 1973), cited by L. Rosenmayr, 'Jugend', in König, *Handbuch der empirischen Sozialforschung*, 2nd edn, vol. 6, p. 256.
[13] B. Schäfers, *Soziologie des Jugendalters* (Opladen, 1982), pp. 79ff.

In the social history of European youth, the altered sexual behaviour of the last two decades must be regarded as one of the most important processes of change. For centuries, according to the norm, young people were excluded from sexual activity, since adults (that is, married people) were regarded as having a monopoly on sexuality. Behaviour patterns, group relations and forms of cultural expression were all shaped by this. All these areas have experienced radical change in the last decades.

One of the more recent highlights of the biography which emerges from the 1981 study is 'consumer autonomy'. This obviously refers to the entitlement in the eighteenth year of life to make large purchases independently, but also the right at 15.5 to make decisions about one's own appearance, which obviously involves buying clothes. Historical precursors of this 'consumer autonomy' might possibly be sought among young people of the upper classes. As a mass phenomenon, it presupposes the affluence of recent decades. Youth as a period of particularly intense consumer activity is certainly relatively new. It also has to do with the sharp increase in leisure time in recent years. In the use of this leisure time, young people have taken on the role of models for society. They are, so to speak, the leisure specialists to whom everyone else turns. Advertising plays strongly on images of youth. Young people could not have become instruments of advertising if they did not have a real and early autonomy as consumers. In the past, however, the purchasing power of young people played a very minor role.

Also connected with leisure and spending is the event of going on holiday independently for the first time, at the age of 17. Of course, travel has a very long history among young people, but it was usually connected with study or work and belonged in a different context from holiday travel. Undertaken alone and without the family, holidays are a sign of an early emancipation from parents. What is surprising is that, according to the 1981 study, this emancipation actually begins a little earlier among young women than among young men. Historically, independent travel was almost exclusively the domain of the male. The levelling-out which has occurred in present times points to a thoroughgoing change in the behaviour of girls, which also has to do with new ideas about male and female roles.

Among the new highlights of youth, the ability at average 19.3

years to own one's own car is certainly of particular importance. A car is far more than a useful means of transport; it symbolizes progress, independence and freedom.[14] It is of great importance for the young person's transition to adult roles. Learning to drive is in our society a major event in adolescent development. As a 'rite of initiation', passing a driving test is endowed by today's teenagers with greater significance than attaining legal majority or being entitled to vote. The right at 16 to drive smaller motor vehicles is seen, so to speak, as a stepping stone to the 'majority' of the full driving licence. Thus motorization, a central factor for social change in the twentieth century, has had a lasting influence also on the course of youth. Alongside the car, or perhaps preceding it, we must take account of the motorbike. Unlike the car, the motorbike has the character of being specifically a young person's vehicle. Furthermore, it has a gender-specific role. A markedly masculine adolescent group-culture has developed around the motorbike, in which the vehicle has taken on a symbolic value. The change of emphasis to the car as the dominant vehicle for young people may indicate that the symbolic relationship between motorization and maleness among teenagers is disappearing.

In contrast to these new milestones in the course of modern youth, some of the thresholds identified in the 1981 survey have roots which go back a long way. To these belongs, for example, the ability to conduct oneself properly in company, which the study places at the age of 16.8. Good manners and social competence are traditionally a very important part of being adult. Historically speaking, this link between social graces and adulthood is a characteristic product of the development which Elias has described as the 'process of civilization'.[15] The adult distinguishes himself from the child by controlling his urges and emotions. It is an important task of adolescence to learn this self-control by means of social discipline. The things which go to make up 'good manners' can be traced back to their origins in the upper classes of society. 'Courtesy' and 'civility' were the norms of behaviour of the nobility and the upper middle class respectively. The standards which they evolved have in the course of later developments gained a universal validity. It seems significant that even today more young people

---

[14] *Jugend '81*, p. 173.
[15] N. Elias, *Über den Prozeß der Zivilisation* (Frankfurt, 1976), vol. II.

from the upper middle class identified this as a milestone in their lives than from the lower middle or lower classes.[16]

Traditionally the acquisition of good manners is closely related to learning to dance. The classical dancing school claimed to provide training in both. For young people from the upper classes, the first dance meant far more than participation in youthful pursuits. It meant being introduced to 'society', which presupposed that one had mastered its conventions. The dancing school provided a preparation for this important stage of growing up. We may regard attendance at dancing school as one of the 'initiation rites' of bourgeois society, if not the decisive one. As the most important point of contact between the sexes in adolescence, dancing also had initiatory features much earlier, in various milieux in old European society, but there the connection between dancing and good social conduct was absent. This had its origin in the training of young lords and ladies, and was furthered by the commercially organized dancing schools of the middle class. Today, more than a half of all teenagers have attended a dancing course before they reach the age of 20, the majority while still relatively young.[17] The average age at which this aspect of youth is completed is roughly the same as that for the ability to conduct oneself socially.

Many European languages make a distinction in the personal pronoun between informal and formal modes of address, as for example French *tu* and *vous*, German *du* and *Sie*, Dutch *jij* and *U*. A parallel distinction is to be seen in the contrast between address by forename and address by title, Mr, Miss and so on. These conventions provide a very old and important method of distinguishing between adults and children, between independent and dependent individuals, between those with authority and those subordinate to them. Among young people, the change in form of address marks a transition in status. In the German survey, young people in 1981 could expect to be addressed by most people as *Sie* from the age of about 18. The way conventional titles are applied to young people vividly reflects how the concept of adulthood has developed historically from independence in terms of domestic law to personal maturity, a development which has been

---

[16] *Jugend '81*, p. 167.
[17] Ibid., pp. 162ff.

so important for the changing meaning of youth. In German, the adult forms of address for a man are *Herr* or in former times *Monsieur*, a borrowing from French. At the end of the eighteenth century it by no means went without saying that unmarried young men in Germany would be called by these titles,[18] yet from the second half of the nineteenth century, it was expected that they would be used from Confirmation onwards.[19] It is interesting that the titles Mister, *Herr, Monsieur*, which originally belonged only to the master of the house, are now extended unaltered to include unmarried males, whereas the female titles undergo a change: Mistress, *Frau, Madame* are only applied to unmarried women in the diminutive forms Miss, *Fräulein, Mademoiselle*. We shall return later to the fact that weddings seem to have been a more decisive turning point for women than for men.

The question of being allowed to go out and come home when one chooses raises what has been a difficult area for young people since ancient times: being free to take part in youth activities outside the home. Here, the tradition of old European society differentiates sharply between young men and women; this varies in rigidity depending on culture and social class, but it is quite clear. Girls always required the permission of parents or someone else responsible in the home if they wished to go out after finishing their work. As a rule, they were only permitted to go out in the evening if accompanied by a chaperon. The reason for this supervision of girls lay in a concern about sexual dangers. In so far as young men were restricted in their activities, it was other factors which were to the fore, such as extravagant spending or alcohol consumption. Today, legislation to protect young people has intervened in this respect, complementing or replacing the supervision of parents. Following the traditional social norms, young men were always permitted free-time activities away from home, albeit starting at a fixed age. In country areas it was not so much the parents as the fraternities of young men who ensured that the younger boys disappeared from the streets before the evening 'angelus' bell. Here, being allowed to go out marked the difference between childhood and youth. In more recent times, supervision for both sexes has taken on this character. True, the 1981 results

---

[18] J. Schlumbohm (ed.), *Kinderstuben. Wie Kinder zu Bauern, Bürgern, Aristokraten wurden 1700–1850* (Munich, 1983), p. 401.

[19] L. Vischer, *Geschichte der Konfirmation* (Zollikon, 1958), pp. 98ff.

did still show gender-related differences, but the process of levelling is well advanced.[20] One of the most striking everyday distinctions between young women and men has thus lost its importance.

As we examine, these 'new' and 'old' thresholds in the 'normal biography' of today's young people from a historical perspective, it becomes clear how thoroughgoing the changes have been which have taken place in the last decades in the social history of youth. Sexuality, leisure, purchasing, driving – in all of these areas fundamentally new dimensions of adolescent life are to be found. But also the examples of traditional turning-points suggest significant processes of change. The most important is the tendency to demolish gender-specific distinctions, behind which presumably lies a general balancing out of the received ideas on male and female roles.

II. Traditional Milestones

The significance of the changes in the twentieth century becomes even clearer if we now make a similar comparison, but start with the thresholds which were valid in early phases of European social development. For the history of youth in Europe it seems particularly significant that the Western Christian tradition did not have an 'initiation' in the sense of a single, all-embracing declaration of adulthood, following the completion of puberty and valid for all areas of adult life. Instead, there was a plethora of partial initiations. The Christian Churches had First Communion and the associated ceremonies of Confirmation or admission to membership as religious thresholds. These, however, had nothing to do with puberty, and there were no political or community rights connected with them. In some areas, such rights would be given to young men of certain ranks when they were made eligible to carry arms. This, on the other hand, had no religious meaning, and did not necessarily coincide with puberty. Various legal thresholds of majority were derived from the granting of arms, but these are only to be seen as minimum ages for the acquisition of domestic authority. Workplace rituals marking the beginning of full employment were common in many milieux, but these again were

[20] *Jugend '81*, pp. 146ff.

not associated with puberty. Likewise, there were rituals connected with joining various groups of adolescents, adults, school-boys, students and so on. They all represent a transition to a higher status, but are again only part of a person's progress to adult society. Some of these part-initiations were extended to carry elements of majority for other areas of life. In more-recent times, that has been especially true of Lutheran Confirmation. But even when a ritual makes a more-comprehensive statement, it is not possible to speak of a rite of initiation in the ethnological sense, with its definition based on studies of fairly homogeneous tribal societies.

The absence of a rite of initiation in Christian/European culture is remarkable in that this institution or something akin to it was known in various preceding and neighbouring cultures. This is true, for example, around the Mediterranean. Like the Egyptians, the Greeks let boys' hair grow long in order to place it before the fertility deities as a thank-offering at puberty. The cutting of hair was for young Athenians part of a ceremony which declared them to have come of age, and which included religious sacrifices, registration in the community-book of Demos, the taking of oaths of citizenship, and the granting of the right to carry arms, symbolized by the formal presentation of a shield and spear.[21] In Rome, the young men received the *toga virilis* at the Festival of the *Liberalia* in the context of celebratory sacrifices. By this they acquired all the rights of citizenship.[22] Of the Germanic tribes, Tacitus describes how the sons of freemen on reaching puberty received their full rights as members of the tribe by the formal presentation of arms.[23] Ritual sacrifice of hair in connection with bestowal of arms is also reported among the Chatti and the Langobards.[24] Among the Franks, the rite of initiation took place at the age of 12. It proclaimed coming of age and, most probably, also entitlement to carry arms. Shorn hair again appears as part of the ritual.[25] Pointers to the

[21] O. Schade, *Über Jünglingsweihen* (Hanover, 1857), pp. 271ff.; R. Zoepffel, 'Geschlechtsreife und Legitimation zur Zeugung im Alten Griechenland', in G. W. Müller (ed.), *Geschlechtsreife und Legitimation zur Zeugung* (Freiburg, 1985), p. 373.

[22] E. Eyben, 'Geschlechtsreife und Ehe im griechisch-römischen Altertum und im frühen Christentum', in ibid., pp. 413ff.

[23] L. Weiser, *Altgermanische Jünglingsweihen und Männerbünde* (Bühl, 1927), p. 31.

[24] Ibid., p. 35.

[25] D. Illmer, 'Zum Problem der Emanzipationsgewohnheiten im merowingischen Frankenreich', *L'Enfant*, vol. II (Brussels, 1976), pp. 148ff.

existence of an initiation rite are also to be found for the early history of the Slavonic tribes. Ritual cutting of boys' hair continued in Poland until the thirteenth century. However, in the period covered by the sources, this took place at the early age of seven, when the responsibility for raising the son passed from the mother to the father. At puberty the young man was then granted adulthood and arms.[26] For the Russian nobility, the cutting of hair is recorded along with the ceremony of horse-mounting as an initiation rite from the Kiev period. This was bound up with recognition as a full adult member of the family.[27]

Of particular interest for a comparison with Christendom are the rules governing majority in the two other monotheistic world religions, Islam and Judaism. Islam certainly knows no general rite of initiation, but puberty is endowed with great significance in both spiritual and temporal spheres.[28] The Koran names two important milestones in the development of the young person, namely *hulum*, the point of psychological maturity, and *asudd*, which brings entitlement to conduct business. The two, however, are for the most part thought of as a unit. They are not fixed at specific ages, but depend on the development of the individual or the estimation of the community, and it is perfectly possible for them to coincide. The social implications of puberty are manifold in Islam. For a start, it gives access to religion and ritual, but more than this, it means the end of orphanhood, the power to administer property, the right to distribute alms, to release slaves, to buy and sell, and to act as a witness in court. Also, finally, it means being subject to the penal code. Whether the young person is also entitled at this point to carry arms depends on his bodily development. All in all, we are dealing here with a comprehensive transition from childhood to adulthood.

The situation in Judaism is very similar to that in Islam. Religious entitlement and legal majority seem to be tightly bound together. Both are reached by a boy at a point which is reckoned to be a minimum age for physical maturity. Shortly after the end of his thirteenth year of life, the *Bar-mitzvah* ceremony takes place

[26] J. Bardach, 'L'Enfant dans l'ancien droit Polonais et Lithuanien jusqu'à la fin du XVIIIe siècle', ibid., pp. 603ff.
[27] M. Szeftel, 'Le Statut juridique de l'enfant en Russie avant Pierre le Grand', ibid., p. 652.
[28] H. Motzki, 'Geschlechtsreife und Legitimation zur Zeugung im frühen Islam', in Müller (ed.), *Geschlechtsreife*, pp. 481ff.

making him a 'son of the law'.[29] There is no documentary evidence for this ceremony before the fifteenth century, but it is certainly very old. It is possible that circumcision, later performed at birth, was originally a part of the *Bar-mitzvah* rite. At any rate, the undifferentiating unity of religious and legal coming-of-age points to a very ancient rite of initiation. Only the right to trade has been separated and made dependent on particular skills. What is also interesting is that the thirteenth year also marks the transition from the elementary school to the higher schools; clearly, Jewish schooling developed in the context of initiation.

The *Bar-mitzvah* ritual is the only genuine rite of initiation to have survived in European history, and indeed to the present day. A couple of variations which arise from the changing social framework are worthy of note. Like the majority of initiation rites, *Bar-mitzvah* was restricted to boys. In Judaism, only men could become full members of the community. In the nineteenth century, however, starting in France and Italy, a *Bat-mitzvah* ceremony for girls came into existence, possibly as a ramification of the contemporary thinking on equality of citizenship. In Germany there was also the influence of Lutheran Confirmation. Such influences were brought to bear especially in the reformed Jewish congregations. In the same context, the age was raised to 16 or 17. In addition to puberty, a certain emotional maturity was prerequisite for the ceremony.

In comparison with preceding and neigbouring cultures, the problem of the absence of a rite of initiation in the social development of Christian Europe raises two main questions. First, why has there been a fundamental separation of the religious and the other legally relevant transitions in status from child to adult? Secondly, why have both been detached from puberty?

The first question has generally to do with the separation of spiritual and temporal concerns in the Christian tradition. Without going into this theme in detail, it should be pointed out that in the first centuries of its development, Christianity was not a state religion. It was therefore possible for completely different criteria to develop for full membership of the religious community than were the norm in the political and social spheres. Certainly, the Church

---

[29] *Encyclopaedia Judaica*, vol. 4 (Jerusalem, 1971), p. 243; *Jüdisches Lexikon*, vol. i (Berlin, 1927), pp. 730ff.

then adopted the norms of Roman Law, which centred on puberty, for the question of eligibility to marry, but in religious life these remained irrelevant. When the medieval kingdoms were founded by the Germanic and Slavonic tribes, the Church with its now Roman legal tradition was once again confronted by thresholds of a quite different origin.

On the second question, it must be considered that Christianity was not originally a tribal religion like Judaism but, rather, a religion of conversion. Belonging to the faith by birth and religious upbringing played no role in the first instance. Adult baptism was originally the normal way of joining the community of faith. It was only later replaced by infant baptism. This shift away from the importance of ancestry may explain the relative lack of emphasis on fertility in Christian marriage. In Judaism it is different. Here fertility is esteemed very highly, and marriage is recommended as early as possible. A particularly strong emphasis on fertility is to be found in all religions with ancestor cults. The continuity of the cult depends on procreation, especially of the male line. Early marriage is encouraged, which in turn necessitates an emphasis on the age of puberty.[30] Christianity has always opposed on principle all elements of ancestor cults wherever they appeared. The absence of a religious significance for reproduction did not encourage early marriage. This was certainly not the reason for the emergence of the European marriage pattern, but it did help to create a climate in which the pattern could become established on this continent and no other. The lack of importance attached to reproduction by Christianity probably also explains how this religion as it developed came by such a belittling attitude to sexuality. Sexual asceticism and religious celibacy are strictly rejected in Islam, for example.[31] Christendom's hostility towards sex is certainly also an important reason why so little attention was paid in Western tradition to the physical processes of growing up.

The absence in the Christian cultures of Europe of a comprehensive status transition rooted in religion to mark progression from childhood to adulthood clears the way for the wide range of thresholds which are found here, differentiating according to age and sphere of life. Among the non-religious thresholds, puberty

[30] See Mitterauer, *Ledige Mütter*, pp. 37ff., for particular developments in the Balkans.
[31] Motzki, 'Geschlechtsreife', p. 500.

may well originally have played a not-inconsiderable role, but it receded in importance relative to other determining factors. For example, in population groupings which had to carry arms it was physical strength not genital development which was decisive for the age at which a youngster would be accepted into the body of fighting men, the exact age depending, of course, on the kinds of weapons involved. Much the same is true in peasant communities of the requirements for physical labour. The only milestones which continued to be connected with sexual maturity were those permitting courting and preparation for marriage. This mattered especially for joining youth organizations; but even that could be left until long after the age of puberty.

Many of the non-religious partial thresholds in European history do show similarities to a rite of initiation. Often they are restricted to young men. Even in intercultural comparisons it seems that female rites of initiation are exceptional. The turning points of youth highlight the major differences between young women and men in the past. To explain this phenomenon of rites of transition concentrated exclusively on male development we must make recourse to what has been offered us by ethnological theory. It seems plausible also to apply to European social history the approach which sees male initiation rites in the context of the strength of the maternal bond, on the one hand, and male dominance in public life, on the other.[32] Starting from a study of the proximity of children's beds to those of their mothers, a comparison of 64 cultures established that in societies in which there is strong bond between mother and child, but in which men dominate adult society, initiation rites for young men are particularly prominent. Unlike girls, boys in such societies must distance themselves from the female dominance of childhood and be introduced into the wider, male-orientated society. Rites of maturity help them overcome this discontinuity.

In European history, the separation of a boy from the female world of the mother happened quite early, during childhood. From about the seventh year of life, children were called upon to help with the work.[33] Boys went with their fathers, while girls remained

---

[32] Cf. H. Kreutz, *Soziologie der Jugend* (Munich, 1974), pp. 138ff.

[33] K. Arnold, *Kind und Gesellschaft in Mittelalter und Renaissance* (Paderborn, 1980), p. 20; B. Hanawalt, 'Childrearing among the lower classes of late medieval England', *Journal of Interdisciplinary History*, 8 (1977), p. 19.

with their mothers. Occasionally this transition was ritualized, as for example with the cutting of hair in the early Polish tradition. For the study of youth, however, such rites of separation are less important than rites of entry. The most significant element of the male rites of passage was the introduction to the male-dominated, sometimes exclusively male, world of adult public life. Tacitus makes this clear in his report of the initiation of young warriors among the Germanic Chatti: '*ante hoc domus pars videntur, mox rei publicae*' ['Until this, they were seen as part of the home, but afterwards, as part of society'].[34] Until this point they were seen as members of the domestic community; now they were regarded as belonging to the tribe. The warrior communities of the Germanic tribes were exclusively male. Girls could have no part in the life of the adult warriors; they remained a part of the *domus* and required no rite of initiation. Many of the institutions of old European society stood in this warrior tradition, keeping public life a male preserve. This is particularly true of the national assemblies of the nobility, but the lower rural and urban courts in the old order were also male forms of public life. A major element of the rites of maturity for young men was to lead into these, or to prepare for them.

Expressed as an ideal type, we may say: whereas the role of the adult male in old European society as master of a house involved him in both public and domestic communities, the housewife had her place only in the latter. In the biography of a girl, then, the principal problems were different from those of a boy. The question of reorientation did not arise in relation to public life, but related instead to the change in the domestic community which occured when she married. This, by contrast is a problem which would not arise for young men in a patrilocal society, as they remained in the parental home. For girls the change of family was, then, the decisive turning-point. Correspondingly, traditional societies often provided a bride with a rich repertoire of rites for leaving home and joining a family. In view of the social conditions in the earliest European history, it has been suggested that the wedding was in fact a form of female initiation rite.[35] This idea should not be rejected lightly. However, the phrase 'initiation rite' refers in normal

---

[34] Tacitus, *Germania*.
[35] Weiser, *Altgermanische Jünglingsweihen*, p. 24.

usage to a celebration of maturity marking the completion of puberty, and in view of the relatively late age at which women have been married in European history we should do well to be hesitant about using it in this connection.

In contrast to many non-religious milestones on the way to adulthood, the religious milestones in European history treated young women and men in the same way, an important fact in understanding the eventual elimination of gender-specific distinctions. Their roots lie not in initiation rites but in the grace-dispensing ordinances of the Christian Churches. Baptism, and the catechumenate in preparation for it, First Communion and Confirmation formed the most important links for later religious rites of growing up.[36] At the time when adult baptism gave way to infant baptism, Baptism, First Communion and Confirmation were a single unit. In the Eastern Church, this unit has survived,[37] showing a concept of the sacraments in which the personal maturity of the recipient is irrelevant. In the West, on the other hand, admission to Communion was made dependent on reaching the *anni discretionis*, the age at which the child has the ability to distinguish between the Eucharist and normal foodstuffs. In 1219 the fourth Lateran Council fixed this at seven years. Likewise Confirmation, which had been separated from Baptism, was pushed back to a later age, yet was never associated with puberty, so that it cannot be seen as an initiation rite.

The Reformation gave rise to a debate on the question of religious concepts of majority in several respects. As a result of the activities of the Anabaptists, adult baptism and renewal of baptismal vows became topics of discussion. Preparation for admission to Communion was developed out of the early Christian catechumenate. *Admissio* to Communion was fixed at a later age than the *anni discretionis*, generally over 14 years. Although the Catholic sacrament of Confirmation (German *Firmung*) was rejected by the reformers, Lutheran Confirmation (German *Konfirmation*) developed out of the ritualizing of a service to celebrate the gaining of a certain religious knowledge and being admitted to Communion.

[36] Esp. Vischer, *Geschichte der Konfirmation*; Ch. Burckhardt-Seebass, *Konfirmation in Stadt und Land Basel. Volkskundliche Studien zur Geschichte eines kirchlichen Fests* (Basel, 1975), pp. 1ff.; R. Metz, 'L'Enfant dans le droit canonique mediéval', in *L'Enfant*, vol. II, pp. 9ff.

[37] *Sacramentum mundi*, vol. II (Feiburg, 1968), p. 40.

This new rite of transition did not become established in all areas at once. For example, in Hessen it was used from the sixteenth century as a defence against the Anabaptists,[38] but it did not appear in some Lutheran territories until the nineteenth century. The main period for the spread of Lutheran confirmation was the second half of the seventeenth century and the eighteenth century. All the subjective denominations which stressed the personal decision of faith, especially the Pietists encouraged the introduction of Confirmation. As the efforts of the Counter-Reformation to win people back to Catholicism were resisted, the idea of a ceremonial public confession of faith before the assembled congregation had a special appeal. Thus Confirmation came to be a clear rite of ecclesiastical adulthood in Protestant lands.

Of all the prerogatives of the adult churchgoer, admission to Communion was the privilege most closely linked with Confirmation. We might also mention eligibility to be a godparent, which is important in permitting 'spiritual parenthood', just as marriage permits physical parenthood.[39] Also significant was the fact that Confirmation in the Lutheran tradition was a prerequisite for receiving a funeral oration.[40] In traditional society, rites of mourning can generally be taken as a reliable indicator of the point at which a person is regarded as adult.[41] A logical consequence of the idea of Confirmation as a stage in growing up was that, in Protestant territories in the 'Age of Tolerance', Confirmation bestowed all the rights of the adult believer.[42]

Just as important as the religious prerogatives granted with Confirmation were the various social rights of adulthood which were linked to it. Since the minimum age for Confirmation was 13 or 14, raised to 16 or 17 in some areas, this ecclesiastical rite of transition provided a very suitable point of crystallization. Its importance is particularly obvious in clothing, a matter which in traditional society indicated extremely poignantly the status changes of the life-cycle. From Confirmation onwards, young people were

[38] E. Schulz, 'Konfirmation', *Hessische Blätter für Volks- und Kulturforschung*, NF 13 (1982), p. 197.

[39] Burckhardt-Seebass, *Konfirmation*, p. 24.

[40] Ibid., p. 27.

[41] Also of interest in this context is the right to choose one's own burial place, a matter of great importance in the Middle Ages. This right was never granted to minors. Cf. Metz, 'L'Enfant', pp. 72ff.

[42] Burckhardt-Seebass, *Konfirmation*, pp. 128ff.

obliged to wear 'decent and respectable church clothes', which would also be used for other festive occasions.[43] Often, boys were given their first long trousers for Confirmation. A typical Confirmation present was the hat, which likewise clearly indicated a new status.[44] From Sweden to Transylvania, we find throughout the Protestant lands the custom that Confirmation marked the point at which young folk began to join the local fraternities or in other ways to spend their leisure time in youthful society.[45] This in turn meant being able to go to dances, being able to begin courting. For young men, it was common after Confirmation to be allowed to visit a public house, and to smoke and drink. Even in working life this was a milestone. It was at this point that many young people went into domestic service.[46] For those who wished to take an apprenticeship or go into commerce, this was the point at which their career was decided. It was expected that after Confirmation, at the very latest, those who remained in the parental home would do a full day's work there. Children from orphanages had to leave the institution and seek work.[47] Sometimes young people who were already working only began to be paid after Confirmation.[48] The new status was unambiguously expressed in the adult forms of address, for which Confirmation was the threshold.[49] In this way, enriched by a variety of facets of secular status, Confirmation took on in some regions the nature of a

[43] Ibid., pp. 59ff.; Schulz, 'Konfirmation', p. 201; Vischer, *Geschichte der Konfirmation*, pp. 89, 127.

[44] Schulz, 'Konfirmation', p. 198.

[45] K. R. W. Wikman, *Die Einleitung in die Ehe* (Åbo, 1937), pp. 17ff.; H. A. Schubert, *Nachbarschaft und Modernisierung. Eine historische Soziologie traditioneller Lokalgruppen am Beispiel Siebenbürgens* (Cologne, 1980), pp. 44ff.; G. F. Meyer, *Brauchtum der Jungmannschaften in Schleswig-Holstein* (Flensburg, 1941), p. 24; B. Petrei, *Die Burschenschaften im Burgenland* (Eisenstadt, 1974), p. 68; R. Braun, *Industrialisierung und Volksleben*, 2nd edn (Göttingen, 1979), p. 122.

[46] Wikman, *Die Einleitung*, p. 23; W. A. Gestrich, 'Jugend in Ohmenhausen, 1800–1918. Eine Sozialgeschichtliche Studie zum Wandel des Jugendlebens in einem württembergischen Dorf unter dem Einfluß der Industrialisierung', Dissertation, Tübingen, 1983; published as 'Traditionelle Jugendkultur und Industrialisierung', in *Kritische Studien zur Geschichtswissenschaft* (Göttingen, 1986), p. 154.

[47] H. Scherpner, *Geschichte der Jugendfürsorge* (Göttingen, 1966), p. 86.

[48] D. Slettat, 'Farmwives, farmhands and the changing rural community in Trondelag, Norway', in P. Thompson (ed.), *Our Common History* (London, 1982), p. 150.

[49] Vischer, *Geschichte der Konfirmation*, pp. 98ff.

comprehensive rite of initiation. In origin, however, it is not. It has never encompassed every form of social transition. And of course, it is not linked to the physical changes of puberty.

The Catholic Confirmation service has never had this kind of comprehensive significance, although here too secular elements are occasionally to be found. This may be seen in some areas with respect to First Communion, especially in those parts of France where First Communion was left relatively late.[50] The membership of the Communion classes formed into the female and male groupings in which young people then spent their leisure hours.[51] After First Communion, girls would begin to gather a dowry. Once again, this rite of transition becomes an occasion for giving significant gifts: jewellery and toiletries for girls, signs of the incipient quest for a partner, and, more recently, 'mopeds' for boys, expressions of their now geographically wider sphere of activity.

If, in more recent times, the religious rites at the beginning of youth mark a point at which many young people begin to part company with the Church,[52] this is also an expression of religious majority. Directly influenced by the individualization of the religious sphere, the modern trend is for youth to become a period of making ideological choices, and increasingly since the nineteenth century, this can mean a reaction against the Church.

Of the non-religious part-thresholds of youth, those connected with military service have always been of special importance for young men. In the tribal law of early Europe, the bestowing of arms was the centre-piece of the rite of transition to adult life. In German, the very word *Mündigkeit* (legal majority) means in its etymological origins the ability to protect oneself and others. This ceremonial arming often happened at a very young age: among the Celtic tribes as early as 10, according to Caesar's report; 10 again in the Anglo-Saxon Law of Kent; between 10 and 12 among the Langobards.[53] The 12-year limit is also to be found among the Franks and other Germanic tribes, and also among the Slavs.

Social majority, which would normally have sexual maturity as

---

[50] A. Van Gennep, *Manuel de folklore français contemporain*, vol. I, part 1 (Paris, 1937), pp. 196ff.

[51] See Y. Verdier, *Drei Frauen. Das Leben auf dem Dorf* (Stuttgart, 1982), pp. 200ff.

[52] Burkhardt-Seebass, *Konfirmation*, p. 153; Verdier, *Drei Frauen*, p. 201.

[53] Illmer, 'Zum Problem', p. 445.

a minimum prerequisite, must in these cases occasionally have preceded it. In a society in which, for want of civil organization and adequate defence, self-assertion and self-protection were all-important, parents would have encouraged their sons to begin training in the use of weapons as early as possible.[54] Carrying arms does not immediately mean mastering them: that requires years of practice. There are a number of clues that in the early Middle Ages there was already a kind of warrior's apprenticeship, which would also end in a rite of transition.[55] The tradition of dubbing among the medieval nobility, by which knighthood is conferred through a stroke of the sword, no doubt has its roots in the second transition which was becoming increasingly prominent.[56] Under the influence of Christian ideas, dubbing became a ceremony of consecration, complete with a colourful ritual. The warrior's apprenticeship continued as the young medieval nobleman gave service as a squire, and this in turn survived in the pages who served in royal houses in more modern times. As late as the eighteenth century, their service commonly came to an end with a ritual celebration.[57] The first transition, however, marking the start of training in arms, became less important as time went on. It manifested itself in many varying forms: by order of the master at arms in one's own household; by service in a foreign court; by attending an officer's school; or by going straight into the army.[58] A kind of 'domestic service' was an important part of the training of young nobles, too. It is not possible to establish a fixed age for the beginning of this training to correspond with the granting of arms in early times.

In the development from the tribal law of early times to the imperial structures of the early and high Middle Ages, the status of the warrior narrowed to include only the nobility. Armed peasants were unusual in European feudal society. Where they did exist, the granting of arms was an important milestone in youth. In the

[54] R. Buchda, 'Kinder and Jugendliche im deutschen Rechte (Mittelalter und Neuere Zeit)', in *L'Enfant*, vol. II (Brussels, 1976), p. 384.

[55] Weiser, *Altgermanische Jünglingsweihen*, pp. 42, 72ff.

[56] H. Delbrück, *Geschichte der Kriegskunst im Rahmen der politischen Geschichte*, vol. 3 (Berlin, 1907), p. 269; Guilhiermoz, *Essai sur l'origine de la noblesse en France* (1902).

[57] Schade, *Über Jünglingsweihen*, pp. 289ff.

[58] A. Corvisier, *Armies and Societies in Europe, 1494–1789* (Bloomington, 1979), pp. 331ff.

cantons of the Swiss Confederation, young men were ready for combat from the age of 16, sometimes from 14.[59] From this point on, they had full political rights in the legislative assemblies. The same threshold was also important for membership of the powerful young-men's fraternities. On the situation in Picardy one commentator writes:

> Here an explicit ceremonial arming of the young man still takes place. At the same time he receives the right to wear a shirt with a blue collar trimmed with red wool, the traditional dress for men in the area. Admission to the fraternity of young men takes place at midnight on All Saints' Day. Only men are present. The lad has to be able to read, and to write his name in the muster. Then he has to demonstrate his skill at swinging the felling axe, binding sheaves, sawing an oak trunk. He must grind a scythe, make bundles of wood, weave a net and build a plough ... after this, he is entitled to begin to look for a wife.[60]

The various components of a comprehensive agricultural rite of passage to adult status, linked also to the carrying of arms, are here clearly to be seen. But even in peasant societies which knew no entitlement to arms, we may reckon with at least a rudimentary form of self-defence which would have been necessary for protection against robbers and wild animals. The knife had wide currency as a peasant weapon. The age at which a peasant lad began to carry a knife in his belt would have been decided carefully. In terms of self-image, this threshold would certainly have had great importance.[61]

As armies of mounted nobility gave way to troops of paid soldiers, the question of an age-limit for entering military service again became relevant for larger sections of the population. Minimum ages for recruitment were occasionally specified in the regulations,[62] but usually physical growth mattered more than age.

[59] H. G. Wackernagel, *Altes Volkstum in der Schweiz* (Basel, 1956), p. 43; R. Wolfram, *Studien zur älteren Schweizer Volkskultur* (Vienna, 1980), p. 71; Burckhardt-Seebass, *Konfirmation*, pp. 12ff.

[60] K. Seidelmann, *Gruppe als soziale Grundform der Jugend*, vol. II (Berlin, 1971), p. 244.

[61] A vivid example of the significance for the adolescence of a young Balkan peasant warrior of receiving a dagger from father or brother is to be found in J. K. Campbell, *Honour, Family and Patronage* (Oxford, 1964), p. 280.

[62] Corvisier, *Armies and Societies*, pp. 51, 56ff., 333ff.

Reaching this age did not bring any rights which were significant for growing up. Soldiering was work like any other and tended to have negative connotations. This situation did not change until the end of the eighteenth century when the idea of compulsory military service for all was first explored. Among the great festivals of the French revolution was the *Fête de la Jeunesse* at which 16-year-olds were solemnly included in the obligation to arms.[63] From the philosophy of the French revolution came the idea that receiving citizen's rights was connected with performing military service, a concept which has influenced debates about the age of majority almost to the present day. The revaluing of military service in social consciousness usually took place in parallel with the rise of nationalistic tendencies. In Germany this can be seen especially in the last decades of the nineteenth century.[64] It was only after completion of military service that one could expect to be treated as an equal in adult society.[65] In rural areas this had the result that membership of some of the fraternities was conditional on the completion of military service, while others had separate groups for those who had served and those who had not.[66] The age for entering military service varied in the different European states. Generally, it was around 20. Whereas in earlier times the granting of arms was the important lower threshold, marking the beginning of youth, military service in the nineteenth century developed into an important intermediate threshold. In some respects it could even be seen as a finale, if we bear in mind that the state-run 'youth work' of the early twentieth century concentrated on the time between compulsory schooling and military service. In all cases, the military thresholds of youth apply only to young men. For females they are only relevant in so far as the degree of militarization determines the width of the gap between the two gender roles.

The military threshold was the centrepiece of the early European concept of becoming adult, and a large number of other thresholds of majority have developed out of it. In studies of youth which start from the perspective of the history of law, these are usually invested with great significance. However, this requires a

---

[63] J. Gillis, *Geschichte der Jugend* (Weinheim, 1980), p. 94.
[64] Gestrich, 'Jugend in Ohmenhausen', pp. 222ff.
[65] Kreutz, *Soziologie der Jugend*, p. 57.
[66] See p. 170.

number of qualifications. In the first place, it is important to realize that in many cases we are speaking of minimum ages which had very little relevance to social reality. When a medieval law book fixes the age of consent at 12 years, that certainly does not mean that 12-year-olds were actually getting married. Reference has already been made to the important difference between attaining legal majority and being free of paternal authority;[67] until the eighteenth and nineteenth centuries, the latter only happened on leaving home. The old German legal maxim *Heirat macht mündig* (marriage is majority)[68] corresponds to the social realities far better than more-complicated phrases such as 'coming-of-age'. Age-related regulations really only became relevant when a father died before his son attained his majority and a guardian had to be appointed. Often, especially in the older legal sources, it is unclear what exactly is meant by majority in a given case.[69] Finally, it must be remembered that the thresholds of majority laid down by tribal or regional law were certainly not intended for the whole population but only for the nobility. In the particularist society of early Europe, thresholds could vary from community to community, from town to town.[70] However, despite these qualifications, the details given about ages of majority do have their importance for social history, for they reflect social conceptions about minimum age limits for growing up with respect to different areas of life.

Diverse as the medieval European thresholds were, a general tendency can none the less be observed, namely, an unmistakable raising of age limits.[71] Where in the old tribal laws the thresholds of legal majority lay at 10 or especially 12, but also 14 and 15, in the high and late Middle Ages they were 18, 20, 21, 24 or 25. In the south and west of Europe, this development took place earlier than in the north and east. There are two possibilities here. Either

[67] See p. 31f.
[68] H. G. Knothe, *Die Geschäftsfähigkeit der Minderjährigen in geschichtlicher Entwicklung* (Frankfurt, 1983), p. 84.
[69] C. Soliva, 'Beschränkte Handlungsfähigkeit – erweiterter Rechtsschutz. Ein Beitrag zur Geschichte der Rechtsstellung Minderjähriger auf dem Gebiet der alten Eidgenossenschaft (13.–18. Jh.)', in *L'Enfant*, vol. II, p. 332.
[70] For the situation in Switzerland, see ibid., p. 331.
[71] Knothe, *Die Geschäftsfähigkeit*, pp. 80ff.; Bardach, 'L'Enfant dans ancien droit', pp. 604ff.; Buchda, 'Kinder und Jugendliche', p. 387; H. Helfenstein, *Beiträge zur Problematik der Lebensalter in der mittleren Geschichte* (Zürich, 1952), pp. 7ff.; G. Köbler, *Das Familienrecht in der spätmittelalterlichen Stadt* (Cologne, 1984), p. 155.

a single threshold was retained but set at a higher age, or it was divided into two separate caesurae. In Saxon law, the old age of majority, 12 years, was kept, but an orphaned son could be under the authority of a guardian until the age of 21.[72] This second solution shows similarities to the legislation in Roman law which provided for a curator who would be responsible from the young person's actual age of majority, 14, until the age of 25. For an explanation of the dramatic shift in the thresholds during the Middle Ages, most writers speak vaguely of an 'increasingly complicated life-style'.[73] One gives us greater detail:

> As the wider use of coinage and the increase in trade altered the economic conditions of the late Middle Ages, a greater degree of maturity was required for participation in the now much more complicated legal transactions, particularly in the growing cities, than had been possible for young people who had attained their majority under the earlier age limits.[74]

These are considerations which are not difficult to understand. In an increasingly complex economic situation the length of training required for commercial activity will of necessity be longer. But there is another line of thinking which can help explain this interesting trend. With respect to the Polish nobility, Bardach has identified a connection between the rise in age-limits and the new divisibility of noble families.[75] These observations suggest that the raising of the age-limits generally may have to do with changes in family form. In complex families with undivided estates, where even a married son remains under the aegis of his father, low ages of majority are possible, since these relate only to marriage and need not at once be connected with full commercial involvement. However, when marriage immediately involves heading a household, the situation is quite different. The young master has the family's estates at his disposal right away. Under these conditions, marriage requires a higher degree of maturity. The shift to higher age-limits could therefore have to do with the spread of the

---

[72] Buchda, 'Kinder und Jugendliche', p. 387; Knothe, *Die Geschäftsfähigkeit*, pp. 82ff.
[73] H. Conrad, *Deutsche Rechtsgeschichte*, vol. I (Karlsruhe, 1934), p. 531.
[74] Knothe, *Die Geschäftsfähigkeit*, p. 80.
[75] Bardach, 'L'Enfant dans l'ancien droit', p. 606.

European marriage pattern and the family system which goes with it, at any rate in those population groups where the higher age was in fact fixed.

It is a safe assumption that the thresholds based on the minimum age for carrying arms were originally also applicable to marriage. The marriage threshold was of course the age at which it was permissible to enter marriage with parental approval; it did not bestow a right to choose independently. The idea that a wedding was valid even without a parent's consent only became established as a result of canon law,[76] and even then marriage without permission was still exceptional. As the ecclesiastical concept of marriage rights gained ground, the age limits of Roman law, 12 and 14, also became accepted. The stages of marital eligibility in Church law, however, have nothing to do with actual marriage practices under the European marriage pattern. In more recent times, the 'age of consent' has generally lain in the 16–20 age band, and has been noticeably lower than the age of majority.[77]

The age limits for liability to prosecution are in the first instance closely connected with civil laws.[78] A father was entirely responsible for the misdemeanours of the children in his household; if he died before they grew up, the guardian was responsible. Changes began to take place when the fine system was dismantled in favour of corporal punishment. For a long time the penal system made no distinction between juveniles and adults. The idea that young people have a lower level of responsibility only came with the concept of adolescence as a time of personal discovery. In France, the first special regulations for young offenders under 16 were introduced in 1971. This Napoleonic *Code pénal* strongly influenced the German legislation of the nineteenth century. The 1871 law book established that a person had no liability to prosecution before the age of 12, a restricted liability from 12 to 18, and full liability only after the age of 18.[79] The limits established by this law were certainly of importance in establishing the

[76] D. Schwab, 'Kind', in *Handwörterbuch der deutschen Rechtsgeschichte*, vol. I (Berlin, 1978), p. 720.

[77] Buchda, Kinder und Jugendliche', p. 392.

[78] G. Buchda, 'Kinder und Jugendliche als Schadensstifter und Missetäter im deutschen Recht', in *L'Enfant*, vol. II, p. 223; Bardach, 'L'Enfant dans l'ancien droit', pp. 631ff.

[79] Scherpner, *Geschichte der Jugendfürsorge*, p. 161.

contemporary concept of 'youth' as opposed to childhood and adulthood in the latter part of the nineteenth century.[80]

Today the threshold of majority is frequently the same as the voting threshold. The history of voting ages shows that there is no necessary correspondence, although there is a certain interaction.[81] At any rate, the right to vote is seldom fixed simply at the age of majority. A connection with the bearing of arms arises where there is a continuous tradition from the old national assemblies. This is the case, for example, in some of the Swiss cantons, where a voting age of 14–16, derived from the medieval military threshold, continued until the time of the Helvetic Republic, and only then was raised. Likewise, in Hungary the sons of noble families were entitled to sit in the Magnate's chamber of the Diet, even after the introduction of the electoral regulations of 1885, as soon as they reached the age of the ancient ceremony of granting of arms. However, political rights in old European society depended more on domestic status than on military considerations. In the public life of many parts of this particularist society, only the father of the house had a say, his dependents being excluded. These old principles continued to have an effect when, with the rise of the modern parliamentary system, political participation became a more widespread matter related to citizenship. In many countries when adult male suffrage was introduced voting ages were chosen which reflected the traditional normal ages of domestic independence. In the early years of the voting system, 25 was a typical minimum age. This placed the voting age well above the age of majority. It was a secondary development which brought these two thresholds into line.

The impact of the legal thresholds of majority on the course of a young person's life has a very complicated history. The linking of majority and arms-bearing marks the beginning of this. If we are right in assuming that the early majority thresholds of the tribal laws are designed to facilitate early marriage, then the beginning and the end of youth were not far apart at that time. The split

[80] L. Roth, *Die Erfindung des Jugendlichen* (Munich, 1983), pp. 98ff.

[81] P. Schmidtbauer, 'Die Erweiterung der politischen Öffentlichkeit im Europa des 19. Jahrhunderts', *Beiträge zur historischen Sozialkunde*, 4 (1974), pp. 73ff.; also, P. Schmidtbauer, 'Hausrechtliche Abhängigkeit und politische Emanzipation. Ein Beitrag zur Geschichte des Wahlrechts im 19. Jh.', Dissertation, Vienna, 1974, MS.

thresholds could be seen in terms of either. At any rate, attaining majority had the character of an upper threshold in those cases in which it actually meant the end of guardianship. With the growth of a new concept of adulthood which had less to do with position in the home than with rounded personality, the age of majority became a target for young people which was not simply seen in legal terms. The fact that, in recent decades, most of the legal thresholds have been reduced is certainly not to be thought of as a shortening of the span of youth. Certain stages of legal respons-ibility, such as the right to vote and to conduct business, or the thresholds connected with crime, trial and punishment can today be reached long before youth has come to an end.

Examples of the ritualizing of the transition from childhood to youth which come close to being an initiation rite are certainly still to be found in recent times. It is no coincidence that the most striking examples come from areas on the edges of Europe. The unusual case of a clear-cut rite of passage for girls on reaching puberty is to be found in the rural areas of Bulgaria.[82] It takes place on Lazarus Day, the Saturday before Palm Sunday, and hence is called *lazarnitza* or *lazarouvané*. Preparations begin several weeks before the festival. The girls gather in groups in houses and practice ritual songs and dances for the occasion. During this time they are not permitted to speak with young men, and sometimes they even withdraw from the village altogether. After this they visit with their songs every house in which there is a young man who is to be married. They present themselves to the whole community in the ritual dance *lazarsko horo*. At the Lazarus feast, everyone attends church together. An important part of the ritual is the donning of new festive clothes which the girls are entitled to wear from now on. The new garb allows them to be easily identified as members of the *svarchenite momi*, the marriageable girls. The costume com-prises a single-piece culotte-dress held together by a belt, and is completed with bracelet, rings, bangles, necklace, head-dress, plaited hair and flowers. The new clothes will later be worn as a wedding dress. The Lazarus Day ceremony bestows on girls who have reached sexual maturity, and only on them, the right to take part in dances and to join in the evening gatherings and festivities

[82] J. Koleva, 'Institut des initiations en Bulgarie', *Ethnologia Slavica*, 5 (1973), pp. 163ff.

of young people. There are similar rites of transition for young men, known as the *koledari*. They too go from house to house singing songs they have practised together, but at a different time of year, at Christmas. They too are introduced to the village community by dance. They too enjoy the characteristic change of costume. In contrast to the girls, however, the newly initiated young men form a group with older unmarried men which will remain together. In these Bulgarian rites of passage, various components are retained which are also to be found in other European cultures, whether singly or as part of something larger, whether ritualized or not, whether marking the beginning of youth or an advanced stage of it. What is missing here, as opposed to comprehensive rites of initiation, is the element of changing status in cultic interests. But certainly there are cultic elements. An important feature here is the fact that at Easter the *lazarki* place red eggs on the graves of the dead. Alongside marriage and love, the dead are mentioned in their ritual songs. Initiation rites often do include the honouring of ancestors. This, however, is a specific element drawn from outside the Christian tradition.

In Hungary we find comprehensive rites of transition with features which are very ancient, sometimes referred to as the 'consecration' of young men.[83] The centrepiece of the ceremony was admission to the youth fraternity, ritualized by a drink and occasionally also a dance. The neophyte had to pay for the wine, sometimes also for cigarettes. The introduction had to be made by a sponsor, one of a number of analogies to baptism. Putting on the belt of the fraternity was often an important element in the consecration ceremony. The new initiate was now permitted to visit the inn or the spinning-room, he was allowed to enter houses where young girls lived, and he could invite girls to dance. If he were attacked, the other members of the fraternity were obliged to come to his assistance. The age at which the ritual took place depended less on sexual maturity than on ability to work, particularly with horses. There was no such formal transition for girls in Hungary. They were regarded as having outgrown their childhood from the point at which they were first invited to a dance. When this happened, a maypole was erected for the girl.

---

[83] K. Viski, *Volksbrauch der Ungarn* (Budapest, 1932), pp. 26, 61; J. Balassa and G. Ortutay, *Ungarische Volkskunde*, p. 656; T. Domotor, *Ungarische Volksbräuche* (Budapest, 1972), p. 85.

These Hungarian rituals also contain much which was typical in traditional societies for the transition from childhood to youth. They had more in common with the traditions of central and western Europe than with those of Bulgaria.

A particularly poignant indicator of the change from child to adolescent is when the new status marked by the rite of transition is characterized by a new term. This is the case in Bulgaria. Of course, the change in terminology need not be linked to a rite of passage. The words used to describe young people in the various European rural societies, which relate strongly to particular aspects of work or domestic service, are expressions of a conceptual distinction which is not necessarily linked to a ceremony of transition.[84] In Central and Western Europe, terminology connected with work seems to have been far more common than that connected with puberty.

In traditional status-conscious European society, a very significant symbol of the transition from childhood to youth, and later from youth to adulthood, was the change in costume. Wherever there were strong rites of passage, as in Bulgaria, this change was linked with the rites. It could, however, demonstrate a change in status quite independently of any ceremonial. In Western and Central Europe, at any rate in modern urban populations, non-ritualized changes in outward appearance are more typical. It is not only clothes which signal status, but also head-wear, jewellery, arms and hairstyle. A typical symbol for the young adolescent girl might be long loose hair with a garland.[85] In many parts of Europe, garlands were signs of virginity. Young girls were often given one at First Communion or Confirmation, and would wear it on festive occasions until they married. The jewellery mentioned in the Bulgarian example played a particularly vivid role in girls' costumes from the Balkans. In France the connection between jewellery and youth is highlighted in the proverb 'no ear-rings, no kisses'.[86] For males, crossing the boundary from childhood was often signalled by a hat. The way this was decorated was also important. Feathers like the cock's plume or aigrette were symbols of the fraternities.[87] Flowers in a hat had specific meanings. In

[84] Cf. for example, Wikman, *Die Einleitung*, pp. 32ff.
[85] H. Bachtold-Staubli, *Handwörterbuch des Aberglaubens*, vol. v (Berlin, 1932–3), pp. 410ff.
[86] Verdier, *Drei Frauen*, p. 254.
[87] See p. 170f.

Vorarlberg in Austria, young men who had just spent their first
summer on the mountain pastures would wear a cigar in their hat
as they drove the cattle back down the hill in the autumn, an
interesting combination of adult symbols to mark the first completed piece of adult work.[88] Costume expressed changing status
in many ways. As a general rule, for females it expressed the
transition from adolescent to woman, while for males it emphasized
that from child to adolescent. We have already spoken in the
context of initiation rites of how the wedding ceremony had a
greater significance for females than for males.

One clear mark of the end of childhood in traditional society
was admission to an organized youth group. As we shall see, the
dominance of male youth organizations made this a predominantly
male threshold.[89] For girls, admission to young people's social
gatherings was more important. Both forms of transition could be
accompanied by varying degrees of ritual. The age for joining
youth organizations varied considerably. Rural fraternities seldom
accepted members younger than 16,[90] and sometimes the age was
fixed at 20. The highest age-limits are found in cases where the
completion of military service is a condition of membership.[91]
Frequently, membership was made conditional on achievement
at work, being linked, for example, to a particular grade in the
hierarchy of domestic service.[92] In the same category belong the
various tests of strength and skill: lifting stones, carrying sacks of
grain or mending fence posts.[93] The importance of physical strength
for age thresholds was stressed particularly in the rural milieu. In
urban journeymen's associations, completion of an apprenticeship
was the condition of membership. This seldom happened before
17 or 18 and was often later. It should not be assumed that, where
admission to membership occurred late, young people were still

[88] Information kindly provided by Dr Edith Hörandner.

[89] See pp. 156ff.

[90] K. S. Kramer, 'Altersklassenverbände', in *Handwörterbuch der deutschen
Rechtsgeschichte*, I, p. 131; Van Gennep, *Manuel de folklore*, p. 198; E. Hoffmann-
Krayer, 'Knabenschaften und Volksjustiz', *Schweizerisches Archiv für Volkskunde*,
8 (1905), pp. 125ff.; Petrei, *Die Burschenschaften*, p. 23; Burckhardt-Seebass,
Konfirmation, pp. 208ff.

[91] J. Peter, *Gasslbrauch und Gasslspruch in Österreich* (Salzburg, undated), pp.
18, 131ff.

[92] Ibid., p. 18.

[93] Ibid., p. 132.

regarded as children up to that point. Admission to a youth organization could be a lower threshold of youth, for example, when it coincided with Confirmation, but it could equally be an intermediate threshold. But whenever it occurred, such important rights for young men as going dancing, making evening visits to girls, visiting public houses, drinking and smoking were all generally tied to this event in rural society.

Rites of entry into youth organizations are mirrored by rites of admission to working fraternities or simply rites marking the beginning of working life. Among the wide diversity of customs for workplace inauguration, some humorous but many coarse, were such activities as beating, soaking with water, crawling through the spokes of a cart wheel, shaving with wooden knives, and so forth.[94] They were supposed to symbolize the discarding of the old identity and the adoption of a new one, and were therefore strongly initiatory in character. For skilled workers, these customs did not take place at the solemn ceremony at which the apprentice was presented before the guild, but rather were connected with admission to the association of young journeymen.[95] In other cases, they usually coincided with starting work. Initiatory customs also had wide currency in merchant circles and among traditional groups of labourers such as miners and sailors.[96] These rites have not survived among industrial labourers. They are important for an understanding of youth in so far as they mark off the beginning of work as the start of a new phase of life. With very few exceptions, these rituals have been restricted to male professions.[97]

The ritualization of working thresholds is to be found in traditional society whenever a person enters a new working community, or whenever membership of a fraternity is conditional on a stated level of achievement. Transitions from one stage to the next within a family business were not ritualized, as they had no importance for the wider community. Such transitions were, however, extremely important for the young person's self-esteem and his sense of being acknowledged by the community. On the farm they also resulted in pay increases. The hierarchy of farm service, especially

---

[94] Schade, *Über Jünglingsweihen*, pp. 410ff.

[95] H. Müller, *Die kleinbürgerliche Familie im 18. Jahrhundert* (Berlin, 1969), pp. 58, 62.

[96] Van Gennep, *Manuel de folklore*, pp. 192ff.

[97] Meyer, *Brauchtum der Jungmannschaften*, p. 46.

as it developed in areas with economies based on large farms, clearly reflects the way the young person gradually climbed the ladder of rank. One author from the end of the eighteenth century attempted to define the various grades of labour and the ages at which they are attained:[98] from ages 9 till 12, a boy must tend the cows; at 13 he becomes a stable boy, and looks after the horses until he is 16; at 16 he is confirmed, which allows more highly qualified work on the farm; from 17 to 20 he works as a junior farm-hand. According to the author, this is the decisive phase of growth. From the age of 21, the 'now strengthened and hardened youngster' can serve as a chief hand. There are agricultural regions in which the stages of farm service were far more strongly differentiated.[99] A precise subdivision was most common in male employment. But even among maids a threefold hierarchy was no rarity. Precise age brackets, like those attempted by the author mentioned above, certainly do not correspond to the social reality. A great deal depended on physical strength and skill. It is reported that one maid completed in five years a career for which others would have required eight or ten.[100] Details like these show clearly to what extent youth was regarded in traditional agrarian society as a time of ascending the hierarchy of labour.

In the small farm, run as a family concern, the boundary between childhood and youth was not marked off by any striking threshold. At a very early age children slipped into a working routine which intensified as they grew up. It is possible to identify a turning-point at about 12 or 13 years of age when children were regarded as able-bodied workers. This is most clearly seen in the fact that a hired maid or stable-boy would be dismissed as soon as a daughter or son reached the age in question.[101] The quality of work undertaken also shows a turning-point at this stage. Until the age of 12 the principle task was tending cattle, traditionally regarded as typical children's work. It was done equally by girls and boys. Only after this point was there a clear gender-specific

[98] Schlumbohm, *Kinderstuben*, pp. 84ff.

[99] M. Mitterauer, 'Gesindedienst und Jugendphase im Europaischen Vergleich', *Geschichte und Gesellschaft*, 11 (1985), pp. 190ff.; 'Formen ländlicher Familienwirtschaft', in J. Ehmeer and M. Mitterauer (eds), *Familienstruktur und Arbeitsorganisation in ländlichen Gesellschaften* (Vienna, 1985), pp. 200ff.

[100] K. Renner, *An der Wende zweier Zeiten*, 2nd edn (Vienna, 1946), p. 117.

[101] Mitterauer, 'Formen ländlicher', pp. 264ff.

differentiation in work.[102] Of course, on the family farm, the division of labour according to age-group was very much dependent both on the physical capacity of the young people and on the limitations of available personnel. We are therefore not speaking here of a rigid age threshold.

Unlike the family farm, the family firm of tradesmen knew no age-related distinctions in the type of work performed. The years prior to becoming established as a master were divided into two periods, first as an apprentice and then as a journeyman. The former lasted roughly three to five years,[103] the latter varying according to the opportunities to become a master. The two phases were qualitatively quite different. The apprentice received no pay; on the contrary, his parents had to pay for his training. The apprentice was subjected far more strongly to the master's authority than was the journeyman. He spent his whole apprenticeship in the same workshop, whereas from the Middle Ages onwards the journeyman was obliged to spend at least a couple of years travelling. The twofold model of apprenticeship and qualified assistantship also relates in principle to the trading house. In contrast to the commercial family firm, there was as a rule a gradation of tasks here. Merchants generally had a larger number of employees, among whom work was divided strictly according to age,[104] so that there could be steady promotion throughout the adolescent years.

In trade and commerce, the transition from childhood to youth was more clearly reflected in working practices than on the farm. The beginning of an apprenticeship, which generally could not be served under one's own father, was obviously a sharp cut-off point. In the eighteenth and nineteenth centuries this often happened between the ages of 12 and 15, most frequently at 14.[105] In the Middle Ages this may have been earlier, but certainly not often

---

[102] E.g., Verdier, *Drei Frauen*, pp. 201ff., 174.

[103] Schlumbohm, *Kinderstuben*, p. 225.

[104] W. Deich, *Zur Sozialgeschichte der Handlungsgehilfen um 1900* (Cologne, 1974), p. 62.

[105] Schlumbohm, *Kinderstuben*, p. 225; H. Möller, *Die kleinbürgerliche Familie im 18. Jahrhundert* (Berlin, 1965), p. 57. The peak between the ages of 13 and 14 has been established by an analysis of the ages of apprentices in various middle European populations in this period in a survey of some 85,000 people, on the basis of a data bank in the *Institut für Wirtschafts – und Sozialgeschichte* at the University of Vienna.

as early as 7 or 8, as some writers occasionally assume.[106] In late medieval England, most children were still living in their parental home between the ages of 8 and 12. In fifteenth-century Cologne there were very few apprentices under the age of 12, and in sixteenth-century France 12 was the average age for beginning an apprenticeship. In the fourteenth century it may have been a little lower there.[107] If the apprenticeship was the form which adolescent labour took in trade and commerce in old European society, work in this setting began at about the same age as on the farm.

The boundary between childhood and youth in trade and commerce is underlined by the fact that apprenticeship was commonly preceded by a spell at an elementary school, and this long before education became compulsory. Consequently, in these milieux adolescent labour was not preceded by child labour but by schooling. With the growth of compulsory education in the eighteenth and especially in the nineteenth centuries, this pattern became familiar for wider and wider sections of the population. Leaving school meant the beginning of work. This was the start of a phase of life quite different from childhood.

The introduction of universal compulsory education was hampered by two factors which mitigated against it, namely agricultural and industrial child-labour. The efforts of the civil authorities against child-labour were not only motivated by an interest in schooling. A fundamental change had taken place in the work expected of children as family businesses gave way to large industries. Although still in the care of their parents, children and young people were placed under enormous additional burdens, even in the relocated home industries which dominated the earliest phase of industrialization. Then, in the large factories, whose owners were not personally known to the children's families, they were quite at the mercy of exploitation. Only after long delays did the civil authorities take any remedial action. The first law to restrict child-labour came in Prussia in 1839.[108] This 'regulation of the

[106] Thus Arnold, *Kind und Gesellschaft*, p. 21. Accepted as a general starting point for entering service by P. Ariès, *Geschichte der Kindheit* (Munich, 1975), pp. 502ff. For a critique of this, see Mitterauer, 'Gesindedienst', pp. 179ff.

[107] Hanawalt, 'Childrearing', p. 19; H. Feilzer, *Jugend in der mittelalterlichen Ständegesellschaft* (Vienna, 1971), p. 196; N. Z. Davis, 'The reasons of misrule', in *Society and Culture in Modern France* (London, 1975), p. 113.

[108] M. Flecken, *Arbeiterkinder im 19. Jahrhundert* (Weinheim, 1981), pp. 90ff.

employment of young workers in factories' prescribed that children could not work regularly in a factory, mine or foundry until the age of nine. A precondition was documentation of three years' schooling or a certificate that the child 'can read its mother tongue fluently, and has made the first steps in writing'. For 9- to 16-year-olds, regular work should be only ten hours a day, with a maximum extension of one hour when necessary. They were not permitted to work night shift, or on Sundays or public holidays. An amendment of 1853 raised the age limit of the prohibition to 12. Work was limited to six hours a day until the age of 14. In 1871 this law was extended to the whole German empire, and in 1891 a further amendment forbade any employment of children within the age brackets of compulsory education. For young people between 14 and 16 daily work was limited to ten hours. In 1938 protection was extended to everyone under the age of 18, and the maximum number of hours was reduced to eight. Even if these various legal requirements did not by any means reflect the social reality, particularly in the nineteenth century, they do clearly show a movement towards two basic objectives: that no paid work at all should be done during the years of compulsory education, and that these should be followed by a period of regulated employment. Like other legal measures to protect young people or improve their conditions of work, these have contributed to the tendency to concentrate our concept of youth on this protected age-group.

The trend of recent decades has been that in practically all European countries the point of leaving school and beginning work has lost its significance as the lower threshold of youth, which it had for by far the largest part of the population at the beginning of the century. The principal reason for this is that more and more young people are opting for secondary and tertiary education. But even without this, the raising of the minimum school-leaving ages combined with the accelerated physical development make it impossible for us any longer to see the transition from school to work as the decisive lower threshold of youth.

In the middle of the span of youth, the completion of an apprenticeship continues to have an important role as a milestone in working life. In the twentieth century this increasingly applies also to girls. In former times, of course, apprenticeship in trade and commerce was almost exclusively for males. There were only a very few trades in which women practised independently and for which they were prepared by a legally regulated apprenticeship. Certainly female domestic and farm service involved training in the broadest sense, in the course of which skills were gained which one would later use as a housewife. There is also another sense in which we might speak of a housewife's 'apprenticeship'. Daughters who did not go into service often prepared for their future roles by short periods of practical experience outside the home. Most importantly in cooking and needlework there were special qualifications to be had. Verdier, in her study of a Burgundian village, has given us the phrase 'a winter with the seamstress' as a tag for this kind of training. She also demonstrates how this time away from home becomes a kind of 'initiation rite' for peasant girls at the beginning of their youth.[109]

Much of the literature takes leaving the parental home and entering service as the principle lower threshold of youth in bygone days. Thus Gillis, for example, says of pre-industrial society:

> What they commonly called 'youth' was a very long transition period, lasting from the point that the very young child first became somewhat independent of its family, usually about of seven or eight years, to the point of complete independence at marriage, ordinarily in the mid or late twenties . . . Beginning at what seems to us to be a very young age, children began to separate from their families and to go to live in other households . . . It was precisely this detachment from family which gave pre-industrial youth its peculiar structure and meaning.[110]

While this statement is quite correct in its assessment of the importance of domestic or farm service for the shaping of youth, it presents a widely held view of the threshold question which needs to be refined.[111]

In the first place it needs to be stressed that the age at which people entered service in traditional societies varied greatly.[112] It

---

[109] Verdier, *Drei Frauen*, pp. 172ff., 205ff., 216ff.
[110] Gillis, *Geschichte der Jugend*, p. 18.
[111] E.g., L. Rosenmayr, 'Jugend', in R. König (ed.), *Handbuch der empirischen Sozialforschung*, vol. 6 (Stuttgart, 1976), pp. 78ff., following Ariès.
[112] A. Kussmaul, *Servants in Husbandry in Early Modern England* (Cambridge, 1981), pp. 70ff., especially illustration, p. 72; R. Wall, 'The age of leaving home', *Journal of Family History*, 3 (1978), pp. 181ff.; Mitterauer, 'Gesindedienst', pp. 188ff.; 'Formen ländlicher Familienwirtschaft', pp. 292ff.

was very rare for children to leave the parental home at 7 or 8.[113] At the other extreme, there were young people who remained in their family of origin until they were over 20 and only then entered service. A threshold which occurs at such a wide range of ages cannot be generalized as marking the starting point of youth. The reasons for this wide variety of ages is to be found on several levels. The economic situation of the family and its need for additional labour was decisive for the question of when children could leave. Rural cottagers and urban day-labourers alike would be glad to have one less mouth to feed as soon as possible. Their labour was not required. It was no rarity to leave home at 10 or 12. Farmers with larger holdings, on the other hand, often found it was in their interests to keep their children at home for as long as possible as cheap labour, even those children for whom there was no inheritance, especially as provision of basic foodstuffs was no problem. An early departure was often brought about by a family crisis, for example being orphaned. On the other hand, family problems could result in a longer stay in the parental home, for example if a sick parent required help. Sometimes children who had left home returned. Leaving home to enter service was not an irreversible transition in status. All in all, the business of leaving home in ancient society was very much dependent on specific family circumstances, especially economic ones. These differing conditions explain the range of ages. It is important to note that the age at which one left home was highly significant in determining one's initial status in the new household. A 20-year-old entering farm service for the first time did not have to start as a stable boy; a 10-year-old, on the other hand, might first be given children's work. The youngest were practically foster children. So, while entering service could be the closing threshold of childhood, it could as easily be an intermediate threshold in youth. Certainly, it is possible to speak of a 'normal age' for entering service.[114] The graph of ages for entering service in agricultural areas usually

---

[113] What it actually meant to leave home young can be seen from some of the biographical records, e.g., M. Gremel, *Mit neun Jahren im Dienst. Mein Leben im Stübel und am Bauernhof 1900–1930* (Vienna, 1983). Cf. also appropriate passages in T. Weber (ed.), *Häuslerkindheit* (Vienna, 1984); T. Weber (ed.), *Mägde* (Vienna, 1985).

[114] On Confirmation as the 'normal age', see K. Tenfelde, 'Ländliches Gesinde in Preußen', *Archiv für Sozialgeschichte*, 19 (1979), p. 222.

reached a clear peak between 13 and 16, that is, immediately after
the age at which young people were expected to take on a full
work-load. However, the deviations from this 'normal age' are so
considerable that it is not possible to speak of a straightforward
connection between service and any particular stage of youth.

The attempt to define youth in pre-industrial times in terms of
entering service also misses the point that even in areas where
service was common there was never a time when the whole of
the younger generation followed this course. Among 20–24-year-
olds, the age group most heavily involved, the proportion was
hardly ever more than two-thirds. A quarter to a half was usual.
Many daughters and some sons only left home when they were
married. For children who were due to inherit, and were responsible
for the continuity of the family home, the question did not arise.
For those who did leave home there were other possible lifestyles,
for example as lodgers or tenants in the city. It must also be remembered that even under the European marriage pattern there
were large areas where domestic and farm service was completely
unknown. This is true of some areas where the rules of inheritance
involved equal sharing, or in areas characterized by wine production or cottage industry.[115] In regions where the 'joint family'
system predominates, there is no such thing as domestic service.
There, the ideal typical situation is that daughters leave home to
be married, while sons do not leave home at all.

The end of the nineteenth and the beginning of the twentieth
century saw the dissolution of domestic service, and the disappearance of this threshold which had been so important in old
European society. In its place came the practice of living at home
but working outside it. Consequently, leaving home came to be
connected increasingly with marriage and with the upper threshold
of youth. The slackening of the link between marriage and setting
up home, brought about by young people choosing to live alone,
is a product of the most recent times.

For a small number of young people in old European society,
leaving home meant entering not service but further education. In
contrast to the local schools which taught writing and counting
in the vernacular, the grammar schools, which had their origins in
religious communities and which taught in Latin, were frequently

---

[115] Mitterauer, 'Formen ländlicher Familienwirtschaft', pp. 229ff.

boarding schools. But even with day-schools, school attendance often meant living away from home, and thus separation from family. The age at which one left home to go to school often varied just as much as the age for entering service. Ariès made a major contribution to our knowledge by calculating that in the grammar schools of the medieval and early modern periods, pupils of very different ages sat alongside one another.[116] The age range at matriculation was correspondingly wide. In the first class of the Jesuit college at Chalôns in 1618–20 there were pupils aged from 8 to 18; at the oratory at Troyes in 1638–9 from 9 to 24; and in the Jesuit college at Caën in 1677 and 1692 from 9 to 17. Not until the eighteenth and early nineteenth centuries were the age groups standardized. As with entering service, there was a normal age for going away to school, despite the wide variation. In the schools mentioned, the most common age for pupils in the first class was 12. Obviously, people did not allow their children to leave home for school significantly earlier than for an apprenticeship or for domestic service. If the move to an advanced school did take place a little earlier, it must be remembered that studying, unlike working, did not require physical strength.

As long as pupils had to go to boarding school, or at least to go and live near the school, pursuing further education involved a radical change in lifestyle. The general move towards day-schools, the increasing number of secondary school and improved transportation networks have together had the effect that most school pupils now live with their families. The threshold of beginning secondary school has therefore become less important. Nowadays, young people are more likely to leave home when they begin university. The degree to which the two thresholds meant a significant new start in life is to be seen in the level of ritualization which was connected with them in traditional society.[117]

Thresholds of youth which arise from the completion of successive courses of study at institutions which are attended one after the other can be traced back historically little more than 200 years. The medieval and early modern periods did not have a school system structured in stages. The various upper and lower schools did not relate to one another and did not represent different

---

[116] Ariès, *Geschichte der Kindheit*, pp. 285ff.; for the data cited, see pp. 324ff.
[117] Ibid., pp. 349ff.; Van Gennep, *Manuel de Folklore*, pp. 233ff.

stages of learning. Courses of study with a planned syllabus as we know them today did not exist. It was possible to matriculate at a university without ever having gone to school. What previous knowledge was necessary could be gained from one of the many private tutors. This situation only changed with the establishment of a state-run school system. In the various countries of Europe, the process of bringing order into the school system took place in quite different ways and at quite different times.

It was in Prussia that the transition from secondary school to university, now a very important threshold of youth, was first regulated by law. In 1788 the *Abitur* was instituted, a combined school-leaving certificate and university entrance qualification.[118] At first, only those who were applying for grants required the certificate, but in time it took on the status of an entrance examination. In 1812 the list of schools to have the status of authorized secondary schools was drawn up. Of around 500 grammar schools which had existed in the mid-eighteenth century, only 91 remained as recognized preliminaries to university. For those young people who foresaw an academic career, passing the leaving exam from one of these schools became the decisive educational threshold. It is no coincidence that this exam has come to be known in Germany as the *Reifeprüfung*, in Austria as the *Matura*, in Switzerland as the *Maturität*. It developed into a kind of 'initiation rite' for the educated middle class.

The growth of state education since the end of the eighteenth century has brought a standardization of the internal structure of secondary schools. A division into 'grades' or 'years' which had to be taken in a particular order had existed since the sixteenth century in the grammar schools, high schools, public schools and the like, but the number of grades and the content of each varied greatly from school to school. The idea that each year-group should represent a particular age-group filtered through very slowly. In the early nineteenth century there were still classes containing a range of different ages. Not until the establishment of state education were regulations introduced to make syllabuses uniform and to

[118] F. Blättner, *Das Gymnasium* (Heidelberg, 1960), p. 191; R. Meyer, 'Das Berechtigungswesen in seiner Bedeutung für Schule und Gesellschaft im 19. Jahrhundert', in U. Herrmann (ed.), *Schule und Gesellschaft im 19. Jahrhundert* (1977), pp. 376ff.; P. Lundgreen, *Sozialgeschichte der deutschen Schule im Überblick*, vol. i (Göttingen, 1980), pp. 66ff.

define age boundaries, thus producing an education process with a universally valid series of stages, each of which was bound to a particular year of life. This principle of school year-groups has become the norm for life in the upper school.

This structuring of youth in terms of educational thresholds was relevant only for a tiny proportion of the population in the nineteenth century, and indeed well into the twentieth. The spread of education, however, particularly in the last few decades, has enormously increased the circle of those affected. In 1921 the proportion of young Germans in the 16–19 age group who were still at school was only 1.82 per cent. By 1937 this had increased to 3.48 per cent, by 1956 to 5.48 per cent, and then a period of rapid growth culminated in the 1975 figure of 16.92 per cent.[119] In other industrial countries in Europe the growth in senior schooling has affected even larger numbers of young people. In terms of the overall proportion of 18-year-olds attending school in 1970, West Germany's 15.7 per cent was bottom of the league of Western European countries. At the head of the table at that time were the Scandinavian states: Norway with 46.5 per cent, Sweden with 40.8 per cent and Finland with 35.2 per cent. In Belgium, too, more than a third of all 18-year-olds were still at school.[120] These figures, of course, include other educational institutions besides secondary schools.

The twentieth century had seen a similarly spectacular rise in the numbers of students. The figures for 20–24-year-olds in Germany were: 1900 0.89 per cent, 1930 1.96 per cent, 1950 4.39 per cent, 1960 6.3 per cent, 1970 13.53 per cent, and 1978 25.46 per cent.[121] The same striking growth has been seen in most other European nations in the last 20 to 30 years. In 1960 there was hardly one of these countries where fewer than 10 per cent of all 20–24-year-olds were students. In 1978 the figure in many countries was more than 25 per cent. Top of the league was Sweden with more than 35 per cent.[122]

Some of the most fundamental changes brought about by the

---

[119] Lundgreen, *Sozialgeschichte*, vol. II, p. 119.

[120] K. R. Allerbeck and L. Rosenmayr, *Einführung in die Jugendsoziologie* (Heidelberg, 1976), p. 117.

[121] H. Kaelble, *Soziale Mobilität und Chancengleichheit im 19. und 20. Jahrhundert* (Göttingen, 1983), p. 200.

[122] Ibid.

spread of education have been in the area of further education for
girls. In 1921 only 0.7 per cent of German girls in the 16–19 year
bracket were in the upper school. Even in 1956 the proportion
was only 3.8 per cent, but by 1975 it had risen to 16.2 per cent,
almost on a par with the male figure of 17.6 per cent.[123] For 19–
22-year-olds, only 1 per cent of German girls were students before
the First world War, and this rose by less than 1 per cent between
the wars. Even in 1955 only 0.8 per cent of girls in this age group
were studying, but this had already risen to 5.9 per cent by 1975.[124]
In Austria in 1984 the number of females matriculating at university had outstripped the number of males.[125] We may say, then,
that until well into the twentieth century the thresholds of upper
secondary and of tertiary education carried weight only for young
men. Today, however, hardly any gender-specific distinctions
remain. The turning-points of a traditionally male biography of
youth now increasingly play an equal role for young people of
both sexes.

The development of the upper school has had the effect of
linking childhood and youth more closely together than was
previously the case. For pupils in the upper school there is no
clear-cut threshold between the two phases of life. The change of
environment which used to be such a significant feature of attending secondary education has disappeared in more recent times.
The concept of childhood as a protected time of life has now been
extended to cover almost the whole of the young person's second
decade. In every way the spread of education has bound childhood
and youth more closely together. Compulsory education has been
lengthened, professional training is partly or wholly carried out in
the schools. Puberty with all its social ramifications now occurs for
all young people during their school years. More and more of
them are released for increasing lengths of time from the need to
do paid work. Starting work no longer marks the beginning of
youth but can come instead at quite a number of different points
in its course. For many, work means that youth has come to an
end. Schooling in its various forms has become the single factor
which determines more than any other the shape of youth.

The decisive upper threshold of youth in old European society

[123] Lundgreen, *Sozialgeschichte*, vol. II, p. 119.
[124] Ibid., p. 150.
[125] *Express Nr.*, 78, February 1985.

was always marriage, the most important transition in life. It is not by chance that even today a person's 'status' is either 'single' or 'married'. The importance of this threshold historically is easy to see. All historical terms for young people exclude those who are married, irrespective of age. The vocabulary for married women and men is quite precisely distinguished from these. A reliable index of social status in the old European world was clothing. In traditional costume we find striking differences between that worn by single and by married people. Usually these differences are greater for women than for men. The most important sign of the status gap between girl and married woman is the bonnet concealing the hair which in youth was left long and uncovered.[126] 'Bonnetting' was often a central component of the wedding ritual. In some European languages, the phrase 'to come under the hood' is still used as a synonym for getting married, while in English, if a woman 'sets her cap' at a man it means she sets out to win him as a husband. Clothing and headwear are an expression of a person's identity, and point to the change of identity which takes place at marriage. Only with marriage has a person achieved his or her purpose in life. Youth, by contrast, is a status of incompleteness. This is vividly seen in the custom, once wide-spread in Eastern Europe, known as the 'marriage of the dead'.[127] If an unmarried man passed away the body would be laid out in wedding clothes. A 'white' and a 'black' bride would follow the coffin to the graveside. Analogous customs were to be found, though less frequently, for girls. In this way the marriage which had been missed in life was symbolically celebrated. Only then was the conclusion of a fulfilled life conceivable.

If marriage is the principal upper threshold of youth, the prevailing social age requirements for marriage will be crucial for determining the span of youth. The average age at which men were married in European history was always about two or three years higher than that for women.[128] It is questionable whether we

[126] Bächtold-Stäubli, *Handwörterbuch des Auberglaubens*, vol. III, p. 1551; Möller, *Die Kleinburgerliche Familie*, p. 179. For Hungary: Balassa and Ortutay, *Ungarische Volkskunde*, pp. 346ff.; for Norway: C. Johannesen, 'Norwegisches Burschenbrauchtum', Dissertation, Vienna, 1967, MS, p. 45.
[127] Petrei, *Die Burschenschaften*, pp. 74ff.
[128] For an overview of the results of detailed local studies, see K. Gaskin, 'Age at first marriage in Europe before 1850; a summary of family reconstitution data', *Journal of Family History*, 3 (1978), pp. 23ff.

can conclude from this that youth lasted longer for men than for women, since there is no comparable universal lower threshold. Besides, it is questionable how meaningful such average age figures for marriage really are. It has already been mentioned that in the seventeenth and eighteenth centuries the mean variation for age at marriage was very wide. The reasons for this lie, on the one hand, in class-related differences in marriage opportunities, and on the other, in the restrictions of family circumstances. Young people who worked for a living generally had to marry later than sons or daughters who stood to inherit, for they and their future spouses had to save enough to be able to afford to set up home. This, of course, is to contrast an artificial pair of opposites, for in practice the financial basis of a marriage was usually a mixture of the two. Similarly, members of the poorer population groups had to wait longer for the opportunity to marry; this reflects the fact that the duration of youth in old European society generally was longer among the lower classes. We shall return to this point when we discuss the question of age dominance in the traditional youth organizations.

The effect of family circumstances on the age at which an individual could marry was strongest in agricultural communities, at any rate under the European marriage pattern. The age at which a heritable farmer's son could marry depended on when the estate was passed on to him.[129] He could inherit the property on his father's death, or it could be transferred to him by contract. The old farmer's state of health was a significant factor in the timing of this transaction. As long as he felt fit, he would be unlikely to agree to relinquish domestic authority. But of course the health of his wife and her willingness to surrender her position were also important factors. If she died, the old farmer would often see that as the right time to move out of the farmhouse into subsidiary accommodation on the farm. However, if he married again, the marriage prospects for the heir apparent would be pushed back a long way. In some areas, the second marriage of a widowed mother had the same effect. But the timing of the transfer did not only depend on the parents; the question of providing for the younger children was also important. By the time the heir was married, as many as possible of his brothers and sisters should have left home.

---

[129] H. Rosenbaum, *Formen der Familie* (Frankfurt, 1982), pp. 70ff.

And finally, the family circumstances of the bride were important. In some areas a girl was not allowed to marry until her older sisters were married. In considering all these factors, it also had to be ensured that the change in personnel resulting from the marriage would not leave the workforce on the farm in disarray. It goes without saying that under these complicated conditions we cannot speak of a 'normal age' for marriage in a peasant community. This would be possible, though with certain qualifications, for agricultural households under the 'joint family' system of East and South-east Europe, since marriage there did not mean becoming head of the home. However, the family system lying behind the European marriage pattern, at any rate in peasant communities, necessarily resulted in a wide variation in the age at which people were married.

The agricultural example which has just been sketched out cannot, however, be taken as valid for all types of family in old European society. In the urban trades, for example, family businesses were often not passed on to the next generation.[130] Neolocal patterns of founding families, as opposed to patrilocal or uxorilocal residential patterns, seem to have been predominant since the Middle Ages.[131] This means that the stage at which a young master-tradesman could be married depended on acceptance by the guild and on his ability to finance a household but not on the circumstances of the family from which he came. Likewise, in the rural cottage industries it was economic factors and not inheritance which determined how soon one could marry, despite the fact that business was structured on a family basis. With the move to individual paid work, the transfer of means of production within the family ceased altogether to be a determinant for the marriage option.[132] It can be demonstrated that in England as early as the seventeenth and eighteenth centuries there was a clear correlation between the level of real wages and the age at which people were married.[133] This provides a very early hint at a trend which would

---

[130] M. Mitterauer, 'Zur familienbetrieblichen Struktur im zünftischen Handwerk', in *Grundtypen alteuropäischer Sozialformen* (Stuttgart, 1979), pp. 98ff.

[131] M. Mitterauer, 'Familie und Arbeitsorganisation in städtischen Gesellschaften des späten Mittelalters und der frühen Neuzeit', in A. Haverkamp (ed.), *Haus und Familie in der spätmittelalterlichen Stadt* (Cologne, 1984), pp. 25ff.

[132] Rosenbaum, *Formen der Familie*, pp. 216ff.

[133] E. A. Wrigley and R. Schofield, *The Population History of England* (London, 1981), p. 267.

become more important as industrialization proceeded. Opportunities to marry were increasingly dependent on the state of the economy and of the labour market. The factors determining the age at which young people get married have thus moved out of the family and into the wider network of society.

In the upper classes of society the factors influencing marriage ages are in many respects quite different. One in particular is worth pursuing. Among the nobility it is noticeable from about the seventeenth century onwards that younger sons heading for careers in civil service married much later than their heritable older brothers.[134] They had to complete a lengthy period of training, then wait for a position which would keep them in a manner befitting their social standing. A similar situation existed in the educated middle class. Here too, marriage was left relatively late, at least for men.[135] With the increase in academic careers and academic education this pattern gained in importance. This was also significant for the development of middle-class concepts of what is the norm. The married student of the present day clearly represents a radical break with this tradition.

If we see marriage as the definitive upper threshold of youth, this raises the question of what we should make of those who remained single all their lives. Do they remain 'young' till their dying day? Historical sources allow quite different interpretations of this. On gravestones in old country church yards it is still possible to read of 'youths' (*Jüngling, Jungfrau*) who died at 60 or 70.[136] Classification by marital status was obviously taken for granted by the community. On the other hand, some of the fraternities had upper age-limits for the participation of single men in group activities.[137] The community life of young people therefore admits the possibility of other contemporary classifications.

The problem of classification arises in a different way in the

---

[134] H. Reif, *Westfälischer Adel 1770–1860* (Göttingen, 1979), pp. 233ff.; M. Mitterauer, 'Zur Frage des Heiratsverhaltens im österreichischen Adel', in H. Fichtenau and E. Zöllner (eds), *Beiträge zur neueren Geschichte Österreichs* (Vienna, 1974), p. 179.

[135] Rosenbaum, *Formen der Familie*, p. 331.

[136] M. Rassem, 'Entdeckung und Formierung der Jugend in der Neuzeit', in *Jugend in der Gesellschaft* (Munich, 1975), p. 99.

[137] A. Lutz, *Jünglings- und Gesellenverbände im alten Zürich und im alten Winterthur* (Zürich, 1957), p. 14; for exceptions, see Van Gennep, *Manuel de Folklore*, p. 206.

case of girls who, as single women, brought a child into the world. In many areas, unmarried mothers were excluded from youth activities. They could not, however, join up with the married women, since in terms of domestic status they were still dependents. Nothing changed in their situation at work either. Unless they still lived with their parents, they were generally not permitted to keep the child with them,[138] so that they did not in fact play the adult role of a mother.

For women generally, it is significant how far becoming a mother marked the end of youth in terms of their actual way of life. For paid employees, motherhood frequently meant giving up work, and therefore income, outside the home. This can be seen from the earliest phases of industrialization.[139] Motherhood was therefore an important threshold in working life. Even today, the birth of the first child means a fundamental readjustment of leisure activities for both parents. Many aspects of youthful activity cannot be continued beyond this point.[140] There are occasional historical references to indicate that young married people without children still continued to participate in the group activities of youth, and were therefore in a kind of intermediate position. In France, these references go back to the late Middle Ages.[141] A different situation arises when young married people are not recognized as full women or men until the birth of their first child, sometimes of their first son. This is found in traditional societies which have a very distinct concept of the importance of fertility, as in the Balkans.[142] In some regions, then, adult status is only achieved through parenthood.

In contrast to the overwhelming importance which marriage had as a great life-event in old European society, it has certainly declined in importance in more recent times. The most important

[138] Mitterauer, *Familienform*, pp. 154, 159, 161ff.

[139] L. A. Tilly and J. W. Scott, *Women, Work and Family* (New York, 1978), p. 126.

[140] E. K. Scheuch, 'Soziologie der Freizeit', in R. König (ed.), *Handbuch der empirischen Sozialforschung*, 2nd edn, vol. 11 (Stuttgart, 1977), p. 62.

[141] M. Grinberg, 'Charivaris au Moyen-Age et à la Renaissance', in J. LeGoff and J. C. Schmitt (eds), *Le Charivari* (Paris, 1981), p. 145; Van Gennep, *Manuel de Folklore*, p. 204.

[142] J. Halpern, *A Serbian Village* (New York, 1956), p. 200; J. Halpern and R. A. Wagner, 'Time and social structure: a Yugoslave case study', *Journal of Family History*, 9 (1984), p. 238. Cf. also K. E. Müller, *Die bessere und die schlechtere Hälfte* (Frankfurt, 1984), pp. 182ff.

single factor here has been the transition from the family economy
to the system of individual paid labour, a process which reaches
back into the Middle Ages, but has been accelerated by industrialization and the growth in bureaucracy. In the family economy,
at any rate under the European marriage pattern, the boundary
between single and married was also the boundary between dependence and authority. For paid employees, white collar workers
and civil servants this is no longer the case. Their status in working life is unaffected by marriage. Consequently, the position of
head of the home is less important, and it too is now increasingly
being separated from marriage. For the man, the domestic authority gained through marriage was often connected with political
rights in the local community or in other forms of public life. With
the demise of the family economy this connection disappears. All
in all, marriage has been 'privatized', its importance being restricted
to the family in the modern sense of the word. All the political and
professional thresholds which used to be linked with marriage
have taken on a life of their own and need no longer coincide
with it. Of the developments of most recent times, the most important factor leading to the decline of marriage as the upper threshold
of youth has been the fact that married people no longer have a
monopoly on legitimate sexual activity. Sex before marriage is no
longer the forbidden exception, and public concepts of what is
permissible are increasingly coming into line with this social reality.
What would in traditional society have been one of the most
important differences between the time before and after the wedding is now disappearing from the picture.

Not only has marriage lost its importance as a decisive threshold
but it has also declined in its influence on the preceding period.
In a society in which, with the exception of priests and religious
orders, a fulfilled life necessarily involved marriage, it was inevit-
able that youth would be shaped by the need to prepare for this
goal. For young women this orientation of youth would probably
have been stronger than for young men. Their future status as
married women would very much depend on which partner they
found. In the present day there is no longer any comparable social
pressure to seek fulfilment in marriage. This has certainly taken a
great deal of the strain out of youth.

If we compare the traditional thresholds of youth with current
ones, a number of general trends appear which are of importance

for the historical development of youth. One trend could be described as a de-ritualizing of status transitions. While comprehensive initiation rites, in so far as they ever existed, disappeared from European society at a very early stage, various milieux did continue to celebrate thresholds in a ritual manner, as for example with the consecration of knights, the elevation of journeymen, various rites connected with starting work, and admission to youth organizations. The clearest instance of a hankering after ritual in old European society is probably the development of Lutheran Confirmation. In the course of time, almost all ritual transitions have disappeared. In the catalogue of today's formative thresholds of youth which was compiled from the results of the 1981 survey, there is not one of this type. The closest which remain are school-leaving exams and marriage, and as we have seen, marriage is not as formative as it once was. The result of this de-ritualization has been that thresholds are no longer as abrupt or as symbolic as they were. The transitions are fluid. Neither for the community nor for the individual concerned are they as easily comprehensible as in former times.

The tendency to distinguish a multiplicity of part-thresholds began early in European history with the distancing of religious and secular transitions. From there, the development can be traced both as a continued separating-out of various spheres of life and as an increasing division of each sphere into a series of stages. This process of differentiation is seen especially in the regulations governing legal majority. It is less-easily traced in the realm of the realization of personal autonomy. The list produced from the 1981 results identified a number of part-thresholds which are very important in this respect. The result of the differentiation process has been that youth has become a phase of life which is not defined by fixed starting- and finishing-points but which instead consists of a plethora of successive and overlapping partial transitions. This may be regarded as a characteristic feature of modern youth.

The earlier and more comprehensive autonomy of today's young people allows us to speak of a tendency towards greater self-determination. In place of a period of virtually static domestic subservience, a process has emerged whereby parents grant responsibility to young people in a series of stages. Whereas in historical times personal self-determination only came with material independence from parents, it is now achieved much earlier.

In scholarly writing, this phase of 'majority without economic means'[143] is often referred to as 'post-adolescence', and treated as a separate phase of life.[144] However, given that young people even in this phase are still involved in youth organizations and youth culture, this division is of no great importance for the realities of social life. It also seems questionable to attempt to define when this point is reached, unless we work on the basis of outward facts, such as leaving home. The ambivalence of our concept of youth, with its twin roots, domestic dependence and the development of an autonomous personality, is once again to be seen in this problem.

Some of the older youth thresholds were strongly dependent on family circumstances and were scattered over a range of different possible ages. In the case of marriage, this has been discussed in detail, but the same is also true of entering service or beginning school. The general historical trend has been for such family circumstances to become less important than wider social factors. It has already been mentioned how macro-economic factors influence the age at which people are married, how this influences society's concept of the 'normal age' for getting married, and how this concept in turn exerts a social pressure which standardizes the ages at which people are actually married. A fixed age-threshold for the whole of society arises when the state enforces this 'normal age' by law. When in the eighteenth century laws were introduced decreeing that entitlement to conduct business independently would be achieved not on leaving home but on reaching an age of majority, this was just such a move away from a threshold which had formerly depended on family circumstances. One threshold defined by the state which did not have a historical predecessor in the family is military service. The most important fixed age-thresholds to be imposed by government were those of the schooling laws. We are thinking here not only of the introduction of compulsory education but of the whole concept of a school system hierarchically divided into age bands. The spread of higher education has meant that in recent years the thresholds of non-compulsory education has become important for an increasing proportion of the population. School life has been the strongest

[143] Gillis, *Geschichte der Jugend*, p. 206.
[144] E.g., *Jugend '81*, pp. 100ff.

contributor to the trend which we might describe as a chronologizing of youth.

To a great extent, traditional thresholds of youth were limited in their importance to particular milieux. The granting of arms was of significance only to the nobility and to armed peasantry. The elevation of a journeyman in trade had no counterpart on the farm. Only religious rites of passage had universal validity. More recent developments have brought a trend towards harmonization. Milieu-specific peculiarities have been marginalized, while thresholds valid for the whole of society have become more central. This again is particularly true in education. This kind of trend towards harmonization does not mean that youth is a phenomenon which is independent of rank or class. When compared to the milieu-specific and regional variants of the past, however, it has certainly become more unified. Today it is perfectly possible to speak of stages which have general validity in the typical biography of a young person, as has been done with the results of the 1981 survey. Class-related differences tend to lie not in the stages which are observed but in the age at which these are reached.

Our analysis of traditional thresholds of youth has shown that many of them were applicable only to young men. This was particularly true of thresholds which had their historical roots in the granting of arms. Like these traditional thresholds, the concepts of youth which are based on them are primarily male in orientation. Male and female youth were so different that until the end of the nineteenth century the concepts relating to the age-group were entirely gender-specific. Only then did a sexually inclusive collective concept of youth emerge. But even so, the turning points of the biography of youth continued to be very different for the two sexes. The trend away from such distinctions, which we have observed repeatedly, is the result of very recent developments. This drawing together of thresholds which were previously strongly differentiated according to gender is certainly one of the most revolutionary changes in the social history of youth.

3
Interacting with the World

Our discussion of the threshold problem has shown that youth as a social phenomenon cannot be measured according to age, but rather is dependent on a person's position within various groupings. Of these different forms of community which determine the social status of young people, the most important is the family. The family is the primary group in which people spend the childhood period which precedes youth. The gradual winning of greater independence within the family, leading ultimately to the breaking of parental ties, marks significant stages in the biography of youth. Marriage, the most important status transition in family life, has been seen to be historically the definitive upper threshold of youth. As a preparation for adult life, the school is a social form which even in childhood played a central role. The growth of schooling in recent times has meant that for more and more people this social grouping has been increasingly influential in the shaping of their youth. For this reason work has receded as a formative influence. Nevertheless, it remains one of the major tasks of youth to find one's feet in the professional sphere, or at least to prepare for this. The fourth level of community which determines the boundaries of youth is the youth group, which has an initiatory function at the beginning of adolescence and which often has to be left at marriage. Other more-comprehensive social forms have also proved significant for the fixing of the historical thresholds, such as regional or municipal community structures, or different levels of becoming or being a citizen. When these wider forms of community decreed the age of majority, or made schooling compulsory, or enacted laws to protect young people in the work place, these were cases of the outside world reaching in and imposing rules which altered the position of adolescents in their primary groups, family, school and work group. Young people do not participate in these higher forms of public life as they do in the primary groups. They are excluded from them, for these are adult social forms. Certainly, wider society has its influence on the pattern of youth in so far as young people are preparing for adult roles. It is not, however, the young person's primary sphere of activity.

A historical study of those social forms in which youth is played out can therefore restrict itself to the four basic types: family, workplace, school and youth group. Thinking of social interaction with adults, we can make a distinction. In the family, the workplace and the school, young people are living together with adults and their activities are to a great extent conditioned by them. These, then, are mixed-age groups. School is included in this category, for although young people are numerically in the majority in the schools, they are far from autonomous in the way they arrange their affairs. However, in the second type of social form, which we shall refer to as single-age groups, we are dealing with the auto- nomous community life of young people. Not all the groupings in this category are exclusively shaped by young people. For example, the organizations which arose out of so-called 'youth welfare' work show strong elements of a social regime. Nevertheless, these are part of the same historical continuum as autonomous single-age groups and must be studied along with them, just as experiments with democratic or pupil-centred schooling belong with the tradi- tional, more-authoritarian pattern of education in the social form 'school'.

I. The Family

In so far as young people today live in a family unit, there is no question of any other role for them than that of daughter or son. Family life for present-day youngsters means life in the family of origin. In the past the matter was not nearly so simple. There were many young people who certainly lived in a family but did not live with their natural parents. As alternative family roles we are thinking in the first instance of domestic or farm service, but also of living with relatives, living as foster children, or taking board and lodgings, in so far as this last arrangement can be described as a family. Children living with their parents were sometimes in the minority. In a random sample survey of Central European cities in the eighteenth and nineteenth centuries, 53 per cent of all 15–19-year-olds were living at home, but only 34 per cent of 20–24-year-olds.[1] These circumstances are, of course, only to be found in countries typified by the European marriage pattern, and even here only in regions and milieux where there was a tradition of entering service. In Eastern Europe and around the Mediterranean it was the custom in the past for children to remain in their own families, just as they do today.

In European history, not only did young people themselves have different positions in their family units than they do today, they also lived with people who today would no longer have a close relationship with them; and in combinations of ages which differ in many respects from those of the present day. Here again we are thinking first of all of servants and farm-hands, but beyond that of the many other types of non-related cohabitation, as well as of living with relatives, which would not be usual today.[2] More-recent history has seen a standardization of the family in the form of the parent–child unit.[3] For the social relationships of young people within their families in the past we must reckon with a far greater variety of family structures. In view of the great importance which must be attached to unrelated persons, it may be helpful to use the terms 'domestic group' or 'household community' instead of family, without, of course, placing in question the familial nature of the cohabitation. In doing so, it would also be useful for the present to include in our discussion those situations in which young people are living in a household to which they have no relationship either by blood or by marriage. These too can display all the features of a family in the widest sense.

Whether young people remained in the parental home, and for how long, varied, as we have said, between social milieux, and depended on numerous factors. The most important were

[1] On this survey, cf. Chapter 2, n. 105.

[2] On types of family roles, and the family typologies which result, see M. Mitterauer, 'Auswirkungen von Urbanisierung und Frühindustrialisierung auf die Familienverfassung an Beispielen des österreichischen Raumes', in W. Conze (ed.), *Sozialgeschichte der Familie in der Neuzeit Europas* (Stuttgart, 1976), pp. 53ff.; M. Mitterauer, 'Familiengrößen – Familientypen – Familienzyklus', *Geschichte und Gesellschaft*, 1 (1975), pp. 226ff.; M. Mitterauer, 'Faktoren des Wandels historischer Familienformen', in H. Pross (ed.), *Familie wohin?* (Reinbek, 1979), pp. 83ff.

[3] H. Rosenbaum, *Formen der Familie* (Frankfurt, 1982), pp. 176ff.

inheritance, labour requirements, ease of provision, need for additional income and educational expectations. Where a house was to be passed on as the basis of subsistence for a family, every effort was made to keep the inheriting child, usually a son, at home until the parents either died or surrendered the house to him. That was true for nobles, for merchants, for skilled workers if they owned a house or had sufficient means of production which could be passed on; it was true for peasant-farmers, and to some extent it was also true for cottagers. Among nobles, merchants and tradesmen with heritable businesses, the inheriting son often had to leave home for a time to be trained for his future tasks, and this often meant entering another domestic group. Leaving home was one of the reversible status transitions of youth. In the case of heritable farmers' sons, such a temporary departure hardly ever happened. In so far as cottagers were ever able to pass on their homes to their children, the family's limited resources usually meant that the future heir could not afford to stay at home and await his inheritance. In all social milieux, the heir of the family had to leave home if the inheritance did not include either a house or a family business. This was typical for both rural and urban day-labourers, for other pre-industrial paid workers, and for a large pro-portion of urban tradesmen. It has already been mentioned that in the trade guilds a simple father–son progression was not common.[4]

The need for extra labour was, particularly in larger peasant families, a factor which tended to keep both daughters and sons in the parental home for longer. Working with one's own children was always cheaper than hiring help. Especially in times of labour shortages, farm children remained at home. In family businesses, labour requirements could have quite different effects. If a family ran an inn, good use could be made of a daughter. The same was sometimes true if the family produced textiles.[5] Generally, how-ever, most skilled labour did not lend itself to the inclusion of the children. Nor was it at all usual for the sons of tradesmen to serve their apprenticeship under their fathers.[6] For the bulk of poorer

[4] Cf. M. Mitterauer, 'Zur familienbetrieblichen Struktur im zünftischen Handwerk', in *Grundtypen alteuropäischer Sozialformen* (Stuttgart, 1979), pp. 98ff.

[5] L. A. Tilly and J. W. Scott, *Women, Work and Family* (New York, 1978), pp. 33ff.

[6] Mitterauer, 'Zur familienbetrieblichen Struktur', p. 117. For England, A. Yarbrough, 'Apprentices as adolescents in 16th century Bristol', *Journal of Social History*, 13 (1979), p. 68.

tradesmen, financial considerations alone made it impossible for adolescent daughters and sons to remain at home.

How long daughters and sons could remain at home depended on how easily the family could provide for them, and this meant a gap between rich and poor. It was an issue for girls particularly. The daughters of wealthier families could remain at home until they married, even if their labour was not required. For them, going into service would have meant a drop in prestige which would have affected their chances of getting married. Daughters of poorer families, on the other hand, had to seek posts as soon as they were physically able.

The phenomenon of adolescent children from poorer families remaining longer in the parental home only really surfaces with the beginning of industrialization, encouraged by the growth of individual paid labour. The more children who were earning, the easier it was for the family to survive. The family now had a financial interest in keeping their youngsters' income as long as possible. This system of collective subsistence is referred to as a family wage economy.[7] If we compare the family wage economy with the earlier family economy we must bear in mind that, whereas the older system was a particular form of structuring work, the new system has more to do with balancing the family budget. Of course, the family wage economy presupposes the decline of the family economy. This method of maintaining the family on the basis of an accumulation of individual incomes is found not only among the early industrial workforce but also in families whose children were salaried, and even among lower civil servants. It in turn declined when the wages of the parents, generally of the father, reached a level where the family was no longer reliant on the income of the children. This system played a very significant part in bringing young people back into the family during the industrial revolution.

Education had a mixed effect on the integration of young people into the family. So long as training meant serving in another household, it took them away from the parental home. This applied not only to the apprenticeship and journeyman years in skilled trades but also to the parallel structures in commerce, and to a certain extent even for the nobility who might serve as squires

[7] Tilly and Scott, *Women, Work and Family*, pp. 15, 104ff.

in other noble families or as attendants at court, or who in more recent times might make the 'grand tour' or attend upper schools which were modelled on religious orders. On the other hand, the newer pattern of education in day-schools, in which it is possible for pupils to live at home, has had the opposite effect of rooting young people in their families of origin. The model of the educated bourgeois family with its extended phase of academic training, in which the children continue to live with their parents throughout their school career, has become the norm at all levels of society.

The process of integrating young people more permanently into their parental families, which was at its most intensive in the last decades of the nineteenth century and the early decades of the twentieth, was brought about not only by these factors but by a whole series of others. A very important point is the disappearance of all the forms of household ties which originated in residential service. This trend can be seen in the fact that since the end of the nineteenth century fewer and fewer apprentices have lived with their master-craftsmen, more and more with their parents.[8] For girls, the disappearance of domestic servants and the rise of the new possibilities for factory or office work have tended in the same direction. A further factor is to be found in the demographic transition. Birth rates dropped, and as families became smaller it became easier to keep children and teenagers in the home. Here again, the turn of the century was a decisive period. And finally, an improvement in housing has certainly also contributed.

This tendency for young people to stay at home longer has certainly passed its peak. In 1981, 71 per cent of all West Germans in the age bracket 15–24 were living with their parents, as opposed to 88 per cent in 1953.[9] This drop is only partly explained by the fact that young people are now starting their own families earlier. In the same years, the percentage of this age group who are married has only risen from 6 per cent to 11 per cent, while the percentage living alone or with other young people has risen from 6 per cent to 18 per cent. The last decades, then, have seen a significant change in the domestic patterns of young people.

[8] In Vienna around 1913, apprentices living with their parents were already in the majority: 50.8 per cent, as opposed to 41.7 per cent living with the master craftsman. See G. Schultes, *Der Reichsbund der katholischen deutschen Jugend Österreichs* (Vienna, 1967), p. 48.

[9] *Jugend '81* (Opladen, 1982), pp. 326ff.

Whether young people lived with their parents depended, of course, not only on whether they were able to stay at home but also on whether the parents were still alive. Today it is not at all unusual for elderly people to see their grandchildren married. A century or two ago it was not always expected that even parents would see the weddings of their children. An analysis of family reconstitution data for the city of Trier between 1730 and 1860 has shown that in this period only 40–60 per cent of parents were still alive when their children were married.[10] The figures were higher in the eighteenth century than in the nineteenth. Class-related differences are striking. In the urban upper classes in the first half of the nineteenth century, 57 per cent of parents died before their children were married. For the lower classes the figure was 72 per cent. This difference can be explained both by the higher age at which working-class people were married and by their lower life-expectancy. The danger of being orphaned was therefore far greater for working-class children than for those in the middle and upper classes. For adolescents to be motherless, fatherless or parentless was not at all unusual in this social setting.[11] The great importance of guardians is to be understood against this demographic back-drop. They were very important figures in the lives of many young people in the past. Their influence extended even to decisions about career or marriage.

The frequent loss of parents meant that it was a common ex-perience for young people to have to live with step-parents. Re-marriage of widows or widowers was most common in agriculture and cottage industry where the proper running of business required a second person. Often the new partner was significantly younger. It was not uncommon for there to be only a minimal age differ-ence between the newcomer and the adolescent stepchild. There were even cases in which, through a second remarriage, 'children' came to be living with 'parents' but had no blood relationship with either of them.[12] All in all, the question of step-parents must

[10] T. Kohl, 'Familie und soziale Schichtung. Zur historischen Demographie Triers 1730–1860', Dissertation (Trier, 1983), MS, pp. 223ff. (Published Stuttgart, 1985.)

[11] M. Baulant, 'La Famille en miette: sur un aspect de la démographie du XVIIIe siècle', Annales, 277 (1972), pp. 959ff.

[12] M. Mitterauer, 'Zur Familienstruktur in ländlichen Gebieten Österreichs', in H. Helczmanovszki (ed.), Beiträge zur Bevölkerungs- und Sozialgeschichte Österreichs (Vienna, 1973), pp. 186ff., 174ff.

have been a source of particular tension in the lives of young people in past generations. Frequently it was this tension which caused them to leave home and enter service.

Another consequence of the loss of parents was that young people often lived with foster-parents. As a rule it was relatives or godparents ('spiritual relatives') who took in orphaned children. This explains why we so commonly read in the old population registers of young people as 'relations'. Adolescents' first entry into farm service was also frequently with relatives or godparents, particularly in the case of girls. This provided a good first step out of the parental home. In this form of family integration, orphaned children who were taken in by foster-parents differed little in status from other young people.

The problem of losing parents, with the consequent involvement of guardians, step-parents and foster-parents, is a particular dilemma of the family system associated with the European marriage pattern, in which the focus of the whole family was a single married couple. In more complex family forms the question does not arise with the same urgency. If a parent died before the children had grown up, aunts or uncles or even grandparents who were part of the same domestic group would simply take over responsibility for the children until they reached adulthood.

Since the middle of the nineteenth century, the problem of orphaned adolescents has become less severe even in the territory of the European marriage pattern. A number of demographic changes can be seen as reasons for this, particularly the increase in life-expectancy and the drop in marriage ages, which together resulted in a closing of the age gap between the generations.[13] The drop in the birth rate is also relevant here. Young children born late in their parents' marriage were most at risk. The 'demographic transition' has led to the smaller number of births being concentrated into the early years of marriage, with a consequent lessening of the average age difference between the generations. The reduced incidence of orphaned children has been a not-inconsiderable factor in the process of rooting adolescence in the nuclear family. In recent decades, however, a sharp rise in divorce rates has had the opposite effect, bringing a new dimension to the difficult question of adolescent–parent relationships.

[13] A. Imhof, *Die gewonnenen Jahre* (Munich, 1981), pp. 164ff.

The changes brought about by the demographic transition have affected not only the ways in which young people live with their parents but also how they relate to brothers and sisters. Dropping birth rates have meant an increase in the number of 'only children' who have no experience of sibling contact. Even in marriages producing more than one child, however, the situation has changed in that both the number of children and the age gap between them have become smaller. In historical times it was common for families to have large numbers of children with wider age differences. These differences were mostly the result of the many gaps left in families by the high mortality rate among infants and children. In some areas only every second child reached adolescence.[14] The high numbers of children are explained by the absence of adequate birth control. Mothers were often still bearing children in the last years before their menopause, especially in the country. Often there might also be step-brothers or step-sisters from a father's second marriage. And even after the last child in a generation had been born, the succession of siblings might be further extended by an older daughter's illegitimate child being brought up by its grandparents.[15] Especially in peasant households, in which older children remained long in the parental home, brothers and sisters with a wide range of ages often lived under the same roof.

With such a broad array of ages, it was possible for older children to take on functions and tasks in bringing up younger ones which would normally have been those of the parents' generation. It was especially common for an elder sister to take on the role of mother. The skills of the mother were often too valuable in the family business for her time to be given over entirely to child-rearing. This task was therefore delegated to an adolescent daughter who was not yet old enough for full adult work. Similar patterns were to be found when the mother went out to work. It was less common for older brothers to be placed in charge of small children: it was when parents died that a brother was likely to take on the paternal role.[16] When brothers and sisters filled the roles of parents, this could lead to close emotional relationships and a strong sense of trust. Certain duties towards younger sisters and

[14] Ibid., pp. 81ff.
[15] M. Mitterauer, 'Familienformen und Illegitimität in ländlichen Gebieten Österreichs', *Archiv für Socialgeschichte*, 19 (1979), pp. 165ff.
[16] Baulant, 'La Famille en miette', p. 967.

brothers often continued even after the adolescent had left the parental home. It frequently happened that those in service would find a place in the same household for younger members of their family.

Sibling relationships in historical times seem to have been much more strongly hierarchical than they are now. The two most important factors were age and sex. In some parts of the Balkans, older sisters were subject to the will of younger brothers.[17] The concept of male domination was here so strong that it even displaced the equally deep-rooted concept of seniority. Sisters were always regarded as being younger. To be taken to such an extreme is, of course, exceptional. The problem of superiority usually arose separately among the sisters and among the brothers. Problems arose, for example, when there was a custom that girls could not be married until all their older sisters had been married in the correct order. The hierarchy of siblings can be firmly undergirded by cultural traditions. This appears to be the case in the Balkans, for example. However, it can also have its basis more in the organization of work, as in agricultural areas where adolescents worked their way through the stages of service on their parents' farm.[18] It is questionable how far the child who stood to inherit the farm had a special position, even in youth. In areas where local custom made the youngest son the heir, the hierarchy would none the less have run according to labour, which would stress age as a criterion. When the eldest inherited, the two would coincide. In noble families, the first-born had a very marked position of superiority from adolescence onwards.

Differences between adolescent siblings which had nothing to do with their hierarchy arose from the behaviour of their parents. For example, in family businesses which required the co-operation of the children, the first children were generally drawn in far younger than those who were born later. Their involvement saved hiring labour, but this did not have the same urgency with subsequent children. Likewise, in the family wage economy it was the earnings of the eldest children which mattered most, as these would

[17] V. S. Erlich, *Family in Transition* (Princeton, 1966), pp. 128ff.; E. Schneeweiß, *Grundriß des Volksglaubens und des Volksbrauchs bei den Serbo-Kroaten* (Celje, 1935), p. 82.

[18] For an autobiographical testimony from South Tyrol, see Kreuztragen, *Drei Frauenleben* (Vienna, 1984), p. 35.

see the family through its financially most-difficult period.[19] As a result, younger children had better educational opportunities. While the eldest son had to begin earning right away, it was easier to afford to buy an apprenticeship for a younger son, or at least to allow him a longer period without an income. Here, of course, there was not only an age-related inequality but also a gender-related one. What a daughter contributed to the family budget often balanced the cost of educating a son.

Differing treatment by parents of their adolescent offspring in matters of work and training provided the material for a great deal of friction. The matters of inheritance and dowries must have placed a particular strain on sibling relationships, particularly in a heritable family business. It has already been seen how deeply all family members in the peasant milieu were affected by marriage and the handing over of the farm. Often, important opportunities for one child could only be grasped at the expense of another. In all milieux where a livelihood depended on the transfer of property from parents to children, the scene was set for conflict between the siblings throughout their youth. The transition to individual paid labour as the primary form of subsistence has lifted a great burden from these relationships.

Of course, being dependent on one another for a living may be a source of conflict but it can also lead to a strong sense of solidarity. There was a whole series of factors which made sibling relationships more intense in the past than they are today. Many of these have their origins in childhood. For example, we might point to children playing together, something which has declined in more-recent times, as even this has been influenced by the trend towards individualization.[20] In family economies, sharing work also led to an intensifying of relationships. Because of the way work was divided between the sexes, this promoted especially the relationships of sister to sister and of brother to brother. Even when the family was not the economic base, sisters had to co-operate in housework. The stronger ties which girls had to the home must have meant that sister relationships were especially intense. These ties existed not only in work but also in the use of free time. Whereas sons looked to the youth group for leisure

[19] J. Gillis, *Geschichte der Jugend* (Weinheim, 1980), p. 133.
[20] H. Hetzer and G. Morgenstern, *Kind und Jugendlicher auf dem Lande* (Lindau, 1952), p. 50.

activities, daughters relied much more on contacts in the home, the neighbourhood, and the wider circle of relatives.[21] There were, however, aspects of leisure activity which brothers and sisters had in common. In the first place, there were dances. Usually the eldest brother would be given the task of introducing the sisters to the youth scene, helping them to make contacts and protecting them. The brother as defender of his sister's honour is an ancient *leitmotif* in traditional societies.[22]

With the changing patterns of work and leisure and of received gender roles, relationships between brothers and sisters have lost much of their power to bind. This is not to say that they have lost their emotional quality, but certainly, the intensity of shared activity and the number of tasks to be undertaken together, which of necessity used to bind families together, have now receded markedly. The process of individualization has taken its toll on adolescent sibling relationships.

In many respects, the second most-important status of young people in families in traditional society, that of servant in a house or farm, differed very little from that of children in their own homes. The similarity was greatest in peasant households. The servants ate at the same table as the farmer's family. Daughters shared sleeping accommodation with maids, sons with farm-hands. The children of the home and the hired workers shared the same tasks and were under the authority of the farmer and his wife in the same way. The same obedience and sense of duty were required of both. Both were responsible to the parents of the home in matters of religion and morality, and parents had the same responsibilities to both, for example to ensure that they attended worship regularly and did not become involved sexually. In so far as the peasant communities had child-raising in our modern sense, both were raised in the same way. The master and mistress of the home even had the right to administer corporal punishment, at least up to a certain age. There was only one real difference: the servant received a wage in addition to board and lodgings, the children of the family did not. This made up for the fact that daughters and sons had a claim to dowries and inheritance. Occasionally, however, it happened that a maid was given a dowry

[21] See pp. 178ff.
[22] B. Schäfers, *Soziologie des Jugendalters* (Opladen, 1982), p. 65.

or a farm-hand remembered in a will. The extent to which farm
servants were integrated into the domestic group can be seen in
the fact that they were often referred to not by their own surname
but by the surname of the farmer or by the name of the farm. They
took their identity from the family in which they lived. This is
quite remarkable when we consider that they often remained for
only one or two years on the same farm.

The social equality of domestic servants and children of the
home which was to be found on the land was certainly not typical
of all milieux. Household servants were to be found at all levels
of society, right up to the royal courts. Certain parallels with the
arrangements in the farmhouse can none the less be observed,
since the two stem ultimately from the same concept of domestic
authority. Differences in the status of servants existed in the
multiplicity of households in which they served. This multiplicity
ranged far beyond the common basic types: the homes of peasants, tradesmen, merchants and nobles. Civil servants took clerical
assistants and secretaries into their homes. In the houses of priests
there were 'servers' who combined church work with education.
The student or young doctor who worked for a professor in return
for instruction was known as a '*famulus*', which is simply the Latin
word for servant. A similar arrangement was once known among
miners, although this was already rare by the late Middle Ages.
The list could easily be extended. It seems that the home community
was the basic working community in the early phases of European
social development. If anyone needed co-workers, he took them
as far as possible into his household. Likewise, learning was
generally done as part of service. Whoever wanted a professional
qualification entered the household of a 'master'.

How far back adolescent service goes in European history as a
constituent part of the family structure is a question which is still
open to research. We can certainly say that there was farm service
as early as the Carolingian period.[23] Following the Frankish
capitulary *de villis*, domestic service contributed to a balancing-
out of manpower between the central manorial courts and the
family farms which were dependent on them. It then spread into

[23] C. J. Hammer, 'Family and "familia" in early-medieval Bavaria', in R. Wall
et al. (eds), *Family Forms in Historic Europe* (Cambridge, 1983), p. 246; L.
Kuchenbuch, *Bäuerliche Gesellschaft und Klosterherrschaft im 9. Jahrhundert*
(Wiesbaden, 1978), pp. 78ff.

wide areas of Europe along with the manorial system of the Frankish empire.[24] This does not, of course, mean that it originally arose in this social context. Nor can it be asserted that the agricultural forms were the definitive roots of all other varieties. Service in noble families may be connected with the warrior entourages of the Germanic tribes.[25] Another possible origin is the tradition of fosterage which is known to be very ancient, particularly in the Celtic parts of Europe.[26] This was a foster-child relationship in which instruction was remunerated.

For more than a millenium, domestic service in its many variations dictated the family status of a large proportion of young people. In the course of the nineteenth and early twentieth centuries it declined and ultimately disappeared entirely. The beginnings of this process can be traced back to the Middle Ages. The following factors should be noted as having contributed. First of all, a general loosening or elimination of the institution occurred wherever it became necessary to organize work on a larger scale, making the organization of labour on a family basis impossible. In mining and construction work this happened in the medieval period,[27] but it only became a mass phenomenon with the Industrial Revolution. The collapse of the family organization of work began in commercial and industrial production, but quickly spread to administration and service industries. In this way, the three principle categories of paid employees emerged: blue- and white-collar workers and officials. Alongside the process of industrialization there was also the process of bureaucratization. And finally, there was a parallel process in agriculture, which led to larger scale organization of labour and a transition to individual paid labour.

Signs of the break-up of the institution of domestic service are also to be seen at the level of the individual family from a

[24] M. Mitterauer, 'Gesindedienst und Jugendphase im europäischen Vergleich', Geschichte und Gesellschaft, 11 (1985), esp. pp. 196ff.

[25] R. Wenskus, Stammesbildung und Verfassung, 2nd edn (Cologne, 1977), pp. 346ff.

[26] F. Kerlouegan, 'Essai sur la mise en nourriture et l'éducation dans les pays celtiques d'après le témoignage des textes hagiographiques latins', Études celtiques, 12 (1968–71), pp. 101ff.; T. Bühler, 'Fosterage', Schweizerisches Archiv für Volkskunde, 60 (1944).

[27] M. Mitterauer, 'Produktionsweise, Siedlungsstruktur und Sozialformen im österreichischen Montanwesen des Mittelalters und der frühen Neuzeit', in Grundtypen, pp. 176ff.; M. Mitterauer, Familienstruktur und Arbeitsorganisation in ländlichen Gesellschaften (Vienna, 1986), p. 30.

relatively early stage. On the one hand, the employer and the closer members of his family can be seen trying to distance themselves from their servants, while on the other, servants showed a desire to withdraw from the comprehensive control of manorial oversight and to win more personal freedom.[28] The tendency of the family to dissociate itself from domestic staff began in the royal courts and homes of the nobility; it spread to the upper middle class through merchants, entrepreneurs and higher civil servants, thus providing the model for the middle-class family, the parent–child group.[29] Symptoms of this are to be seen, first, in the exclusion of servants from the family meal; then in the deliberate separation of the children of the house; in the move from payment in kind, such as food and clothing, to money; and finally, in physical distancing, with clearly segregated accommodation for staff and a general separation of living and working areas. This trend could run against the interests of the servants, for example when it made their position in society less secure, but on the other hand it could work in their favour, as when they became freer in the use of their spare time or in their choice of personal relationships. As early as the late Middle Ages, journeymen were seeking freedom from being compelled to eat at the master's table,[30] though with no success, for in the early modern period the paternalistic domestic forms were strengthened among tradespeople. In the nineteenth century there was a sharp decline in the availability of housemaids, as factory work promised more personal freedom though less social stability. Generally, two trends can be seen in this loosening of the ties: it came sooner to male personnel than to female (urban housemaids were the last major group to remain integrated in the family) and it came sooner to older than to younger personnel (apprentices were less likely to be emancipated from domestic subordination than were journeymen). This reflects an overall tendency in the loosening of family ties on young people.

In dislodging domestic servants from their place in the family circle, the trends which have been outlined reveal a variety of

[28] H. Stekl, 'Hausrechtliche Abhängigkeit in der industriellen Gesellschaft. Das häusliche Personal vom 18. bis ins 20. Jahrhundert', *Wiener Geschichtsblätter*, 30 (1975), pp. 301ff.

[29] Rosenbaum, *Formen der Familie*, pp. 261ff., 301ff., 367ff.

[30] K. Schulz, 'Die Stellung der Gesellen in der spätmittelalterlichen Stadt', in A. Haverkamp (ed.), *Haus und Familie in der spätmittelalterlichen Stadt* (Cologne, 1984), p. 314.

possible sets of relationships for the young employee within the
family. As an ideal type, the young servant placed on the same
social level as children born in the family was less applicable in
large households than in small ones, less in the cities than in the
country, less at the highest levels of society than in the middle
class where employer and employee were closer in their social
origins. In one very important respect, however, the social relationships of servants within the family had always been different from
those of the children of the home: the servant was not subject to
the same incest taboo which existed between parents and children
or between brothers and sisters. As a result, sexual relationships
could occur within households which included servants. Domestic
subordination could become sexual exploitation. The master–maid
relationship was particularly delicate in this respect,[31] but the
relationship of the maid with the son of the house is to be seen
in the same context. Relationships between farm-hands or journeymen and the daughters of the house seem to have been less common. Sexual relationships between male and female servants were
most common on the large farms. The problem of young people
who are members of a household, but are not protected by the
incest taboo, is uniquely European, and help to explain why this
culture developed such especially rigid sexual norms.

Presumably it was precisely this moral threat which caused parents to ensure that their daughters did not move too far from home
when they entered service. We can observe how farm-girls, particularly young ones, travelled much shorter distances than their
male equivalents. Daughters were more often sent to relatives or
godparents than were sons. When a girl from the country went into
service in the city, parents would attempt to find someone they
trusted to act as a contact person, both to keep control and to offer her support. The mobility of female servants was generally not
as great as that of males. Travels like those of the journeymen were
never undertaken by girls. Farm-girls and housemaids were therefore always within much easier reach of their natural parents. This
had the not-insignificant ramification that they were more liable
to be called upon to use their earnings to support their family of
origin.

The decline of domestic service in its traditional forms has meant

[31] M. Mitterauer, *Ledige Mütter. Zur Geschichte unehelicher Geburten in
Europa* (Munich, 1983), p. 165, n. 253.

that from the early part of the Industrial Revolution, alternative living patterns developed for young people which were less influenced by domestic authority. There were, for example, lodgings, board and lodgings, and tenancy.[32] Lodgers had only the right to a place to sleep. 'Board and lodgings' was a similar arrangement with meals included, although not always with the same family. The tenant rented a room in a private house. The possibilities of part-board and of differing use of space meant that between these three main types there were any number of variations. It therefore makes sense to treat all of them together.

Lodgers were almost exclusively male. Certainly, 'lodging girls' were not unknown, but even when there was a great shortage of accommodation this was regarded as quite unsatisfactory.[33] The vast majority of lodgers were in their twenties. We are speaking, then, of the latter stage of youth,[34] and mostly of single people. The same was true of tenants, although here the proportion of young women was greater.

Originally, most lodgers were journeymen who were unwilling or unable to live with the master. In the early industrial period there were also many unmarried workers who could not afford a room of their own, but only a bed. As apprentices lost their status in the master's household, they too became lodgers. Lodging was particularly common in cities with large numbers of immigrants and serious housing shortages.[35] But even young people who stayed in their place of origin often chose this lifestyle if they wished to be free of parental control.

A wider variety of people became tenants. Whereas lodgings were only offered by families in the lowest social classes for whom every opportunity to earn a little extra was important, the letting of rooms occurred at all levels of society. This form of accommodation was especially popular among students. Unlike lodging, group tenancy was common.

---

[32] J. Ehmer, 'Wohnen ohne eigene Wohnung. Zur sozialen Stellung von Untermietern und Bettgehern', in L. Niethammer (ed.), *Wohnen im Wandel* (Wuppertal, 1979), pp. 132ff.

[33] J. Ehmer, 'Frauenarbeit und Arbeiterfamilie in Wien. Vom Vormärz bis 1934', *Geschichte und Gesellschaft*, 7 (1981), p. 455.

[34] Ehmer, 'Wohnen', p. 140; L. Stone, *The Family, Sex and Marriage in England, 1500–1800* (London, 1977), p. 28.

[35] A. G. Darroch, 'Migrants in the nineteenth century: fugitives or families in motion', *Journal of Family History*, 6 (1981), p. 269.

It is not possible to give a general answer to the question of how far lodgers and tenants were assimilated into the families in whose homes they lived. Integration was certainly more likely when the family's meal was shared. Intermediate forms occurred when the arrangements included only breakfast and Sunday dinner with the family.[36] It must be remembered that it was not uncommon for young lodgers, boarders and tenants to be related to the families which housed them.[37] Young people who travelled to the cities often sought a contact of this sort. Again, a young person might take accommodation with compatriots, or there might be a professional contact. Frequently there was some social connection which went far beyond the simple contract of rent. In the case of groups of young people who rented a room together, the members of the group often had family, ethnic or professional backgrounds in common. This kind of communal living may not have had a family structure, but it did involve close social relationships.

The lack of social relationships was certainly one of the main problems for many lodgers. If they were not permitted to enter the premises during the day, they had no contact there at all. They had no choice but to spend their time on the street or in the public house. It is widely reported that alcoholism was common among lodgers.[38] And in other ways too they showed symptoms of impoverishment and deviant behaviour. The youth welfare work begun in the second half of the nineteenth century made it a priority to combat this situation. It attempted to bring relief by building hostels for apprentices, journeymen and unmarried people.[39] These stood in the tradition of the hostels which had long been run by some of the journeymen's associations. Even factory owners occasionally set up dormitories for unmarried workers.[40] However, the problem of accommodating the unmarried workforce had in the course of industrialization reached such proportions that measures of this kind made little impact. Immediately prior to the First World War there were in the German Empire about 200,000 lodgers aged between 15 and 30,

[36] Ehmer, 'Wohnen', p. 145.
[37] Ibid., p. 146.
[38] *Handbuch für Jugendpflege* (Langensalza, 1913) pp. 20, 74.
[39] Ibid., pp. 22, 296.
[40] Ibid., p. 20; H. Lessing and M. Liebel, *Wilde Cliquen* (Bernsheim, 1981), p. 60.

and in the inter-war years young lodgers represented a very serious social problem in many large cities.[41] The problem was only solved when changing family size and living conditions made it possible for young people to remain longer in their parental homes.

The tendency which we have seen for young people to remain in their families has led to a general standardization of young people's living patterns. The high point of this development seems to have been reached in the 1950s. Then it was the norm for young people to stay in their parents' household until they married. Fairly recently, however, some very significant changes have occurred which have brought about a variety of different residential patterns for young people. The new forms have little in common with their historical predecessors. They are clearly seen if we take, as an example, students, who have a certain leadership role in young society, and compare their actual living patterns with the patterns they would most prefer. A study conducted in 1979 in Germany gave the following picture:[42]

	Actual (%)	Desired (%)
Own flat	30	50
Communal flat	18	31
Hall of residence	13	13
Rented room	15	4
Parental home	22	6

Similar trends were isolated in an Austrian study in 1984, in which the category 'own flat' was divided between single people and young couples.[43] The actual figures lay at 17 per cent and 20 per cent respectively, much the same as five years earlier in Germany. The combined figures for 'own flat' as a preferred option, however, were now up to 75 per cent. Unfortunately, the figures for couples sharing a home do not distinguish between married and unmarried couples.

The statistics provided by these studies clearly demonstrate that, at any rate in the later years of youth, the trend is away from the parental home. A return to the situation of the 1950s is not to be expected. Other traditional patterns seem to be on the way out,

[41] Tilly and Scott, *Women, Work and Family*, pp. 108ff., 183.
[42] *Jugend '81*, p. 106.
[43] *Express* Nr., 78, Feb. 1985, p. 22.

particularly the rented room, but also the student residence, although this has changed its ethos in the last couple of decades. The future for young people seems to lie in three residential patterns: the single person living alone; the couple living together; and the group living in community. All three allow the realization of aims which reveal some of the central basic trends of modern youth.

A tendency to individualism, reflected in the desire for private space, can also be seen among young people who are living with their parents. For most adolescents in the parental home it is taken for granted that they will have a room of their own from an early age.[44] Having one's own space makes it possible to develop one's own sphere of individuality. We may certainly see a continuity between this early physical separation and the later desire for an independent home. Occasionally there is an intermediate stage in the form of a cellar or attic which has been turned into a semi-independent flat within the home,[45] giving a greater degree of freedom from parental control. This freedom is often the main reason for leaving the family home. Sometimes it may be achieved with the setting-up of an incompletely autonomous household. Major tasks such as washing or cooking may continue to be done by parents.[46]

Historically, it is a very recent thing for young people to have their own room in their parents' home. Its earliest occurrence was among the upper middle class. As a mass phenomenon it only came with the rapid improvements in housing and the reduction in family size during the last decades. The growth in schooling had its own functional requirements. School pupils need separate working space if they are to study without disruption in their parents' home. Certain features of leisure activity also encourage the separation of space. Record-players and cassette recorders are obvious examples. The development of youth music would have been inconceivable without the marking-off of individual spheres for young people. The whole development of the modern youth culture has been strongly dependent on the availability of space, and on the freedom to make creative use of it.[47] It is a product of

[44] *Jugend '81*, pp. 327ff.
[45] Ibid., p. 159.
[46] Ibid., pp. 335ff.
[47] Schäfers, *Soziologie des Jugendalters*, pp. 152ff.

the modern consumer society that young people, as individuals
within a family unit, have so much personal property. In various
respects, individualization has been achieved long before the move
away from the parental home is made.

The development of an individual sphere finds its logical conclusion in the founding of an autonomous one-person household.
It is historically a completely new phenomenon for a young person to be in charge of a home. The traditional pattern is based
on the fact that setting up home coincided with marriage. But this
link is increasingly being broken. It is therefore possible to have
an independent home long before reaching the normal age for
marriage.

Living alone is socially acceptable for young women as well as
for young men. Indeed, if anything, one-person households are
more common among females, presumably because received
gender roles equip them better for the purpose.[48] Living alone,
of course, does not rule out the possibility of a relationship with
a partner. It is likely that one-person households are often founded
precisely in order to have the freedom to develop this. The
boundary between living alone and living as a couple is not at all
rigid.

By 'partner households' we mean especially the situation which
the French call *cohabitation juvénile*, where two young people
who are not married are living permanently together. This is a
social phenomenon which has increased greatly in recent years
and for which there is no satisfactory terminology.[49] 'Common-law
marriage' misses the mark, since a marriage structure is precisely
what this is not. Equally, terms like 'trial marriage' or 'engagement'
are inadequate, since they imply preparation for a future wedding.
'Living together' or 'cohabitation', the phrases most commonly used
in English, are really too general, since they could include any
attempt at intensive group-living.[50] Even 'partner household' is
lacking, as it requires an adjective like 'juvenile' to distinguish it
from extra-marital forms of partnership in later life. But at least this
term captures the nature of the relationship and its structural
characteristics.

[48] *Jugend '81*, p. 160.
[49] A. Bejin, 'Ehen ohne Trauschein heute', in P. Ariès et al., *Die Masken des
Begehrens und die Metamorphosen der Sinnlichkeit* (Frankfurt, 1982), p. 197.
[50] Ibid.

Living together with a fixed partner in the juvenile period is historically a totally new phenomenon. Certainly, relatively long-term
premarital sexual relationships were known in the past, especially
in regions which had a graduated form of courting, as with the
Scandinavian custom of regulated night-time visits.[51] Even the most
tolerant societies never permitted premarital relationships to reach
the stage of moving in together in a shared household, however.
Nor can the historical concubinate be seen as a precedent. In the
nineteenth and twentieth centuries this related to forbidden marriages among adults, not to the sexuality of youth.[52] The fact that
forms of premarital cohabitation with a fixed partner now meet
with widespread social recognition indicates a radical change in
attitudes to sexuality and marriage, at least in some sections of the
population. This, of course, applies equally to partner relationships of young people living alone or in groups, but it is expressed most clearly in the practice of cohabitation juvénile.

But there are other social changes which are important for the
'juvenile partner household'. If the relationship is to be easily
severed at any time there can be no material dependency of one
partner upon the other. This kind of household is based either on
the paid work of both partners, or on parental handouts on both
sides.[53] The latter presupposes higher levels of earnings than would
have been possible even a few decades ago; the former presupposes real career opportunities for women. If both partners are
working, this has a knock-on effect on the division of household
chores. Cohabitation juvénile has undoubtedly brought about a
more general sharing of housework. The idea of bringing a greater
degree of independence and self-sufficiency into the living pattern
is clearly linked with the process of individualization which has
already been discussed.

The social prerequisites which have been identified for the young
couple living in a partner household generally also apply to the
group household, the third new residential pattern for young
people. What is historically new about this is not that groups of
young people live in a communal dwelling: that has always been
possible, in the most varied milieux. What is new is that these
are now mixed-gender groups. Here there is a parallel with

[51] More detail in K. R. W. Wikman, Die Einleitung in die Ehe (Åbo, 1937).
[52] Mitterauer, Ledige Mütter, p. 106.
[53] Bejin, 'Ehen ohne Trauschein heute', pp. 199ff.

cohabitation juvénile. Like the partner household, the group household may include couples with long-term relationships. The significant difference is that here these are slotted into a more-comprehensive group context. The group household combines two objectives which society had previously always kept strictly separate: it is both a household and a youth group, a youth group in which members of both sexes have equal status as is usual in modern youth culture.[54] The shared life of the peer group becomes so central that the group constitutes a household in its own right. What we see here is a tendency which works against the trend for young people to remain in the parental home, namely a growing interest in an intensive participation in adolescent group-culture. This development is just as powerful in the one-person household and the partner household. Participation in adolescent group-culture contributes significantly to the fact that partner households are not simply de-institutionalized marriages, but rather are a specific phenomenon of youth.

One-person households, partner households and group households are specific living patterns of later youth. A French study, for example, has shown that life in a *cohabitation juvénile* becomes most common among young women at the age of 20–21, among men at 22–23.[55] It is not yet possible to say on the strength of developments thus far that these forms are a phase in the life cycle which is part of the experience of young people generally. In some countries, Sweden for example, the signs do point clearly in this direction.[56] What can be said with certainty is that the old sociological model of the immediate transition from the 'family of orientation' to the 'family of procreation' no longer does justice to the present day social realities. It belongs to that period when the number of young people remaining in the parental home was at its height.

If, having looked at the ways in which young people lived in families or other domestic groups in the past, we now wish to consider the factors which shaped their relationships with their parents, thinking especially of the quest for greater personal autonomy and the tension which this caused in parent–child relationships, we must begin by stressing that a large proportion

[54] See pp. 232ff.
[55] Bejin, 'Ehen ohne Trauschein heute', p. 197.
[56] Ibid.

of young people at the age in question were not living in the
parental home at all. That is especially true of members of the
urban and rural lower classes, who entered service at an early age,
but also of the children of most tradesmen and many agricultural
workers, altogether more than half the juvenile population in some
areas. For all of them, we may wonder how they dealt with the
typical sources of adolescent conflict in the absence of the person
with whom they had a close relationship in childhood. Frankly,
historical sources which can help us here are rare.

The clearest contrast to the determinants of modern adolescent
parent–child relationships are certainly to be found in the classical
agricultural family economy. This was fundamentally shaped by
the decisive role of property and work. The right of the father, or
of the parents, to control inheritance and dowries ensured the
authority of the older generation over the younger until questions
of property were settled. On this basis it was always possible for
them to demand obedience. The same was true of young people
in other milieux in which the existence and maintenance of social
status was secured by control of the means of subsistence, especially
among the nobility and the property-owning middle class. We
have already seen how closely the transfer of property was linked
to marriage in peasant communities, where the whole family was
affected by the choice of a partner. It was therefore required that
parents' wishes should be taken into account at this juncture. This
created a potential for major conflict towards the end of youth.
Individual, free choice of partner was for a long time unknown in
traditional rural society. Even in areas where the rural youth fraternities had a strong influence on the regulation of courting, things
still as a rule proceeded strictly in accordance with parental expectations.[57] Likewise, in other population groups in which inheritance was important, young people were given little influence over
the choice of a partner. In groups which regarded bloodline as
important, the principle of equal birth also had to be considered.
This was certainly not restricted to the nobility. Even in peasant
societies, the preservation of a family's honour by an appropriate
marriage could prove very important. This kind of thinking was
far stronger in the Balkans than in Central Europe.[58] Wherever group

[57] Wikman, *Die Einleitung*, p. 137.
[58] See, for example, J. K. Campbell, *Honour, Family and Patronage* (Oxford,
1964), pp. 268ff.

identity was more prominent than personal identity, it was expected that young people would marry according to honour and rank. This potential conflict has almost completely disappeared in our modern achievement-orientated society. Likewise, the rise of individual paid labour has meant that inheritance has lost much of its importance as a factor influencing relationships between the generations.

A special modification of the inheritance factor as a problem between the generations arose in peasant societies wherever it was the custom for the farm to be passed on to the next generation while the parents were still alive. Here, it was possible for the heir to achieve the desired autonomy without waiting for the father's death. At what point the farm was passed on would depend on the old farmer's fitness for work. The question of the individual's contribution within the family economy not only made the children answerable to the parents, but also the reverse.[59] Work was generally a central category in relationships across the generations in the farming milieu. Just as affection and emotions are generated by good working relationships, so dissatisfaction with the children's work would be a latent cause of tension. The desire to get as much work as possible out of adolescent offspring, and for as long as possible, could cross the boundary of exploitation. For example, during the time of the great drift of populations to the cities, many peasant-farmers kept their grown-up daughters on the farm so long that they missed their chance to marry.[60] There is no other social milieu in which adolescent labour caused such tensions between the generations as in farming. Cottage industry, as we have seen, never relied so heavily on the work of the children.

It was in the trade guilds that the problem of career choice first arose as a potential area of conflict between parents and children. It seems unlikely that 12–14 year olds were often given much say in the choice of an apprenticeship. Rather, we may assume that it was at the end of the apprenticeship that they began to think

---

[59] W. A. Gestrich, 'Jugend in Ohmenhausen, 1800–1918. Eine sozialgeschichtliche Studie zum Wandel des Jugendlebens in einem württembergischen Dorf unter dem Einfluß der Industrialisierung', Dissertation, Tübingen, 1983; published as 'Traditionelle Jugendkultur und Industrialisierung', in *Kritische Studien zur Geschichtswissenschaft* (Göttingen, 1986), p. 121.

[60] *Handbuch für Jugendpflege*, p. 4.

independently about work. The future employment of the sons of tradesmen certainly did not run in automatic continuity from their training. The beginnings of a completely free choice of career, however, are to be found not in the lower middle class but in the educated classes. The originally theological concept of career as vocation, the ideal of personal self-determination, but also the practical opportunities afforded by a relatively long and broad education, all point to this group. The bourgeois model of the free choice of career then spread to the whole of society. The chances of being able to put the idea into practice varied greatly in traditional society. They were always better in the city with its multiplicity of alternatives than in the country; they were always better in the upper classes, where a final decision could be postponed through a long period of education, than in the lower classes, where financial considerations made it necessary to grasp the first opportunity which came along; and they were always better for men than for women because of the strict differentiation of working roles. Even in the twentieth century, many country girls had no alternative to farm work other than to become seamstresses.

Personal choice of career also means personal choice of social status. As the old society began to decline, the educated middle class became the first group for whom the social position of an adult depended very much on personal achievement in youth. As a result, young people came under great pressure to fulfil their parents' expectations. That was true at school, at university and at the beginning of working life. Here was a new source of conflict which had never existed in a society where status was decided primarily by birth. The wider the population group in which educational achievement dictated social position or facilitated social climbing, the sharper this conflict became. The educational explosion of recent decades has made this a central problem between parents and adolescents in more and more families. Being forced by external and internal pressure to meet the demands of parents is an expectation which never existed in this form for the young people of old European class society.

If it was in the middle class that the threshold of modernity linked achievement with social status, it was in the early industrial proletariat that achievement became the basis of a contribution to the family budget. In the system of the family wage economy the status of young people within the family depended very much on

what they brought in. If the adolescent son earned well, he had
a strong position which might even place him in competition with
his father, who might be earning less. This could place a further
strain on a relationship already complicated by the father's 'secondary patriarchalism', a kind of compensation for his subordinate
position in the workplace. Daughters were involved as earners in
the family wage economy even more than sons. The traditional
female role expected a greater degree of self-sacrifice for the sake
of the family, and this meets here with processes of exploitation
within the home. It is a phenomenon not restricted to workers,
but is common also among salaried employees. Even adolescents
no longer living at home were often called upon to contribute:
housemaids, for example. This pattern of the younger generation
supporting the older has undergone a radical change in the twentieth century. Generally the situation has been reversed.[61] Young
people remain financially dependent on their parents for a considerable time. Support frequently continues beyond leaving home
and setting up a new household. Both patterns can give rise to
conflict, the first by limiting the purchasing power or economic
autonomy of the youngster, the second by raising the possibility
that parents may use their economic superiority to exert their
authority.

Young people's spending is undoubtedly a very ancient and
widespread source of conflict in their relationships with their parents, and would have played a role since the days of the traditional peasant communities. In milieux where it was merely a
question of giving the son pocket-money for visits to the inn,
however, it would not be of fundamental importance. It becomes
a problem with the rise of a consumer society,[62] particularly in those
population groups for whom young people's spending may be
thought of as endangering the family's ability to meet its basic
needs. The main points of conflict are not only the autonomous
control of the young people's own income or their claim on a
share of their parents' finances, but also the kinds of consumer
goods which they purchase. The growth of youth fashions in
clothing has combined conflicts about spending with conflicts about

    [61] G. Baumert, 'Einige Beobachtungen zur Wandlung, der familialen Stellung
des Kindes in Deutschland', in L. von Friedeburg (ed.), *Jugend in der modernen
Gesellschaft* (Cologne, 1971), p. 316.
    [62] R. Sandgruber, *Die Anfänge der Konsumgesellschaft* (Vienna, 1982).

youth values, attitudes and behaviour patterns. Since the purchase of consumer goods like clothing is closely linked with the quest for personal identity, willingness to allow young people independence in this sphere is not only a question of financial resources but also one of recognizing young people's individuality. As a result, it has come more easily in those population groups which were the first to respect the trends of individualization.

Consumer autonomy for young people is closely connected to freedom in the use of leisure time. This area of tension is also very old, but has become more important in recent times because of the enormous increase in free time and in the possible ways of using it. Traditionally, it was not activities within the house but those outside it which were controversial, especially for girls. An indication of this has already been seen in the restrictions on going out, which to the present day is a major issue in adolescent self-determination. The efforts of parents to regulate the company their children keep correlates with the influence they had historically on the choice of a partner. This issue has doubtless receded. Meanwhile, however, another issue has been gaining in importance. Since the family has changed from being a work group to being a social group sharing primarily the use of leisure time, family and peer group have found themselves in competition in a way in which never happened in traditional society. The competition between family and peer group does not only lie in the demands of time; the rivalry of different sets of values, historically a minor matter, is now highly significant.

Conflicts of views and values between parents and their adolescent offspring were meaningless in the past as long as young people grew up into an environment with a homogeneous outlook. Where no other point of orientation existed there could be no ideological tensions. Traditional peasant societies were relatively free of this. In the cities, alternative philosophies were possible at a much earlier stage. The middle-class demand for individuality and autonomy makes a fundamental deviation from the parents a possibility, but we should not overestimate the importance of the element of ideological controversy in the bourgeois family. Even distinct protest movements of middle-class youth were not necessarily directed against their own parents. So it was, for example, with the German Youth Movement at the beginning of the twentieth century, whose most influential supporters frequently came from critical liberal homes.[63] Looking at society as a whole, value differences between the generations have certainly increased in recent times. The tempo of social change and the insistence of the adult generation on values which were developed in the context of another age make it probable that these differences will become even more marked. However, differences in outlook need not cause conflict. How far conflict can be avoided depends very much on whether we can learn to live with these differences.

II. The Workplace

The history of the organization of work in Europe may be characterized as the development from the co-operation of the family economy to the marketing of individual paid labour. In the course of this development, the social relationships involved have altered radically. Relationships in a commercial company are far more objective than those in a family concern. Indeed, as the burden of production has been removed from the family, family ties have become more emotional, making the contrast between family and business relationships even more striking.[64] Unlike in the traditional family business, work in the factory or office is not built on close personal co-operation. Individual paid labour always involves a danger of isolation. The development of the large business has brought with it a comprehensive process of social disciplining. Work is regimented and heteronomous. Elements of self-regulation, for example making one's own decisions about the amount of time spent in work and in recreation, have disappeared. The structures of authority in the workplace have taken on a completely new character. The immediate supervisors of the work process are themselves subordinate to others. Intermediate authorities liaise between those who make decisions and those who implement them. Management is no longer directly accessible, the relationship is anonymous. Elements of personal responsibility therefore lose their importance. The security of the employee's position is no longer guaranteed. The 'moral economy' which shaped working relationships in the traditional family structure is

---

[63] H. Giesecke, *Vom Wandervogel bis zur Hitlerjugend. Jugendarbeit zwischen Politik und Pädagogik* (Munich, 1981), p. 30.
[64] Summarized in Rosenbaum, *Formen der Familie*, esp. pp. 279ff.

now replaced by relationships which contain the potential for exploitation and social uncertainty. All these changes which have accompanied the growth of individual paid labour affect paid employees generally, but they affect young workers to a greater degree for two reasons: first, because their position as beginners in the system is weaker; and secondly, because they are having to adapt to social relationships which are new to them. The gap between the worlds of family and work has widened steadily since the decline of the family economy system. Bridging this gap is one of the tasks of youth which European social development has made especially difficult.

It was a characteristic of the family economy, the basic working unit in old European society, that production and reproduction were closely related. In other words, the family economy system relied on members of both sexes and of two or more generations working together. Certainly, there were exceptions to this basic rule when a couple remained childless or a marriage partner died. However, the frequency of remarriage and of the adoption of 'substitute children' in traditional family businesses shows that the co-operation of husband and wife, and of parent and child, was indeed very much the norm.[65] Working relationships, then, depended on roles allocated according to age and gender. With individual paid labour, the link between production and reproduction is broken. The organization of labour no longer has to take account of the age and sex combinations which are dictated by the processes of having and rearing children. Certainly it is still important that a person's two roles, at work and in the family, are compatible. It is, however, no longer the task of those who organize the workplace to ensure that this compatibility is achieved. The relationship of the young person to adult work has been deeply affected by the separation of work and family. This process has in many respects been different for women and for men, a difference which has had a lasting influence on the status of young women and men at work.

The institution of domestic service created a special type of family economy in European history. Service has been described as a kind of 'retrospective birth control',[66] and indeed, taking in servants did represent a break from a total dependence on the

---

[65] Mitterauer, 'Auswirkungen von Urbanisierung', pp. 62ff.
[66] The phrase originates with E. A. Wrigley.

genetic lottery. It was possible to shape the family's work force in terms of age and sex as was necessary for the work in hand. Family economies which were restricted to the co-operation of relatives were not so flexible. Under these circumstances the workforce could only be enlarged by marriage and childbearing. Furthermore, in patrilineal family systems it was only the marriage of male members of the family which would increase manpower. This made it very difficult to be sure of having adequate personnel. The situation could be eased when several married couples lived together. The 'joint family' system is an economic necessity wherever cultural traditions make the addition of individual workers impossible. Cultural patterns of this kind must be seen as underlying any situation where the family economy is limited to patrilineal relatives and their wives.[67] Equally, the European marriage pattern and the family system which goes with it was only possible where there were no such cultural restrictions. The extension of the family economy by individuals who are not necessarily related provides a far freer system of recruitment than the joint family. Its flexibility means that it is open to the further development of more comprehensive ways of organizing work. Large households with many servants are in a number of cases to be seen as the first stage in the development of large-scale industry. There is therefore a continuity between some types of domestic service and modern paid labour. Within the traditional family economy, the main importance of domestic service was that it had a decisive influence on the shaping of specifically adolescent forms of work.

Division of labour according to age groups is first and foremost a question of growth and physical strength. In a society where production of the staples of life required heavy physical labour, this factor was extremely important for the division of work. In 1780, around 65 per cent of working people in Central Europe were employed in the physically demanding agricultural sector, as opposed to 9 per cent in 1970. In the service sector, which required relatively little heavy work, the figures were 16 per cent and 43 per cent respectively.[68] The movement of personnel from the one sector to the other has by itself resulted in an enormous change

---

[67] M. Mitterauer and A. Kagan, 'Russian and Central European family structures: a comparative view', *Journal of Family History*, 7 (1982), pp. 124ff.

[68] H. Kaelble, *Soziale Mobilität und Chancengleichheit im 19. und 20. Jahrhundert* (Göttingen, 1983), p. 248.

in the importance of bodily strength. Even more important has been the energy revolution which has meant that tasks which previously required great strength no longer do. Against this background it can be clearly seen how muscle power was the basis for working roles. The development of the physical potential of young people in the course of their adolescence can be illustrated by a set of figures published in 1913.[69] Muscular power, measured in kg, averaged at that time:

Age	Females	Males
12	45	70
13	55	80
14	60	90
15	65	105
16	68	112
17	70	115
18	70	122
19	70	135

Girls, then, were 17 years old before they had the strength which boys had at 12, and at that they had reached their peak. Boys, on the other hand, could expect their strength to double between the ages of 12 and 19, after which they would be able to do twice as much as was possible for a girl. Physical requirements alone would have made age and gender distinctions necessary in the apportioning of work. The spectrum of work undertaken by young people therefore ranged from very light duties, which might be given to a child, through to the heaviest, which would be required of a man in possession of his full adult strength. At the lower end of the scale were various forms of boy-labour such as running messages or delivering goods;[70] at the upper end, handling horses or felling trees. The hierarchy of adolescent work was most clearly seen in the stages of farm service. The development down to the present day show a tendency to level out the differentials between the various stages of youth, and between youth and adulthood. Physical strength develops earlier nowadays, people start work

[69] *Handbuch der Jugendpflege*, p. 68.
[70] On boy labour see Gillis, *Geschichte der Jugend*, pp. 131ff.

later; there are very few jobs left which require such physical exertion that young people would be unable to take them on.

The second reason for dividing labour according to age was a social one. Young people, being single, were more mobile than adults. It was easier for them to deal with tasks away from the home, they could cope more easily with a prolonged absence, they could cope more easily with a separation of living and working quarters, and they were freer to change jobs if necessary. Mobility was also a factor in which there was a difference between women and men.[71] The care of children meant that married women were restricted to work which kept them in one place. For single women this was not yet the case, but with a view to their future roles as housewives they were generally assigned analogous tasks even before marriage. Furthermore, in addition to this matter of continuity from girlhood to womanhood, there was another element which was equally important. Girls' geographical sphere of activity was restricted in order to protect them from sexual risks. This aspect carried particular weight in those areas which attached the greatest importance to virginity, for example in large parts of the Mediterranean countries. In areas which attached less significance to virginity, girls could take on responsibilities further away from the home. A good example of this is the work of the dairymaid on the Alpine pastures. For all that the female radius of activity was always more limited than the male, the younger girls were more likely than the older ones to be given tasks which required mobility. The same is true of the division of work between single and married men. Under the European marriage pattern, the phase of life in which this roving work could be done lasted a relatively long time both for women and for men.

The linking of production and reproduction in the traditional family economy meant that the sharing out of tasks was closely related to the social status of those who undertook them. Consequently, in this system adolescent work was always subordinate work, since it was carried out by individuals who were subordinate under domestic authority. On the other hand, adult work was always self-regulated. The same was to a great extent true even of the developing cottage industry, although here the adult worker's

[71] M. Mitterauer, 'Geschlechtsspezifische Arbeitsteilung in vorindustrieller Zeit', *Beiträge zur historischen Sozialkunde*, 11 (1981), pp. 77ff.

independence was already restricted by the regimentation of a more-comprehensive working unit. In the family economy, then, there was a clear break between the subordinate work of youth and the independent work of adulthood. In the modern context of individual paid labour, however, this qualitative leap is no longer present. All employees are subordinates. The development of paid labour has brought about a closing of the gap between youth and adult in the work situation.

The levelling of differences in the social quality of work done by young people and adults can be understood in terms of the growth of paid work. In European history, individual paid labour has to a significant extent developed out of specifically youthful forms of work, namely those connected with domestic service. In agricultural paid labour, this process can be traced particularly far back. The term *Seldner*, which in many areas of Austria is used to refer to small peasant-farmers doing paid labour for others, seems to have its roots in *Selde*, meaning sleeping quarters. The original reference is to service on large dairy farms, in which domestic servants were housed in their own quarters near the farmhouse.[72] The trend for servants to be moved out of the family itself can be traced in rural areas from the early Middle Ages through to the nineteenth century, both in farming and land-owning households. In sparsely populated areas especially, there were frequently dependent smallholdings clustered around farms, in which former farm servants were allowed to live in return for work. In working relationships, the sense of domestic subordination often continued into adulthood, so that this was rather a patron–client relationship than paid labour in our modern understanding.[73] Alongside this, however, at an early stage in history there were also agricultural workers whose working relationships with their employers were more objective. The forms of paid work which developed out of farm service are diverse. One example would be forestry workers. Reference has already been made to a parallel early development among miners.[74]

[72] P. Fried, *Herrschaftsgeschichte der altbayerischen Landgerichte Dachau und Kranzberg* (Munich, 1962), p. 195.

[73] N. Ortmayr, 'Ländliches Gesinde in Oberösterreich 1918–38', in J. Ehmer and M. Mitterauer (eds), *Familienstruktur und Arbeitsorganization in ländlichen Gesellschaften* (Vienna, 1986), p. 346; N. Ortmayr, 'Beim Bauern im Dienst', in H. C. Ehalt (ed.), *Geschichte von unten* (Vienna, 1984), pp. 107ff.

[74] See p. 100.

Analogous developments from service to paid employment can be seen in the trades. In building and transport, for example, journeymen ceased very early to be part of the master's household. Trades which underwent the transition to large businesses while remaining closed household communities were mainly to be found in rural areas. This applies, for example, to smithies, mills and breweries. But even in the cities in the early period of industrial-ization there were growing industries where the owner and his unmarried workers still shared a traditional household pattern. Manorial dependence was certainly not the only historical root for the social situation of the early industrial work force, but it was a very significant one.

For the majority of white-collar workers, it was the role of the merchant's assistant which was formative. Commercial assistants who had been promoted were withdrawing from the household even before the mid-nineteenth century.[75] In the second half of the century, this became the norm. With the growth of the commercial house to the structure of a large business, the number of independent merchants declined as a proportion of the total number of people in commerce. Service in the commercial household was no longer a phase of youth, but became instead a career pattern for life.[76] Other groups of employees followed this pattern.[77] As examples of learning situations which have developed directly out of domestic service, we can mention pharmaceutical dispensers and surgical registrars.

In the periods of transition from forms of service to forms of individual paid labour, the groups of employees concerned were often young, unmarried people, so that it is possible to see early paid labour as a specifically juvenile form of work. This influence of the young and the unmarried carried through into the political action and behaviour of the early working class. For our present purposes, the link between adolescent labour and the development of paid labour is mainly of interest because of the social factors

[75] R. Engelsing, 'Die wirtschaftliche und soziale Differenzierung der deutschen kaufmännischen Angestellten im In- und Ausland', in *Zur Sozialgeschichte deutscher Mittel- und Unterschichten* (Göttingen, 1973), p. 105.

[76] W. Deich, *Der Sozialgeschichte der Handlungsgehilfen um 1900* (Cologne, 1974), p. 90.

[77] A. Baryli, 'Zur Sozialgeschichte der Angestellten in Österreich', *Beiträge zur historischen Sozialkunde*, 13 (1983), pp. 116ff.

which brought it about. When paid work was first introduced into the tradition of domestic service, the payment of labourers on an individual basis made it very much more difficult for young people to set up their own homes. The extremely high age of marriage among such groups is a result of this. With the move out of the household community, all the security which the 'whole house' (*das ganze Haus*, the extended domestic community) traditionally offered its members was lost, especially security in case of sickness or shortage of work. Many of the problems of early paid labour can be understood as the consequences of domestic service existing without family ties. If we think of service as adolescent work, we are in a sense speaking of a lengthening of juvenile dependence, which now becomes a more-general, lifelong social dependence. Taking service out of the family community resulted in the development of a lower class. What had been a subordinate position within the family as a transitional phase of life now became a permanently subordinate social status.

The connection between adolescent work and subordination can also be discussed with reference to other types of work which did not have their origins in household service. Military life may be taken as an illustration. From the rise of paid soldiery in the Middle Ages until the introduction of general military service in the nineteenth century, fighting men can be regarded as a special kind of paid worker. Indeed, until the state took over control of the army in the age of absolutism it was an extremely capitalistic form of work. In the late Middle Ages and early modern period, mercenary activity was one of the most lucrative forms of enterprise.[78] At the same time, it was specifically an activity of the young. Soldiering required total mobility and was therefore almost exclusively the preserve of the unmarried. Soldiers and mercenaries certainly could get married but there were immense difficulties involved.[79] The requirements of strength and agility also encouraged a situation in which most paid soldiers were young. In this form of work there were other elements of dependency in addition to the obvious one of payment. These arise from the functional

[78] F. Redlich, *The German Military Enterpriser and his Work Force* (Wiesbaden, 1964–5); R. van Dülmen, *Entstehung des neuzeitlichen Europa, 1550–1648* (Frankfurt, 1982), p. 357.

[79] A. Corvisier, *Armies and Societies in Europe, 1494–1789* (Bloomington, 1979), pp. 174ff.; A. Corvisier, 'La Société militaire et l'enfant', *Annales de démographie historique* (1973), p. 328.

necessity of military discipline. The mass armies of the early modern period were certainly very important settings for developing new forms of discipline, and it is worth considering how influential these were as models for the organization of the first large factories. At the very least, the rise of industrial paid labour must be seen in the context of a more comprehensive social discipline which took its cue partly from military precedents. Important parallels between military discipline and other forms of juvenile subordination are to be seen in the nineteenth century. The militarization of schooling led to school discipline being based on military disciplines. The idea of the army as the 'school of the nation' was very important at that time for shaping the dependent relationships of young men. However, military service had by this time long since lost its importance as a specific form of young persons' employment.

The contrast between dependent, subordinate adolescent work and independent adult work seems historically to be restricted to the traditional family economy. In the wage-earning society of more recent times it no longer applies. All paid work is dependent work. In the struggle to modify these dependent relationships the situation of young employees has improved at the same rate as that of adults. The achievement of worker participation in factories has come to both at the same time. In fact, the right to express opinions seems to have been granted earlier in working life than in national and political life.

A particular aspect of the dependent nature of adolescent work is its character as a learning process. Vocational training in old European society was always by hands-on experience, never by abstract teaching methods. It has already been seen that domestic service was the classical framework for this. In principle, every form of service was based on learning by participation. Even the work of the farmer had to be 'learned' in this way. The most progressive form of learning in the context of domestic service was developed in the trade guilds. Training here was divided into two periods. The apprenticeship was the period of learning (French *apprendre*) in the strictest sense, in which knowledge and skills could be gained in a stable relationship with a master-craftsman in return for a fee. The journeyman then sought to improve his qualifications by studying the working methods of as many masters as possible before becoming a master himself. The structure of training was very similar in the commercial house. Here there was no counterpart to the master's certificate examination. The stages of qualifications in training were more rigidly graded, though they were not separated by marked thresholds. Even before the industrial revolution, the senior school played a role in the merchant's education.

The industrial age has seen great changes in the learning component in young people's work. In the first place, the growth of factory work dramatically increased the amount of work which required no training. Certainly, there was unskilled labour in the pre-industrial period, but it did not have anything like the same significance. Unskilled work now became available not only in production but also in the expanding service industry. Changes were also taking place in the trades. The increase in the number of apprentices often had less to do with more-intensive training than with building up a cheap workforce. The unscrupulous herding of young people into apprenticeships which offered no prospects, a system sometimes known as the 'apprentice factory', was therefore often a backward step for adolescent vocational training. Between skilled and unskilled work there now arose a middle type, known as semi-skilled work,[80] which did have a very short period of training, but which did not involve sustained training throughout youth. Semi-skilled workers became very important in the tertiary sector.

The decline in opportunities for learning in the workplace may be set against the growth of learning unconnected with work. The separation of the learning process from paid employment happened through the institution of the school. Vocational training in schools and colleges has grown enormously since the second half of the nineteenth century. Alongside professions for which the preparation is entirely academic, there are now jobs for which training is mixed. In this two-fold system of education we find the technical colleges which stand alongside the traditional apprenticeship. Study at these colleges was initially on a voluntary basis but became obligatory as they gradually took the place of training at work. The rapid growth in higher education in recent decades has created a trend towards completely institutionalized vocational training and away from mixed forms.

[80] H. Kluth, 'Arbeiterjugend – Begriff und Wirklichkeit', in H. Schelsky (ed.), *Arbeiterjugend gestern und heute* (Heidelberg, 1955), p. 67.

It is difficult to give a general answer to the question of whether youth and adult work are still distinguished by learning components, since so much learning has been taken out of the working sphere. Where vocational training still takes place in the context of paid work, the distinction seems to hold good. However, it could disappear as continuing in-service training for adults becomes more widespread. When work-related training accompanies the whole course of a career, there is a far greater degree of continuity from youth to adulthood.

A third aspect which distinguished adolescent work from adult work in the traditional family economy has to do with a characteristic of youth which has already been discussed, namely mobility. Young people, being single, are more readily able to change both their type and place of work, while adults, being married, are geographically more fixed. In traditional society this meant a further element of discontinuity, which varied in importance according to social class, region, gender and status within the household.

In the family economies of Western, Central and Northern Europe, domestic service provided special opportunities for mobility. But even in regions in which the family system did not permit this form of changing household and workplace, travel did occur in connection with work. In Russia these travels were known as *otchod*. Here even young married men would leave home for the summer months, occasionally even for several years; early factory work was widely based on this system.[81] In regions of Central Europe which have little tradition of service, a number of forms of seasonal migration have developed. This happened, for example, in the areas of partible inheritance in Switzerland: Vorarlberg and West Tyrol. It was mainly done by young people.[82] Travel related to work, therefore, did not necessarily mean separation from the family of origin, as was usual with domestic service.

Domestic service in the farming situation seems to have been

[81] R. E. Johnson, 'Family relations and the rural–urban nexus: patterns in the hinterland of Moscow, 1880–1900', in D. L. Ransel (ed.), *The Family in Imperial Russia* (Urbana, 1978), pp. 264ff.

[82] O. Uhlig, *Die Schwabenkinder aus Tirol und Vorarlberg* (Innsbruck, 1978); A. J. Fitz, *Familie und Frühindustrialisierung in Vorarlberg* (Dornbirn, 1985), pp. 184ff.

characterized by a particularly high incidence of moving from one place of service to another, especially among young men in the latter stages of youth.[83] The working relationship was established in the first instance for a year, and at the end of this period many farm-hands looked for a new position. The main reason seems to have been the opportunity to improve one's position. The chances of a change in service that would lead to a promotion in the farming hierarchy, bringing both better money and higher prestige, were greatest in areas where service was very common. It was often in the period of most rapid physical growth that the possibilities of improvement from year to year were best. The decision to stay or move was also influenced by other factors, such as the quality of food, satisfaction with treatment by the farmer, relationships to other farm hands and so on. The farmer, too, could terminate service at the end of the year if he were dissatisfied. He might also do this if an adolescent child of his own were able to replace a maid or farm-hand.

The area in which farm servants might travel was in the first instance limited to the immediate vicinity of their birthplace, either within their own parish or in the neighbouring perishes. The radius of operation was wider for farm-hands than for maids. However, it also frequently happened that girls from rural areas would go into service in the nearest small town. From there the way was open to larger towns and cities. Usually, the degree of migration of servants would be proportional to the centrality of the community.[84] Those in the later stages of adolescence were more likely to move away from their place of birth than were younger ones. It could be that this change of social milieu became a regular progression in the course of youth. Whereas the first stage of youth was spent in the country, the later years were the time for experiencing an urban environment. Marriage could then lead back into the country. At any rate, there was a concentration of young workers in the cities, males in the commercial quarters, females in the residential areas of the upper classes where they served as housemaids. If the countryside was referred to as the

---

[83] A. Kussmaul, *Servants in Husbandry in Early Modern England* (Cambridge, 1981), pp. 49ff.; M. Mitterauer, 'Formen ländlicher Familienwirtschaft', in Ehmer and Mitterauer (eds), *Familienstruktur*, pp. 282ff.

[84] B. Ankarloo, 'Agriculture and women's work: directions of change in the West, 1700–1900', *Journal of Family History*, 4 (1979), p. 119.

'cradle of industry',[85] it was to a certain degree also the cradle of pre-industrial work in the cities.

In the urban trades, the length of time a young worker remained in one place varied greatly. While apprentices were bound to one master for the whole of their apprenticeship, journeymen changed their place of work frequently. It was unusual for them to remain for a whole year. The journeyman years were spent moving from town to town. In commerce, apprentices were bound in the same way to a single workplace. Older commercial assistants, because of their position of trust and the necessary knowledge of the practices of an individual business, had a greater degree of continuity than a journeyman in the crafts.

In all forms of employment which culminated at the end of the youth phase in self-employed activity, the contrast between the mobility of youth and the stability of adulthood was fairly clear. In careers which did not lead to independent status this contrast did not exist, even in pre-industrial times. The 'day-labourer', as the phrase implies, had only short-term employment. There was no difference here between adult and adolescent work. However, young day-labourers were not common before the industrial revolution. Day-work usually only arose when a person moved away from a domestic working situation.

The changes in the workplace in the industrial period have mitigated against the distinction known in the traditional family economy between mobile adolescent work and stable adult work. The numbers of independent people declined in proportion to dependent individuals.[86] The early industrial period had a great need for unskilled workers. In the tradition of day-work this led to short-term contracts, especially for women. But even entering skilled employment did not necessarily mean workplace continuity in the setting of capitalist paid labour. Equally in the tertiary sector, there were many new kinds of work which offered no long-term prospects. In this way the spread of individual paid labour destabilized adult work. The working conditions typical of the early period of industrialization, with frequent changes of workplace and home, only began to change when employers became interested in having a permanent, qualified workforce, and

[85] J. Mooser, *Arbeiterleben in Deutschland, 1900–1970* (Frankfurt, 1984), p. 36.
[86] Data for France and Germany in Kaelble, *Soziale Mobilität*, p. 249.

employees were able to win a greater degree of job security. These achievements had their effect also on adolescent work, so that the working life of individual paid employees generally came to have a more continuous pattern.

The consequences of the decline of the family economy for adolescent work in the industrial period are different for females and males. Paid work, which was now appearing in quantity, was primarily work outside the home. The separation of home and workplace is one of the most important ramifications of industrialization and of the changing work patterns which accompanied it. Work outside the home, however, means quite different things for single women than for married women with children. The latter can only take up employment away from home if someone else takes responsibility for the children. Women's paid work outside the home was therefore concentrated on the unmarried.[87] This was equally true for factory workers and office workers, among whom married women were a minority. Consequently, women's work outside the home was characteristically young people's work, as is clearly seen from the contemporary terminology. One spoke of 'working-girls', 'mill-girls', 'factory-girls' and 'shop-girls'. On getting married or having a child, young women often did not leave paid work but instead continued it at home. This increased enormously during the industrial revolution. Marriage, or the birth of the first child, was therefore a major threshold in the lives of working women. There was very little continuity between adolescent work, outside the home, and adult work, within the home. Certainly some women, especially in the textile industry, continued to work for the same employer, but none the less the change to home working meant a radical alteration in working conditions and in social conditions. In cases where a career was given up altogether, all continuity was broken. The question of how far the old contrast between mobile adolescent work and geographically static adult work survived the transition from family economy to individual employment can only be meaningfully answered for that minority of women who were able to continue working outside the home after getting married and having children. For them, the answer is similar to that for men.

[87] Tilly and Scott, *Women, Work and Family*, pp. 87, 184; Ehmer, 'Frauenarbeit und Arbeiterfamilie', pp. 454ff.

The transition to individual paid labour radically altered the relationship of adolescent and adult work, and this change was different for men and for women. In the traditional family economy, adolescent female work was a consistent preparation for adult roles. This was equally true for the daughter of the home, the housemaid and the milkmaid. The skills they developed could be used later when they became housewives. With the shift to individual employment, the work of adolescent girls became a dead end. Their experience with the spinning-machine or in the tobacco factory, as shop assistants or telephonists was completely useless after setting up home. The exceptions were those types of work which could be done from home, and those such as dress-making which were also useful in the family. These exceptions apart, girls' employment outside the home offered no longer-term prospects. It was from the outset seen only as a temporary phase, since the real objective was to become a housewife and mother, which in principle meant staying at home. Because women's paid employment was seen to have this temporary character, there was for a long time no systematic training. They had to be content with short phases of practical learning.[88] In the tertiary sector of employment, the introduction of proper training for girls came first in office work. In Germany this happened around the beginning of the twentieth century.[89] At about the same time there were renewed attempts to establish proper training schemes for girls in the industrial field.[90] These were important steps for the emergence of female career possibilities in the sense of continuing employment with long-term prospects.

In many respects adolescent and adult work have increased in similarity as modern employment patterns have developed, so that areas of conflict and tension in the workplace no longer run primarily along the generation line. From the situation in the family-economy system of work, in which adolescent work and dependent work were identical, fundamental changes have taken place. Then,

---

[88] G. Wellner, 'Industriearbeiterinnen in der Weimarer Republik: Arbeitsmarkt, Arbeit und Privatleben, 1919–1933', *Geschichte und Gesellschaft*, 7 (1981), p. 542.

[89] Deich, *Zur Sozialgeschichte*, p. 79.

[90] A. Schlüter, 'Die Entwicklung weiblicher Lehrverhaltnisse Anfang des 20. Jahrhunderts aufgezeigt am Verband für handwerksmäßige und fachgewerbliche Ausbildung der Frau in Deutschland', in *Die ungeschriebene Geschichte. Historische Frauenforschung* (Vienna, 1985), pp. 259ff.

conflicts resulting from subordinate positions at work were at the same time problems between the generations, even when the age gap between the parties in conflict was not especially wide.

In the family economy, family conflicts and work conflicts could not really be separated. There were, however, some conflicts which only affected children born in the household, and others which only affected those in service. Problems of inheritance, which were the central area of potential conflict in the agricultural family economy, did not touch the maids or farm-hands. On the other hand, the question of levels of wages was not a source of dissatisfaction for daughters or sons, but it was a very major issue for young people in service. Payment in cash was not always the most important thing here. Food, accommodation and clothing were equally significant wage components. The quality of food was crucial. Many maids and farm-hands changed their place of service because the cooking was not good or because there was not enough to eat. In some areas it was regarded as a legitimate form of protest for farm servants to throw poor-quality food at the farmer's wife.[91] Because of the difficulty of calculating the exact value of payment in kind, standards for a 'moral economy' were developed which were under the supervision of the local authority.

The other areas of difficulty between master and servant were very little different from those between parent and adolescent children. Completion of allocated work was important, and there were no limits to the length of the working day. But the leisure activities of young people in service were also completely under the control of the householder. There was no difference between maids and daughters in the restrictions on going out. If a maid had a romantic involvement, this was supervised. In service there was no such thing as a private sphere independent of working relationships.

This comprehensive subordination of the servant, extending far beyond the realm of work, was in earlier times equally common in urban households. For housemaids it continued with slight modifications until the collapse of manorial work patterns. For male servants, however, as early as the Middle Ages there was a tendency to define a working relationship in the strictest sense and to question the competence of the master outside this area.

[91] Ortmayr, 'Ländliches Gesinde'.

This struggle for emancipation was strongest among the journey-men in the crafts, who supported each other through their frater-nities. These journeymen's associations were the first attempt at the collectivization of the grievances of dependent workers, which previously had to be dealt with individually. In the conflicts be-tween masters and journeymen a number of themes emerged which were later to be major issues for paid employees: levels of pay, working hours and working conditions. Apprentices were not drawn into this development. For them, the comprehensive mano-rial dependency continued in principle until, in the nineteenth and twentieth centuries, they ceased to be part of the master's household. An expression of this all-embracing subordination was the right of corporal punishment, which put a particular strain on master–apprentice relationships. A specific problem for appren-tices arose when, in addition to service in the workshop, other domestic chores were demanded. Because of the apprentice's complete integration into the household, this abuse was wide-spread. Another classical problem for apprentices, which is closely connected with this, arose when proper training was neglected.

Since, even in the industrial period, the numbers of apprentices trained under master-craftsmen far exceeded those required for the continuation of the trades, many of the traditional problems of apprenticeship remained major grievances. The exploitation of apprentices as cheap labour, without providing the relevant pro-fessional training, became more acute in the industrial period with the system of 'apprentice factories'. It is therefore not surprising that protest movements of young workers often began with this group. The *Verein der Lehrlinge und jugendlichen Arbeiter*, from which the German young workers' movement developed, was founded in 1904 when the suicide of a Berlin apprentice, who had been mistreated by his master, created a wave of indignation among Germany's working youth.[92] To begin with, the trade unions did not welcome the idea of separate organization for young workers. In their view, the class problem of work already embraced the specific problems of young workers, and this was a fair analysis of the situation. The development of paid employment in the course of the industrial revolution had had the result that the problems of dependent workers had become a matter of class conflict which

[92] W. Laqueur, *Die deutsche Jugendbewegung* (Cologne, 1982), p. 80.

went far beyond the difficulties of youth. However, from the emergence of an independent movement for young workers we may gather that until this point the workers' movement had taken too little account of the questions which were important for young people.

Stormy relationships across the generation gap have, through their radical transformation in the period of industrialization, developed differently in the workplace from in the family or school. The parent–teenager or teacher–pupil type of relationship has no immediate counterpart in the world of work. The relationship between young employees and their superiors is not significantly different from other authority and dependency relationships in the professional sphere. The traditional battlefields of dependent work – levels of pay, working hours and working conditions – are no longer, as in the family economy, problems of youth. Rather, they affect all employees and have therefore ceased to be the points at which the generations conflict.

III. The School

Like the social forms of the working sphere, those of the school have much in common with family and household structures in their origins in European history. Like them, their development has taken them far from this original similarity. Today, school and family are two fundamentally different types of social institution. The values taught in the family are overwhelmingly particular, while those of the school are more universal. The role of the young person in the school is, as in the workplace, firmly geared towards achievement; in the family, this aspect is not to the fore. Relationships in the family are based on affection and emotion, whereas those in the school are largely objective. The further we go back in history, the more these contrasts become blurred. On the one hand, the social form household appears in many ways as the root and model of the social form school. On the other, education in the family has come increasingly under the influence of the school. This characteristic process whereby school and family have grown apart while at the same time interacting with each other, is of great importance for our understanding of social relationships in the school and their historical origins.

From the very beginning, the European school was strongly influenced by household structures. The senior schools of the Middle Ages developed out of religious houses, monasteries or cathedral chapters.[93] Future monks were often given over to the monasteries while still only boys. These *pueri oblati* made up the core of the monastic *schola*. Alongside the actual novices, however, many monasteries also took in outsiders, boys who were not destined for the order, but were to be educated together with those who were. The same was true of the cathedral schools. They too served first and foremost for the education of young canons, who made up their *schola interna*. But here again there was also a *schola externa*, in which poor boys would be taken in to be trained as secular priests. The chapter provided them with a bed and meals, in return for which they were obliged to serve as choristers.[94] This is an example of a pattern which was fairly widespread in medieval society: being taken into a household to receive an education in return for services rendered. However, in addition to training for ecclesiastical careers, the church schools also admitted members of the laity for instruction. This is the decisive point at which they went beyond the usual pattern of household education. The *schola externa* of the monastery or cathedral, under a *magister* or *scholasticus*, was not restricted to the education of members of the same station. Unlike the skills and insights passed by a craftsman or merchant to his apprentice, the knowledge handed down in the religious house was of more-general significance to the whole of society, so that it was possible here for an institution to develop as a subsystem of the household community, which could claim to offer a broad education.

The monastery and cathedral schools became the model for the other grammar schools which arose in varying numbers during the course of the high and late Middle Ages. As urban life began to unfold, the initiative for setting up these schools came to rest more and more with the municipal authorities. But even then, the religious houses provided an important link. Urban schools were

---

[93] Cf. F. Paulsen, *Geschichte des gelehrten Unterrichts auf den deutschen Schulen und Universitäten vom Anfang des Mittelalters bis zur Gegenwart*, 3rd edn, vol. I (Leipzig, 1914), pp. 13ff.; H. G. Good, *A History of Western Education* (New York, 1947), pp. 69ff.; H. Feilzer, *Jugend in der mittelalterlichen Ständegesellschaft* (Vienna, 1971), pp. 98ff., 221ff.

[94] Paulsen, *Geschichte des gelehrten Unterrichts*, vol. I, p. 16.

generally attached to the parish church of the town. To begin with, the instruction would have been principally that which the parish priest offered for his choirboys.[95] If the numbers of town children interested in the lessons increased, a full-time school-master might be engaged. In these schools the pattern of the domestic group had for the most part already been lost, but it continued to have a strong structural influence. The magister, for example, would have the same kind of comprehensive authority as the father of the house. An obvious expression of his 'paternal' status was his right to administer corporal punishment. The rod turns up again and again in the Middle Ages as the typical symbol of the schoolmaster.

In the medieval town, a second type of school developed. It came later than the urban grammar school and was certainly influenced by it in structure. With the development of commercial accounting and of written transactions in trade, literacy and numeracy were becoming increasingly important. To meet this need, vernacular schools of counting and writing were established throughout Europe, mainly in the fourteenth century. The clergy were also very important in the teaching of this elementary know-ledge. Many of the vernacular counting and writing schools were attached to priests' houses and monasteries. Sometimes, however, they were run by laymen. Here we may detect echoes of com-mercial structures, for example in the training of the teachers who would first have been apprentices and journeymen, or in the way that school-'masters' combined in guilds. However, teachers did not take trainees into their homes in the way usual in the trades. These elementary schools were as relevant in youth as in childhood since, like the higher schools, they did not have fixed-age classes and frequently had children and adolescents sitting together.[96]

In higher education, universities developed out of cathedral and monastery schools in the Middle Ages.[97] Universities and gram-mar schools differed in their legal standing. In educational content they frequently overlapped. Well-developed grammar schools of-fered a large part of what the university arts faculty taught by way of preparation for study in the three higher faculties: theology, law

[95] Ibid., p. 19.
[96] P. Ariès, *Geschichte der Kindheit*, p. 418.
[97] H. Denifle, *Die Universitäten des Mittelalters bis 1400*, vol. I (Berlin, 1885); G. Kaufmann, *Die Geschichte der deutschen Universitäten*, vol. I (Stuttgart, 1888).

and medicine. Likewise, in the social and living conditions of pupils and students (the Middle Ages called them all 'scholars') they were frequently akin. The basic structure of the university as a corporation of all teachers and scholars was co-operative. In its internal structure, however, various types of family patterns certainly played their part. As in other higher schools, a recurring problem was how to integrate those under instruction into households. From the household communities of pupils and students, who in turn took on teaching and tutoring functions, there frequently arose new forms of domestic organization, the influence of which worked back in to the development of the schools.

One of the most important of these forms of organization was the college,[98] which became widespread in the fourteenth and fifteenth centuries, mainly in England and France, and long influenced the lifestyles of senior school pupils and students. The original idea was not unlike the hall of residence. At their foundation they were provided with endowments which covered the living costs of a certain proportion of their members. College members lived on the premises of the establishment in a manner comparable to a religious community. They shared their religious observance, they ate together, they were subject to a common household order, every detail of their daily life was regimented.[99] The model was the canonical seminary attached to the cathedral. Places in the college were often reserved for people at particular stages in their education. Since older pupils or students generally gave tuition to younger ones, the teaching component in the colleges was present from the very beginning. In many colleges the founder made provision for a magister who, in addition to his teaching duties elsewhere, also gave lessons within the college itself. Although never designed to be teaching institutions, colleges became more and more places of study. In some areas they covered the whole range of subjects, from grammar upwards. Having become centres of teaching, however, the colleges lost their strict residential character and began to admit external students to their classes.[100]

[98] P. Moraw, 'Zur Sozialgeschichte der deutschen Universität im späten Mittelalter', *Gießener Universitätsblätter*, 2 (1975), p. 47.
[99] Kaufmann, *Die Geschichte der deutschen Universitäten*, pp. 291ff.; Ariès, *Geschichte der Kindheit*, pp. 244ff.
[100] Ariès, *Geschichte der Kindheit*, p. 256.

A similar development from pupils' residence to teaching establishment is to be found in the history of the pensionary. These were not founded on the model of the religious community, but rather had their origins in lodgings rented to pupils, either individually or in groups.[101] If the presence of pupils became a permanent state of affairs, a teacher would often be engaged for them. It can be demonstrated that, long after the end of the Middle Ages, the organized cohabitation of pupils or students led time and again to the introduction of teaching within their ranks. This meant that once again domestic and academic social forms overlapped.

As late as the nineteenth century we find the phenomenon of teachers and clergymen, both of whom had by virtue of their education the same qualifications for the purpose, taking in pupils as pensionaires. The instruction they provided could enhance or even completely replace what was provided at school. In such cases a very thorough domestic integration took place, which in turn, in keeping with the social order of the day, meant elements of domestic service.

What was even more common than pupils living in the homes of their teachers in old European society was the opposite idea, that of teachers moving into the homes of their pupils' parents.[102] This phenomenon is principally to be found in the upper classes of society, among the nobility and the richer bourgeoisie. Here too, the social relationships were based on household patterns, albeit of quite a different sort from when the pupil left home. Here the teacher was part of the domestic staff. Rather than drawing authority from being head of a household or claiming some analogous position, he was himself a servant. Consequently, he was closer in age to his pupil. Private tutors of this kind were generally young people who had only just completed their own education or possibly were even still studying. At any rate, they were not married. The phenomenon of adolescents being taught by adolescents may be seen frequently in old European society.

[101] Paulsen, *Geschichte des gelehrten Unterrichts*, vol. I, pp. 22, 260; Ariès, *Geschichte der Kindheit*, p. 242; Kaufmann, *Die Geschichte der deutschen Universitäten*, vol. I, p. 211.
[102] Paulsen, *Geschichte des gelehrten Unterrichts*, vol. I, p. 339; W. Roessler, *Die Entstehung des modernen Erziehungswesens in Deutschland* (Stuttgart, 1961), pp. 138ff., 383ff.; H. H. Gerth, *Bürgerliche Intelligenz um 1800* (Göttingen, 1976), pp. 51ff.

Thus, for example, older pupils were constantly employed as teachers' assistants,[103] while in communities of pupils or students living together the more advanced gave tuition to the others. Teaching was certainly not simply a question of knowledge being passed from one generation to the next. Teaching relationships among adolescents were perfectly normal. This is not only true of theoretical learning. In the trades, apprentices learned as much from journeymen as from master-craftsmen.

In the early modern period, an interesting special form developed out of the tradition of private tuition in the households of the nobility: the Grand Tour.[104] On completing their education in the parental home, young noblemen would make an educational journey which would take them through various European countries. They visited royal courts or the homes of noble friends in order to perfect their courtly manners, they matriculated at universities, mainly to learn law, and they used their time abroad to acquire languages. This idea of learning by travelling has parallels in the training of young artisans and merchants. As with them, it was always connected with entering new households, but it had additional domestic components. The tutor, a member of the young nobleman's own household, accompanied him on the journey. Often, two brothers who had been educated together made the Grand Tour with their tutor. It was then a whole group who left the noble's home and in the course of their journeys attached themselves to others. In the eighteenth century, an attempt was made to replace the Grand Tour by a form of schooling which incorporated its most important elements.[105] These schools for young gentlemen, with their emphasis on social skills, physical training, modern languages and science, represented a completely different kind of education from the (Latin) grammar schools with their roots in the religious orders.

Apart from this, the work of the private tutor in the noble household only ever made the most tentative steps towards a school-

---

[103] Paulsen, *Geschichte des gelehrten Unterrichts*, vol. I, p. 295.

[104] Ariès, *Geschichte der Kindheit*, p. 304; H. Kühnel, 'Die adelige Kavalierstour im 17. Jahrhundert', *Jahrbuch des Vereins für Landeskunde von Niederösterreich*, 36 (1964), pp. 364ff.; Reif, *Westfälischer Adel 1770–1860* (Göttingen, 1979), pp. 364ff.

[105] Paulsen, *Geschichte des gelehrten Unterrichts*, vol. I, pp. 514ff.; Ariès, *Geschichte der Kindheit*, pp. 305ff.

based pattern of education. Occasionally sons of noble families of the same age living in the same area came together to take instruction from a shared tutor. In this way a class could form.[106] Shared education of young nobles was more common in the courts of princes than in the homes of individual noblemen. When the sons of princes were educated together with young nobles who had entered the prince's household, school structures frequently developed. Famous court schools evolved in Italy in the Renaissance.[107] Schools for pages and sons of the nobility are included in this category of schools which grew up out of the courts.[108] Important as these establishments were, however, they did not develop into a tradition of high-level schooling. In the last analysis, court education could not compete with religious models. Both in content and in social form, European schools received their most formative influence not from the nobility but from the clergy. The religious household would therefore also be the more important as far as the domestic roots of schooling are concerned.

Home tutoring was not only important for young men in old European society; it was equally so for young women. For them, too, it was limited to small groups of nobles and rich bourgeoise. Teachers were taken in as part of the household staff to provide the daughters with instruction in religion, foreign languages, music and refined handwork.[109] These forms of private tuition for girls provided important adolescent social relationships. For the development of schools, however, they had little significance. We can mention pensionaries for daughters of upper-class families where teachers continued in their own homes the instruction which had been begun in the pupil's home. These forms of schools, however, differed little from the family/small-group structure of identifiable household communities. The same is true of other forms of education for girls, in convents and church foundations. Only the teaching orders of nuns, especially the Ursulines and the *Englische Fräulein* founded in the sixteenth and early seventeenth centuries, clearly broke out of this pattern.[110] As a rule, the

[106] G. Heiß, 'Konfession, Politik und Erziehung. Die Landschaftsschulen in den nieder und oberösterreichischen Ländern vor dem 30 jährigen Krieg', in *Bildung, Politik und Gesellschaft* (Vienna, 1978), pp. 22ff.
[107] Good, *History of Western Education*, pp. 130ff.
[108] Ariès, *Geschichte der Kindheit*.
[109] L. Voss, *Geschichte der höheren Mädchenbildung* (Opladen, 1952), pp. 50ff.
[110] Ibid., pp. 53ff.

education of young women was constantly marked by the characteristically strong domestic ties which have frequently been noted, and this prevented the development of larger forms of schooling. It would not have been possible for girls to rent accommodation, let alone travel around from school to school.

The growth of extensive units, numerically far beyond the limits of the family group, is an important feature of the school as a social form. This development in scale started in the households of the religious orders. The monastery or cathedral chapter, as a subsystem of which the school began, represents a large and complex form of household which, for all that it was built on domestic models, none the less differed considerably from family forms. As an institutional household it was not based on internal reproduction. It was not restricted in selecting its next generation and certainly not in the choice of those young people who were to be educated alongside the new generation of the house. There were quantitative limits imposed by the capacity of the building, but even these limits could be exceeded when external pupils not integrated into the community of the house were admitted for instruction. Even in the Middle Ages there were occasionally schools with several hundred pupils.[111] The higher schools, the universities, sometimes attracted large numbers of students. On the other hand, there were also small schools where it was possible to get to know all the pupils and where there was a family atmosphere.

The tension between large-scale schooling and instruction in small units runs right through the early history of school life. In periods of reform a reduction in the numbers of pupils to small units was always demanded in the interests of teacher–pupil relationships. So, for example, the Jansenists in the seventeenth century propagated schools with eight to ten pupils per teacher.[112] In the early twentieth century the German *Jugendbewegung*, the Free Youth Movement, produced reform models in which the 'school community' was divided into 'families' in order to create an affectionate, emotional social climate. No one has ever succeeded in putting these ideas into practice on a lasting basis. Despite every effort, secondary schools have developed the structures of large

---

[111] Good, *History of Western Education*, p. 148; Ariès, *Geschichte der Kindheit*, p. 287.

[112] Ariès, *Geschichte der Kindheit*, p. 377.

organizations. The expansion of education since the middle of the twentieth century has intensified this trend to a degree never known before. Classes have multiplied. Schools with more than a thousand pupils are no rarity. The structural analogy to large businesses becomes increasingly obvious. In this respect, school does prepare young people for the social relationships of working life. The contrast with the relationships within the family becomes greater as intimate emotional ties become more important there. By comparison, the upper school is becoming more objective. This is particularly true of teacher–pupil relationships. In relationships between the young people, the conditions for close personal contacts have improved as the class has developed into a fixed group which remains together. In the colleges of higher education, on the other hand, comparable groups do not form, since relationships between students are those of the mass organization.

The development of higher education into a large social organization led to problems in areas which we from our present-day perspective would class as not belonging to school life at all. In the past this was seen differently. As long as pupils or students were integrated into household communities, their behaviour outside classes was also under control. All forms of school which admitted external pupils were faced with the problem of how to supervise them. The majority of these external pupils did not live in the vicinity of the school and therefore were not under parental care, but were in rented accommodation or pensionaries. The responsible school authorities therefore attempted time and again to draw these pupils into some domestic structure. The resulting households which then took on a secondary teaching function have already been described. However, such attempts were not always successful. The travelling scholars of the Middle Ages represented a serious social problem. Often there were some very young adolescents among them. The much-cited life of Thomas Platter, from the early sixteenth century, shows clearly the lifestyle of such a travelling pupil.[113] In the school itself there was a host of disciplinary problems. Visits to taverns, fights with other youngsters, immoral behaviour, all these were recurring themes. Sometimes there were also political questions, as in Germany in the *Vormärz* period (1815–42). Gatherings of pupils in private

[113] Ibid., pp. 356ff.

houses were carefully monitored because of a perceived danger of conspiratorial tendencies. All in all, the control of pupils in the upper school in matters not directly related to their education was a continual source of tension. One possibility of increasing this control was provided by the growth in boarding schools, which was at its height in the second half of the nineteenth century.[114] The fact that this trend was later reversed has already been seen in connection with the development of the family. The new role of the family led to a sharing of authority and responsibility between parental home and school. Teachers were no longer responsible for all aspects of the lives of their pupils. The school came to have a restricted competence which did not include those parts of adolescent life unconnected with education. This contraction of the school's jurisdiction was very important for the emerging right of pupils to shape their lives autonomously.

The growth of the higher schools into large organizations also caused problems of social control in their internal running. They inherited a comprehensive disciplinary apparatus from the religious households in which, unlike in other groups organized on a family basis, it was necessary to develop a general and lasting system of ordered cohabitation. In particular, the regimented rhythm of the day had its roots far back in the tradition of religious houses. Communal prayers, communal meals and communal work made a strictly enforced time discipline essential. But there were other areas, too, in which the monastery or cathedral chapter influenced social discipline.[115] Various types of homes or asylums which developed out of the religious households adopted their forms of discipline. The school is one of these, and even when it no longer has a household structure, this heritage continues to be formative. So, for example, the forms of punishment used in schools are in the same tradition. The close contact between school and monastery meant that in the course of history new patterns of discipline in the religious houses were passed on to the schools. This is especially obvious in the case of the Jesuit schools. Like the order itself, the schools which it ran placed great emphasis on personal

[114] Ibid., p. 401.
[115] H. Treiber and H. Steinert, *Die Fabrikation des zuverlässigen Menschen. Über die 'Wahlverwandtschaft' von Kloster- und Fabrikdisziplin* (Munich, 1980), pp. 53ff.

discipline; where this failed, a system of pupils spying on and denouncing one another was typical.[116]

A second source for the social discipline of young people in the school which has grown in significance in more recent times is the military. Hyppolyte Taine poignantly characterized the boarding school of his day as a combination of monastery and barracks.[117] After the reforming of secondary education under Napoleon, the French *collèges* increasingly adopted regimental methods and barrack-square style. The use of the pea-whistle became standard, as did assembling in lines and drilling in formation. School uniforms made this changed social climate visible.[118] In Prussia about the middle of the nineteenth century a new type of teacher modelled on the territorial army officer began to oust the older model of the humanistic Greek enthusiast.[119] Here too the influence of military-style authority began to make its mark. Such a move towards military forms of discipline in the secondary schools, however, was restricted to those countries where public life generally was becoming more militarized at that time. Comparable trends are not to be found, for example, in Great Britain.

The development of the school from a subsystem of the religious house to a large social organization necessarily involves a division into manageable units. The basic unit of pupils today is the class. The class is also one of the most important social forms in adolescent life, so that it would seem helpful to look at the question of how it arose.

Classes, in the sense of groups of pupils of the same age who together are confronted with a predetermined body of knowledge, did not exist in the early period of schooling, nor was there any system whereby groups were regularly promoted to a higher level. When in the medieval grammar schools several programmes of instruction were offered in parallel, these were arranged in a much more *ad hoc* fashion into sections known as *lectiones*.[120] The number of these sections depended principally on the number of available teachers. It must of course be remembered here that advanced pupils were frequently deployed to teach beginners.

---

[116] Good, *History of Western Education*, p. 163.
[117] Ariès, *Geschichte der Kindheit*, p. 401.
[118] Ibid., pp. 381ff.
[119] F. Blättner, *Das Gymnasium* (Heidelberg, 1960), pp. 192ff.
[120] Paulsen, *Geschichte des gelehrten Unterrichts*, vol. I, p. 23.

The groups taught by teachers or senior pupils were not permanent and stable units. It seems to have been left for the most part to the pupils themselves to opt for participation in this or that group. Spatial considerations also seem to have worked against the emergence of permanent groupings.[121] The different *lectiones* were usually accommodated together. Cases were recorded where nine or even twelve teachers at once had to give instruction in the same room.

The teaching methods of the Middle Ages, reciting, repeating together, and learning by rote, made it possible for relatively large numbers of pupils to be taught together. This fact alone makes it seem unlikely that communal learning would lead to strong community bonds. The constant fluctuation was another factor of importance. Some pupils remained only a short time at one school before moving on again. The poorer pupils often had to earn their own living by service in the households which had taken them in and were therefore not in a position to take part in lessons regularly.

The first attempts at a division of the higher schools into classes were made in the sixteenth century.[122] This was part of a general move towards the systemization of the content of lessons. School constitutions specified a degree of successive ordering of material according to levels of difficulty. The grading of material began with the separating off of the grammar pupils, that is, the junior classes, but soon it spread to the school's whole programme of lessons. Only in the university faculties did studies remain ungraded, a difference which has a continuing influence on the present-day situation. In the new academies founded in the sixteenth century, however, even the philosophies, corresponding to the university arts faculties, were included as the final classes. Likewise, the *studia superiora* in the Jesuit schools were ordered into classes representing years.[123] Here for the first time we find the concept of the annual promotion examination.[124] Only when the pupil demonstrated positive results could he proceed to the next class, another important step in the development of classes. At about the same time it was established that one teacher would be appointed to each class. In the French colleges, the principle of linking a teacher

[121] Ariès, *Geschichte der Kindheit*, pp. 279ff.
[122] Ibid., pp. 269ff.; Paulsen, *Geschichte des gelehrten Unterrichts*, vol. i, pp. 342ff.
[123] Paulsen, *Geschichte des gelehrten Unterrichts*, vol. i, p. 423.
[124] Ibid., p. 432.

to a class was generally accepted by the end of the sixteenth century. At this time, however, school classes still did not have their own separate space. The medieval single-roomed school continued. The number of pupils in a class was considerable. According to biographical records, the fluctuation continued to be very wide. Even after the introduction of classes, we cannot assume that the pupils of a class formed a closed group bound together by their shared experience.

After the grading of material, the second important stage in the development of the modern system of classes was the ending of mixed-age classes.[125] In the Middle Ages and well into the modern period it had been virtually a feature of the system that older and younger pupils learned together, the former often being in charge of the latter. Mixed-age groups of adolescents were the norm in the most varied spheres of life. Among brothers and sisters in a family it was dictated by nature, among the servants in a large household it was required by the structure of labour. In the historical fellowships of young men the distribution of ages was just as wide. Conformity of age played no part in social interaction. Likewise, within a school class there could be a difference of as much as ten years in the ages of the pupils.[126] The educational principle that pupils of the same age should be confronted with the same standards was argued as early as the seventeenth century, but its realization was still a long way off. Classes made up of pupils all of the same age were not achieved until structured systems of state schooling were set up in the nineteenth century.[127] The introduction of year groups was of immense importance for the social life of young people. In the decades which followed, it influenced not only the social relationships that pupils enjoyed within the school, but also the groups they formed outside. The social life of adolescents came to be based more and more on particular age-groups, less and less on the idea of a range of ages. Only at this stage did the idea of a 'peer group' in the strictest sense emerge. As school attendance became more usual, young people increasingly came to build their contacts on this pattern.

A number of factors in the development of higher schooling

---

[125] Ariès, *Geschichte der Kindheit*, pp. 285ff.
[126] Ibid., pp. 324ff.
[127] See pp. 75ff.

were crucial for the emergence of the class as the pupils' social base. In the day-schools, an important issue was the stabilization of what had been a fluctuating pupil population. In the boarding schools, which were increasing in numbers until the middle of the nineteenth century, this fluctuation had never been as strong. Another important issue was class size. In the seventeenth and eighteenth centuries classes of over 100 were no rarity, especially for the younger pupils in the higher schools.[128] In the nineteenth century these class sizes were generally reduced, either as a result of the educational beliefs of the head teacher or because of standardizing regulations from government. In large schools this involved running parallel classes. The system of having appointed class teachers also helped to keep the class together. This was first known in the Jesuit schools. In the early nineteenth century it was usual for the *ordinarius* to teach most, if not all, subjects to his class.[129] This person provided a point of reference which helped to unite the class.

The nineteenth century, however, brought important changes which challenged the universal competence of a single teacher for his class. There were already voices arguing that teachers should not be responsible for the behaviour of their pupils outside the school. Within the school there was a move towards a system of subject teachers. The class teacher who dominated the secondary schools in the first half of the century were for the most part qualified in philology. In the era of the new humanistic education, classical languages stood in the forefront. The philologist was seen as the embodiment of the teacher who, like the theologian in an earlier period, seemed ideally suited to give instruction in all disciplines.[130] Classics had, in the humanistic academies, almost replaced religion as the subject for shaping pupils' world view.[131] However, as the university arts faculties became increasingly differentiated, it became impossible to maintain the idea that a general education with classics should be the prerequisite for the study of any other subject. In a slow process which was for the most part only complete in the second half of the nineteenth

[128] Cf. Ariès's examples, *Geschichte der Kindheit*, pp. 324ff.

[129] A. Beer and F. Hochegger, *Die Fortschritte des Unterrichtswesens in den Kulturstaaten Europas*, vol. I (Vienna, 1867), pp. 42, 328.

[130] Blättner, *Das Gymnasium*, p. 146.

[131] Ibid., p. 124.

century, the standardization of teaching qualifications made disciplinary specialization obligatory.[132]

Authorization to teach was now granted only for a narrow group of subjects, not in a more general form. In this way subject teachers became the norm in secondary schools. This was of great importance for the social relationships between pupils and teachers. There was now no longer any question of a single teacher with a dominant personality being the sole influence on a class. Pupils were increasingly confronted by a number of role models, offering the very important opportunity of choice in personal orientation. For the teacher, there arose the dilemma whether to feel responsible for the whole education of the young person or to concern himself only with the imparting of specific subject knowledge. The tension between educationist and specialist has been familiar to teachers ever since. The restriction of teachers to their subject has contributed to the objectification of the social climate which has made the school more like the professional world, with its organized division of labour. With the breaking up of the teacher's overall responsibility for the life of the pupil, a structural analogy both with the role of the parent and with that of the primary teacher disappeared.

In tertiary education things developed quite differently. A unified graduation of material, which could have led to the formation of groups not unlike school classes, for the most part never happened. Again, there was never a trend for students studying together to be of the same age. There was no lasting connection between a group of students and a teacher: a multiplicity of teaching personalities was the norm. The fluctuation of the student population does seem to have varied at different points in history, but there has been no fundamental change. In the universities, then, many of the conditions are missing which in the secondary schools led to the development of classes as a social form. Students have less social contact with one another while under instruction. Instead, other forms of social interacting stand in the foreground, such as fraternities, clubs and residence groups. These are not directly influenced by the teaching structures.

An essential difference between the religious house and other domestic social forms concerns the gender mix. Because of the

---

[132] Ibid., pp. 152ff.

law of celibacy and the vow of chastity, religious houses were always made up of members of a single sex. This structural feature has had far-reaching consequences for the development of secondary schooling in European history. Higher levels of education were as a matter of principle either offered to males and females separately or restricted to males only. Early attempts at co-education are to be seen in the court schools of the Renaissance, which had their origins not in the religious houses but in courtly training.[133] Similar experiments were sometimes made by families who had private tutors. However, in the long term, the pattern of court education did not lead to a more general trend towards young women and men being educated together. The military component in the education of the nobility worked against this. On the level of vernacular writing and counting schools, co-educative patterns can be traced back a long way. This was not justified on the basis that the pupils in this type of school were all below the age of puberty; in the early modern period the age mixture was still very wide. When for example a master was recommended to exclude girls from lessons because the presence of older lads threatened their virtue, it is clear we are speaking of co-education for adolescents.[134] However, it is true that these elementary schools developed into schools for younger children. When compulsory education was first introduced, it only affected people below the age of puberty. In some countries, such as France, co-education was rejected even for this age-group.[135]

The introduction of co-education at secondary-school level had at least two historical preconditions. The first was the move to day-schools. In no country did mixed-sex education begin in the boarding schools. The second was that the content of lessons desired for young men and women became the same. Only when an equal standard of secondary education was made available to girls could integration take place. The demand for equal educational opportunities therefore had first to be acknowledged by society. In the older schools run by nuns and in the schools for young ladies in the first half of the nineteenth century, this was certainly not the case, as the knowledge imparted was never intended as a basis for further study.[136] Secondary schools for girls which were

---

[133] Good, *History of Western Education*, pp. 130ff.
[134] Ariès, *Geschichte der Kindheit*, p. 418.
[135] Beer and Hochegger, *Fortschritte des Unterrichtwesens*, pp. 99ff.
[136] Voss, *Geschichte de höheren Mädchenbildung*, pp. 62ff.

envisaged as a preparation for university were not opened until the second half of the century. How far these led to co-educative forms varied from country to country. In England, mixed education began soon after the foundation of the first girls' secondary schools. By the end of the First World War, more than one-fifth of all English secondary schools were already co-educational.[137] In the Scandinavian countries, schooling for adolescents of both genders began with the *samskolan* in Stockholm in 1876.[138] Co-educational secondary schooling spread very quickly in Scandinavia. In Germany, on the other hand, it was quite unknown in the nineteenth century. The first beginnings came in the early twentieth century, partly influenced by the ideas of the German Free Youth Movement.[139] In France, as in the other Romance countries, segregated education at secondary level was particularly resilient.[140] Varying cultural traditions governing the separation of the sexes in adolescence are thus echoed in the school systems.

With the expansion of schooling in recent decades, the principle of educating males and females together has found wide acceptance. Only now has the proportion of girls in secondary schools increased so rapidly that mixed classes have become a general necessity. The resulting situation, seen against the history of secondary education, represents a radical change. In the phase of life in which those sections of the population who traditionally sent their children to school always placed special emphasis on the separation of the sexes, learning together is now a matter of course. It no longer requires the ritual of the dancing school to provide the first contact with the opposite sex. Relationships are made easy and natural by doing everyday things together in the school. Communication in the school influences social life in free time. If, in contrast to past ages, young women and men tend to play down gender-specific differences in their behaviour and activity, this can surely to a great extent be attributed to co-education.

In all social forms which historically have taken their basic structure from the household pattern, attempts at democratization face strong opposition from the received social relationships. This

[137] H. C. Barnard, *A Short History of English Education from 1766 to 1944* (London, 1949), p. 193.
[138] P. Barth, *Die Geschichte der Erziehung in soziologischer und geistesgeschichtlicher Beleuchtung*, 6th edn (Leipzig, 1925), p. 720.
[139] Ibid.
[140] E. J. King, *Other Schools and Ours*, 4th edn (London, 1973), p. 125.

was true of manufacturing industry, of various forms of institution, and equally of the school. Participation presupposes a co-operative element. The traditional household, on the other hand, is primarily founded on a power structure. The basic pattern for social relationships is domestic subservience. Like the father–child and the master–servant relationships, the teacher–pupil relationship also belongs socio-historically in this context.

The developments in secondary schooling since its medieval origins have not exactly encouraged pupils to claim more autonomy in the school. At first, any new influences which modified and reformed the social relationships within the school began in the religious orders. The Jesuits were particularly important here. When a large proportion of the secondary schools in the Catholic lands were taken over by them, these were drawn into a rigidly centralized system of hierarchically structured dependent relationships. The influences which flowed from an all-embracing power structure must also be taken into the reckoning when discussing the shaping of dependent relationships within the school. The process of bureaucratization of schooling, which came about when the state authorities took administrative responsibility in the nineteenth century, had similar results. Here again it produced a comprehensive system of structured subordination. In some countries this was accentuated by periods of militarization. The degree of subordination of young people in the school must always be seen in the context of these wider features of the school system.

A first attempt at pupil participation was offered by the so-called monitor system, which had its origins in the Middle Ages. It was based on the idea of entrusting older pupils with tasks which were of assistance to the staff. As a rule, the monitor system was used as an instrument of social control. In exceptional cases, however, it could become a means of participation. So for example in the Paris *Collège de Sainte Barbe* at the end of the seventeenth century, pupils holding the office of 'tribune' were present as pupil representatives at the weekly staff meetings at which matters of censure and punishment were decided.[141] Likewise, in some of the reformed schools of the seventeenth and eighteenth centuries there were tentative moves to grant pupils more autonomy, to encourage group work, and to create a climate of co-operation

---

[141] Ariès, *Geschichte der Kindheit*, p. 377.

between teachers and pupils. Initiatives of this sort came particularly from the academies of the English dissenters, in Germany from the philanthropic educationalists, and in France from the Jansenists and the schools they founded.[142] In the classroom there was an attempt to get away from traditional rote learning and to encourage the independent acquisition of knowledge.[143] In language teaching, the introduction of conversational methods altered the pupil–teacher relationship.[144] Attempts to introduce debating into the learning process and to organize study groups also created new forms of communication.[145]

In the nineteenth century the first models of self-administration were explored, again with the British schools leading the way. Special mention must be made here of the Hazelwood School founded in 1819.[146] Here the attempt was made to build all school activity on the co-operation of the pupils. They were given a certain freedom to choose the content of their studies, a right which was otherwise unknown below university level. As the basis of self-administration, a written school constitution was drawn up. Punishments were imposed by the pupils themselves. Older pupils were given responsible duties. This school experiment was particularly important in its influence on the reforming of the public schools. The prefect system, styled on the older monitor tradition, served here to strengthen the sense of responsibility of individuals and groups.

The idea of giving pupils more responsibility and a greater say in school life found its way into the German schools much later than in Britain. At the beginning of the twentieth century the German Free Youth Movement, the *Jugendbewegung*,[147] provided an important stimulus which encouraged the idea of self-determination for young people. At first, this was merely the programme of a generation of pupils who were sharply critical of the existing schools and their authority structures. However, the

---

[142] Good, *History of Western Education*, pp. 175ff.; Ariès, *Geschichte der Kindheit*, p. 373.

[143] Paulsen, *Geschichte des gelehrten Unterrichts*, vol. II, p. 155.

[144] Good, *History of Western Education*, p. 228.

[145] Ibid., pp. 176, 228.

[146] S. J. Curtis, *History of Education in Great Britain* (London, 1948), pp. 70ff.

[147] Barth, *Geschichte der Erziehung*, pp. 650ff.; T. Koebner, R. -P. Janz and F. Trommler (eds), *'Mit uns zieht die neue Zeit'. Der Mythos Jugend* (Frankfurt, 1985), pp. 224ff.

Youth Movement produced a series of educational theorists, some of whom attempted through radical experiments to put the ideas of the movement into practice in schools. The various reform movements which strove for the realization of the work-school idea were also influenced by the ideas of Free Youth.[148] In particular, they aimed mainly at greater independence for pupils in planning their studies. The principle of responsible participation in school life gained new impetus after the First World War through the growth of pupils' unions modelled on the workers' movement.[149] The social climate of the Weimar Republic, however, was not ripe for the democratization of secondary education.

Forms of pupil participation generally only arise at those points in the history of schooling when the wider social framework favoured co-operative autonomy. Consequently, attempts to give pupils a right to a say in their affairs are particularly common in Britain, the classic land of 'self-government'. The degree of autonomy and shared authority in the religious community influences the forms of participation in schools. It is significant that the progressive impulse in England was to be found in the schools of the Puritan dissenters.

Decisions to introduce pupil participation in recent times are also to be seen in the context of wider democratic trends in society. They are concerned mainly with questions of school organization. On the other hand, the history of schooling shows us that participation in determining the content and methods of instruction are also very important for pupil autonomy. In both areas, the further development of participation rights will be of the greatest significance. The expansion of education has meant that more and more young people are affected for longer and longer by dependency relationships in schools. This makes it all the more essential that the received historical patterns of domination be abolished.

[148] Blättner, *Das Gymnasium*, p. 245; J. V. D. Driesch and J. Esterhues, *Geschichte der Erziehung und Bildung*, vol. ii (Paderborn, 1951), pp. 412ff.
[149] Barth, *Geschichte der Erziehung*, p. 741.

4

Brotherhoods and Sisterhoods

Obviously, young people today relate to each other, as they always have done, at home, at work and most of all at school. But social interaction in these groupings is controlled by adults. By 'youth groups' we mean those social forms in which young people are 'by themselves'.[1] The principal subjects of our investigation are autonomous youth communities. Of course, we must also take into consideration those organizations which are created by adults for youngsters in an attempt to meet their real or perceived needs, and in which elements of self-determination emerge only secondarily. The main examples of this are the organizations which arose out of youth welfare work.

Nowadays communal youth activity is clearly placed in the category of leisure. Historically speaking, however, free time is a relatively recent phenomenon which has evolved alongside the modern patterns of paid employment and school. A large part of the activity of youth groups in the past was not 'free time' activity in the sense that one chose to spend one's available, uncommitted hours in a particular way. Participation in the realm of cult and custom, for example, was to a great extent obligatory. The activities of historical youth groups were sometimes closely connected with work. Such an integration is to be found, for example, in the classical model of spinning-room conviviality; here it is well-nigh impossible to distinguish between leisure and work.

The concept which today we regard as self-evident, that youth groups are voluntary alliances of young people, cannot simply be applied to the past. In early times, and more recently in areas with a strong sense of tradition, involvement in youth groups was not optional. In this respect it can be misleading to refer to traditional youth groups as 'associations', with the implication that people

[1] G. Wurzbacher, *Gesellungsformen der Jugend* (Munich, 1965), p. 9.

choose to associate. Historians researching youth have been making this mistake for too long. The principle of free choice certainly goes back a long way in the cities, but it only gained a wider acceptance with the development of the middle-class club, and it developed much later for adolescents than for adults.

Autonomous youth groups have played a very important part in European history, certainly more important than in most cultures beyond Europe. This was encouraged by the specifically European attitude to marriage. The European marriage pattern resulted in a long period of youth, which meant that at any one time the proportion of adolescents or young adults in the total population was very high. However, a long period of youth does not automatically mean that young people have a more intensive community life. The development of an autonomous company of youth depends far more on the extent to which young people are integrated into the primary groupings of the adult world, particularly the family, and how far they are able to emancipate themselves from these. In this respect, European history shows a fundamental difference between women and men. The latter always had a far greater degree of independence, and were therefore well ahead in their community life. There were also significant variations according to social milieu. In the upper middle class and in the nobility, adolescents were generally subject to their families to a greater degree. However, despite these distinctions, to which we could add regional and period variations, it can safely be said that the degree of adolescent independence in Western and Central Europe was generally relatively high, no doubt because of the institution of domestic service. Correspondingly, we find autonomous forms of youth communities very early in these areas. We may regard this as a characteristic feature of the whole of European social development.

Expressed at its simplest, youth groups in European history may be categorized as belonging to three main types: the local youth group for a parish or other geographical area; the gathered, organized association; and the informal youth group. These three basic types correspond to the stages of the development of social forms generally, and in particular the development of the leisure culture,[2] albeit with phase displacement. In rural areas the ancient

[2] Cf. W. K. Blessing, 'Fest und Vergnügen der "kleinen Leute"', in R. van Dülmen and N. Schindler (eds), *Volkskultur. Zur Wiederentdeckung des vergessenen Alltags (16–20. Jahrhundert)* (Frankfurt, 1984), p. 353.

forms generally lasted far longer than in the cities, so that in a comparison of milieux the different stages may be observed to run parallel. As the three basic types influenced one another, a multitude of modifications and subdivisions appeared. The basic types themselves took on quite different forms as the social framework changed.

I. In the Country

The history of local rural youth groups has been thoroughly researched by folklorists. The multitude of names by which these groups were known provides many interesting pointers to their form, composition and function.[3] The simplest are names which define a subgroup of the rural community marked off by age and rank. Into this category fall such terms as *iuniores, iuniores innupti, adolescentes, Burschen, Buben, Knaben* (these latter two being used to mean young men, not children), *Knechte* (usually means servants, but here includes sons of a household), *die Ledigen* (singles), *die jungen Gesellen* (youngfellows), *garçons, garçons de village, jeunes garçons, garçons de la paroisse* (parish boys), *varlets* (grooms, knaves), *jeunesse, gioventu,* and so on. Terms like these are widely spread throughout the regions of Europe. At this stage in history there was no need for more specific names for these youth groups. Within the local community, a terminology specifying age and rank was adequate. For those outside, the group could be identified by naming the locality. That these youth groups, characterized by simple collective names, were indeed forms of community can be seen from a second category of terms which in some areas go back as far as the Middle Ages. These include, for example, *valeterie, garçonnage, societé, societé de la jeunesse,*

[3] Various names for rural fraternities are gathered in K. S. Kramer, 'Altersklassenverbände', in *Handwörterbuch der deutschen Rechtsgeschichte*, vol. I (Berlin, 1971), p. 138; E. Hoffmann-Krayer, 'Knabenschaften und Volksjustiz', *Schweizerisches Archiv für Volkskunde*, 8 (1905), p. 125; B. Petrei, *Die Burschenschaften im Burgenland* (Eisenstat, 1974), p. 41; N. Z. Davis, 'The reasons of misrule', in *Society and Culture in Early Modern France* (London, 1975), pp. 104, 300; D. Dünninger, *Wegsperre und Lösung* (Berlin, 1967) pp. 243ff., 96; C. Johannesen, 'Norwegisches Burschenbrauchtum', Dissertation, Vienna, 1967, MS, pp. 11, 15; J. Peter, *Gasslbrauch und Gasslspruch in Österreich* (Salzburg, undated), p. 149. For Sweden, see K. R. Wikman, *Die Einleitung der Ehe* (Åbo, 1937), p. 32.

confrérie des garçons, bachellerie, compagnons, compagnie, compagnia del mats (the Grisons), *Knabenschaft, ledige Gersellschaft* (Switzerland), *Bursch* (Franconia, Thuringia, Rheinhessen, Styria), *Borsch* (Luxembourg), *Zeche* (drinking fellowship, Innviertel, Upper Austria), *Irten* (Upper Austria, from MHG *urte*, band), *Ruden* (Upper Austria, from *Rotte*, gang), *Passen* (Salzburg, Salzkammergut, refers to any group of people or animals which belong together), *Konta* (Slovenia), *Bruderschaft, Bubenbruderschaft, Burschenverein, Sodalität* (Eifel), and so on. *Burschenschaft* is now the usual German word, normally represented in English as 'fraternity'. These terms refer almost exclusively to groups of young men. This indicates that, at least on the level of the local community, male forms of youth groups are the older and more dominant form. A number of terms point to the organizational structure of the groups, such as *abbaye, abbaye de la jeunesse, capitanage, Königreich*. These terms indicate that an 'abbot', 'captain' or 'king' held the leadership of the group, which was free to appoint its own office-bearers.

A certain amount about the main functions of the groups can also be deduced from some of the names. In France and Belgium, the terms *varlets à marier, compagnons à marier* or *fils à marier* have a long history. They indicate that seeking a marriage partner is the principal task of the age-group. The form in which this quest is conducted may be gleaned from the Norwegian *nattelöpere* (night-runners), *nattefrier* (night-suitors), and the term current in Switzerland and Vorarlberg, *Nachtbuben* (night-lads). A similar tale is told by the name *Gassenledige* (alley singles). It is the night-time visit to the girls (*das Gasslgehen, Fensterln*) which is the group's main preoccupation. *Stubatbuben* (chamber-lads) may refer either to the girls' sleeping accommodation or to the room where they gathered in the evenings to spin. The Lower Franconian *Gunkel* (distaff, an implement in traditional spinning), rather an odd name for a male youth group, has this idea in mind. *Hualevjonken* (twilighters), the name used in Schleswig, indicates the time of day when the young men would gather. The drinking culture typical of rural fraternities lies behind such terms as *Gelage* (carouse) or *Robischburschen*. This last name, used throughout Burgenland and parts of Lower Austria, is derived from the Slavic *rovŭs*, the slate on which the wine consumed by the fellows was marked up. New initiates into the fraternities were obliged to buy wine for the others, hence the custom in Lower Austria of referring to the group as *die Eingekauften*, those who have bought themselves in. Dancing as group activity is emphasized by the name *Reih* (line-up, Eifel). A widely used term for social gatherings of young men is *Fastnachtsknechte*; at *Fasching*, the Shrovetide Carnival, the activities of the fraternities reached a peak. Another high point of the year was *Kermis*, the annual church fair, so that such titles as *Kirchweihknaben*, *Kirtagsburschen* or *Kilbebuben* were very common. This festival of the patron saint of the local church was very important in traditional society for building group identity. The local youth fraternities played a leading part in it. The association of the rural fraternities with the *Kermis* festival shows how the parish church and its community had become the standard territorial unit for the group structures of young men.

The importance of the church for the group activities of traditional rural youth cannot be stressed enough. The church was the one place where the whole community met together at regular intervals. The manner in which they gathered displayed the basic structure of the community with its subgroups for all to see. A description of the ordering of Protestant congregations in Transylvania makes this clear:

Men and women sit separately on opposite sides of the central aisle. The eldest on each side sit at the front, with decreasing ages towards the back. The confirmed, unmarried 'lads' and 'maids' sit in their own areas, the girls in front of or beside the rest of the congregation, the boys usually at the back or in the gallery. The order within these groups is again determined according to age. These correspond to the formal and informal local groups: the formal structure of the local community is made up of married men, the confirmed lads having a parallel but subordinate organization in their 'brotherhood'. Until the nineteenth century, neither the girls nor the women were organized on an inter-family basis, but they met together informally. The smaller children, who have not yet been confirmed, being closer to their families, are permitted to sit together, usually near the altar, although they too are ordered by gender and age, the boys and the older ones always towards the front.[4]

[4] H. A. Schubert, *Nachbarschaft und Moderniesierung. Eine historische Soziologie traditioneller Lokalgruppen am Beispiel Siebenbürgens* (Cologne, 1980), p. 44.

These strict status differentiations in the congregation do not apply generally to all times and places. However, the idea of separate seating according to gender, family status and age is a common pattern in both Protestant and Catholic areas. Both female and male youth are to be seen as a section of the church community; not a group to be joined, but a status which is automatically bestowed by the various rites of passage.[5] In this sense the girls are a subgroup of the community just as much as the boys. The formal organization of the male subgroup, in this case as a 'brotherhood', is a significant intensification of the internal group contact. It means far more than just sitting together in church. The variety of activities and the intensity of communication had the result that male youth groups at parish level developed a far stronger community life than female ones. As a status group in the traditional rural parish, however, girls must be taken equally into account, just as groups of boys are important even when they did not develop into organized fraternities.

Gathering in church had the effect of strengthening the sense of community. In addition to the Sunday services there were many other reasons for coming together in the church, such as the religious instruction which was often obligatory for young people, or rosary prayers, or Sunday School. The spectrum of possibilities varies according to denomination, period and region. But this always provided opportunities for contact: one walked together on the way to church, often in single-sex groups, one conversed in the churchyard after the service, or even during it. As early as the seventeenth century, complaints were recorded in the Tyrol about the village lads who were standing around outside the church during the Mass.[6] Weddings and funerals were also occasions when the young people of the parish, or at least some of them, met at the church. If an unmarried person died, it was usually unmarried people who carried the coffin. Young people had an even more important role at weddings, which were, after all, the occasions when two of their number parted company with the

---

[5] Cf. W. A. Gestrich, 'Jugend in Ohmenhausen, 1800–1918', Dissertation, Tübingen, 1983; published as 'Tradionelle Jugendkultur und Industrialisierung', in *Kritische Studien zur Geschichtwissenschaft* (Göttingen, 1986), p. 155.

[6] A. Dörrer, 'Das "Gasslgehen" ging im "Fensterln" auf. Zur Sprach- und Kulturgeschichte einer vorehelichen Brauchgruppe der Burschen', in *Festschrift H. Amman*, vol. II (Innsbruck, 1954), p. 130.

group. *The socii sponsi et sponsae* are known to have been present at weddings as early as the Middle Ages. Throughout Europe, single friends of both partners have a major part in the wedding ritual. One striking tradition which is widely known from France to Eastern Europe is that of barring the way:[7] visitors at the wedding were required by the boys of the bride's home village to pay a fee, a clear symbol of the claim they felt they had on the girl. This payment to the *valeterie* of the parish is attested in central France as early as 1402.[8] Again, it was the parish youth who protested against the remarriage of widows and widowers by means of the *charivari*, the banging of pots and pans in mock serenade, a custom attested since the late Middle Ages.[9] The parish, then, has long been the territorial frame of reference for celebrating marriage, and the geographical unit within which the adolescent contacts leading to marriage take place. In considering the importance of the parish for the social life of young people, one other major factor must be taken into account. Elementary education generally developed as an offshoot of church structures. The school catchment area was the church parish. Thus with the intensification of schooling, boys and girls were increasingly brought into contact with one another on this territorial level from childhood on, and these contacts carried over into the social groupings of adolescence.

The idea that young people represented a subclass, so to speak, within the congregation of the parish church provides us with a basis for some conclusions concerning the age and distribution of rural youth groups. In attempting this we must of course take account of a number of limiting factors. In the first place we need to pursue the question of the relation between parish and administrative district. These do not always coincide. It is therefore important to note that the civil administrative ward could also have influenced the formation of social groups, especially for young men, for example in connection with local defence. Manorial structures must also be taken into consideration. Feudal dependency could place people under pressure to enter a particular marriage, with the result that the parish was not the basis for selection.

[7] Dünninger, *Wegsperre und Lösung*.
[8] Ibid., p. 245. Cf. also A. Burguière, 'Pratique du charivari et repression religieuse dans la France d'Ancien Régime', in J. LeGoff and J. C. Schmitt (eds), *Le Charivari* (Paris, 1981), p. 183.
[9] Ibid., pp. 183ff.

Indeed, the prevailing regulations on marriage always do affect the opportunities of young people to come into contact with each other. In comparisons between the rural areas of Rumania and those of the neighbouring south Slavic regions, for example, it becomes apparent that in Rumania the habit of marrying within the local community corresponded to the presence of strong youth fraternities; complex families were absent there.[10] In the south Slavic countries, on the other hand, the spread of the *zadruga*, a patriarchal complex family form, corresponded to the principle of exogamy; the young men there generally sought brides from outside their own village.[11] Youth groups analogous to the Rumanian fraternities did not exist there. Such parallels point to fundamental structural contexts and enable us to make assumptions about the age and distribution of rural youth groups. Wherever there have been distinct forms of ecclesiastical and secular local communities since the high Middle Ages, we may assume that fraternities had already formed. On the basis of current research, the main areas of distribution seem to have been France, Germany, Switzerland, Northern Italy, Austria, Hungary, Rumania and the Scandinavian countries.[12]

Although church congregations frequently provided the social framework within which rural youth groups operated, this is not to say that religious activities were their main function. On the contrary, religion played only a minor part in group activities. In this, there were major regional differences. In many areas of northern France, a parish boys' group under the patronage of St Nicholas was matched by a corresponding girls' group whose patron was St Catherine.[13] At the festivals of the two saints, 25 November and 6 December, the promotion of youngsters from childhood to youth was conducted with all due ceremony.[14] It was the influence of the church which caused these two groups to run parallel and to be given equal status. Where organized girls' groups

[10] D. Chirot, 'The Romanian communal village: an alternative to the Zadruga', in R. Byrnes (ed.), *Communal Families in the Balkans* (London, 1973), p. 153; O. Buhociu, *Die rumänische Volkskultur und ihre Mythologie* (Wiesbaden, 1974), pp. 44ff.

[11] J. Halpern. *A Serbian Village* (New York, 1956), p. 190.

[12] Davis, 'The reasons of misrule', p. 109.

[13] A. van Gennep, *Manuel de folklore français contemporain* (Paris, 1937), p. 208.

[14] Y. Verdier, *Drei Frauen. Das Leben auf dem Dorf* (Stuttgart, 1982), pp. 216ff.

existed, involving all the adolescent females in the rural community, these frequently had their roots in the religious sphere. Usually they were secondary foundations. Attempts to bind youth groups more firmly into church life go back at least to the sixteenth century, both in Protestant and in Catholic countries. In France, these seem to have been relatively successful.[15] These *confréries* in France were far stronger than the church-based *Bruderschaft* in Germany. But in Germany too there is evidence of the transformation of a youth group into an ecclesiastical order of brothers as early as the end of the fifteenth century. According to its constitution of 1645, this *Bubenbruderschaft* of Mittenwald was ordered as a Christian brotherhood in honour of St Mary and St John, yet retained strong features of a rural youth group.[16] In Catholic areas it sometimes happened that youth fraternities acted as standard bearers in processions.[17] Occasionally the regular church attendance of the members of the fraternity was monitored by its leaders. In Protestant areas of Switzerland the statutes of some youth groups prescribed penalties for any group member who attended church with uncleaned shoes or dusty clothes, who forgot his hymn-book, or who laughed or slept during the service.[18] The Transylvanian fraternities were preserved in their ancient form by being taken into the church structure.[19] But these are all formations which have been superimposed; they are, so to speak, attempts to churchify groups which in their traditional values, norms and activities often ran counter to the church's practice and teaching. This is most obviously the case with the traditions of courting, the often quite liberal sexuality of the spinning-room, the *charivari*, the drinking culture, and the continuation of pre-Christian cultic forms. In general it can be said that the Reformation and the Counter-reformation, and also revivalist and ascetic movements within the churches, were strongly opposed to the rural youth fraternities. In many areas this caused ancient traditions to fall into disuse.

[15] Davis, 'City Women and Religious Change', in *Society and Culture*, 75; E. Shorter, *Die Geburt der modernen Familie* (Reinbek, 1975), pp. 236ff.

[16] H. Usener, 'Über vergleichende Sitten- und Rechtsgeschichte', *Hessische Blätter für Volkskunde*, 1/3 (1902), p. 51.

[17] H. Schauert, 'Die Fahnengesellschaften im oberen Sauerland', *Rheinisch-westfälische Zeitschrift für Volkskunde*, 2 (1955), pp. 119ff.; Blessing, 'Fest', p. 357.

[18] Hoffmann-Krayer, 'Knabenschaften', p. 141.

[19] Usener, 'Über vergleichende Sitten- und Rechtsgeschichte', p. 49.

On the other hand, it is also one-sided to seek the origins of the cultic functions of the rural fraternities exclusively in pre-Christian tradition. German-language scholarship on this theme has long concentrated solely on pre-Christian traditions. Its attempts to draw connections between rural youth lore of recent times and the secret cultic societies of Germanic antiquity have brought it deservedly into disrepute. Certainly, it would be rash to ignore the conclusions of past researchers simply because of their political implications. When a recent study by a prominent Italian scholar who had no knowledge of the German tradition of scholarship sees the origins of the *charivari* in the youth group's representation of the 'wild hunt', this must give us cause to ponder.[20] It seems certain that the rural youth groups did indeed preserve many pre-Christian cultic traditions. As in other respects, they are here a very conservative social form. However, it is difficult to argue plausibly for a direct line of continuity from the cohorts of young men in Germanic tribal society to the youth fraternities of more modern times. The wider social frameworks are simply too different.

The central function of the rural fraternities in traditional society was the regulation of sexual relations in adolescence by ritualized forms of courting. This was a major task wherever the age of marriage was relatively high for both sexes. Early marriages arranged by parents for their children make such arrangements unnecessary. Traditions of autonomous adolescent courting, on the other hand, always imply a degree of participation in the choice of a partner. Where the sexes were strictly separated for moral reasons in adolescence, as in the Mediterranean countries, these customs did not arise. Instead, there was frequently a tendency to marry young. Consequently, the control of courting by the fraternity was practically known only in Western, Central and Northern Europe. It could take very different forms. The night-time visit to the girls, variously know as *Kiltgang* (dusking), *Fensterln* (windowing), *Gasslgehen* (alleying) and so on, was known throughout the Alps and in many parts of Germany, it was very common in Scandinavia and the Baltic countries, and occasionally occurred in England and France.[21] Sometimes it was done individually, sometimes in small groups. If geography allowed, the

[20] C. Ginzburg, 'Charivari, associations juvéniles, chasse sauvage', in LeGoff and Schmitt (eds), *Le Charivari*, pp. 131ff.
[21] Details in Wikman, *Die Einleitung der Ehe*, esp. map, p. 164.

whole local fraternity would gather at the start of these evening excursions. At any rate, the group as a whole would be informed of any contacts which were made, and would regulate these according to their received norms. Thus, although this custom did involve a step-by-step lifting of sexual restrictions, it never amounted to wanton promiscuity. What contact was allowed to whom, and at what age, were questions which were subject to strictly observed rules. None the less, the regions where night visits were institutionalized in this way did suffer from relatively high rates of illegitimacy.[22]

Another form of courting, which can overlap with the first, was the so-called *Mailehen* (May-feu). The girls of the village were allocated to the members of the fraternity for a certain time and with certain rights, in particular, rights to dance and entertainment. This was the practice in the western parts of Germany, in The Netherlands, in the bordering regions of France, occasionally in the north and east of Germany, and also in Denmark under the name *gadelamsgilder*.[23] The girls were distributed by the May King, the leader of the fraternity, often by means of an auction. In some areas of France, the *donnage* was carried out by popular acclamation of the gathered crowd of youngsters.[24] On the other hand, the matching up of couples could be left to chance, for example the first boy a girl met on St Valentine's Day in England or on the first working day after Christmas in Norway.[25] These were social institutions which virtually forced adolescents into contact with the opposite sex. The problem of breaking out of the phase of sexual latency was thus solved in a highly ritualized yet standardized and obligatory form. After the phase of general separation of young males and females there came about a social interaction of the whole adolescent population of the rural community. The roles of the sexes remained quite separate. The active role fell to the males. The decisive processes of communication took place on their side. The girls met them as individuals; in this form of courting there was no room for a girls' group with a parallel function.

[22] M. Mitterauer, *Ledige Mütter. Zur Geschichte unehelicher Geburten in Europa* (Munich, 1983), pp. 55ff.
[23] M. Panzer, *Tanz und Recht* (Frankfurt, 1938), p. 125; Johannesen, 'Norwegisches Burschenbrauchtum', p. 65.
[24] Shorter, *Die Geburt der modernen Familie*, p. 157.
[25] Johannesen, 'Norwegisches Burschenbrauchtum', p. 65.

The territorial principle which is so characteristic of the rural youth fraternities is connected with the claim they felt they had on their 'own' girls. Suitors from outside the locality who appeared at the girls' windows were likely to be beaten or ducked in the well. Likewise, on the dance floor the girls would be defended from any advances by outsiders. Such disputes were frequently the occasion for brawls, which could lead to stabbings and sometimes ended fatally. In particular, *Kermis*, when young people from several parishes came together, was the occasion for conflicts of this kind. Brawls at church fairs are recorded from the late Middle Ages on.[26] The peaceful solution to such territorial claims, the 'barring of the way' by which the bride was 'purchased' by another community, can also be traced back to the medieval period.[27] But the strongly territorial nature of the rural fraternities and the resulting aggressive competition with the neighbouring groups were more than simply vying for the local marriage market. The adult men always had responsibility for establishing the boundaries of the community and defending them from intrusion from without. This adult role was developed in adolescence. Competing interests of neighbouring communities, for example for the use of woods and pastures, can be observed from the Middle Age,[28] and these were foreshadowed in the earlier phase of life. Furthermore, the rural fraternities' territorial struggles can be seen as having a symbolic value which was of great importance for group identity and solidarity.

The dance was of great importance in courting traditions. For boys, permission to attend dances was generally granted on admission to the youth group. From this point on, dancing was often not only a right, but an obligation. For girls, the first invitation to accompany a boy to a dance, or at least the first which her parents allowed her to accept, was the clear sign that she was no longer a child. The organization of dances at *Fasching*, Easter, May Day, Pentecost (Whitsun) or *Kermis* was one of the most important tasks of the fraternity which required special arrangements, office bearers, and especially money and produce. Donations were often

---

[26] A. Lutz, *Jünglings- und Gesellenverbände im alten Zürich und im alten Winterthur* (Zurich, 1957), p. 56.

[27] Cf. Dünninger, *Wegsperre und Lösung*.

[28] K. S. Bader, *Das mittelalterliche Dorf als Friedens- und Rechtsbereich* (Graz, 1967), p. 50.

gathered for the purpose by a solemn procession which paraded from door to door. In some areas there were particular dances which were organized not by the fraternity but by the girls, like the French St Catherine's Day Ball or the German *Jungferntanz*.[29] This involved an *ad hoc* organization of girls, which sometimes conducted a 'collecting parade' of its own. However, these were exceptions, for the active role in courting was male. The importance of the dance for the young men's fraternities was so great that in some cases the dance step or tune was taken up as the symbol of the group, for example the *Landler* (a primitive waltz) in the *Zechen* of the Innviertel. Here the dance was seen to epitomize the fraternity, courting being pushed a little into the background.[30]

The dance had a special role at the other end of courting, in the wedding ritual. Often the transition from one status to the other was enacted in the custom that the bride first danced with all the unmarried guests, then with all the married ones. Sometimes a representative from each group sufficed.[31] The ritual parting from the youth group often involved separate farewell parties for bride and groom. One example of this was the *Polterabend*, at which crockery was smashed to bring good luck, hence another of the fraternities' names, *die Polterer*. The participation of single people in the wedding ritual was also known in parts of Europe which had no organized youth fraternities, as in the British traditions of stag nights, best men and bridesmaids. Striking parallels to the wedding ritual are to be found in the funeral traditions for those who died unmarried, the so-called 'wedding of the dead'. The 'black' and the 'white bride' have already been mentioned. The youth group played an important role in this occasion.[32]

The second major complex of activities of the rural youth fraternities can be gathered under the heading 'censure'. This rich vein of tradition in the old rural community was connected with

[29] Verdier, *Drei Frauen*, p. 217; Panzer, *Tanz und Recht*, p. 129.

[30] R. Wolfram, in *Österreichischer Volkskundeatlas*, vol. 5 (Vienna, 1974), pp. 25ff.

[31] R. Wolfram, *Die Volkstänze in Österreich und verwandte Tänze in Europa* (Salzburg, 1951), pp. 119ff.; Johannesen, 'Norwegisches Burschen brauchtum', p. 47; Panzer, *Tanz und Recht*, pp. 113ff.

[32] H. Bächtold-Stäubli, *Handwörterbuch des deutschen Aberglaubens*, vol. I (Berlin, 1932–3), p. 1008; H. P. Fielhauer, 'Die "Schwarze" und die "Weiße Braut" beim Begräbnis Lediger', *Das Waldviertel*, 19 (1970), pp. 72ff.

courting to the extent that a major area of censure related to the sexual behaviour of girls.[33] Girls regarded as too free with their favours were exposed and denounced by symbolic actions such as the hanging of a straw doll in a public place. Similarly, the fraternity would censure widows or widowers who took a younger person as a second spouse. *Charivari*, strictly speaking, relates to the denunciation of second marriages, and in France goes back as far as the Middle Ages.[34] The remarriage of a parent often meant that the transfer of a farm was postponed, and this had a seriously detrimental effect on the prospects of the heir's becoming independent and marrying. It is hardly surprising that this was a sensitive issue for the fraternities. Beyond this, the group's disciplinary jurisdiction covered sexual matters generally. Traditional gender roles were carefully maintained, an important matter for young people who were growing into these roles. A French scholar has gathered together a list of potential victims: hen-pecked husbands; misers; tight-fisted godparents; strangers who failed to pay their dues; vain girls; adulteresses; incurable drunkards; violent or disruptive people; informers; in short, anyone who offended against the public opinion of the village.[35] The main form of censure was public derision, expressed in processions after nightfall with mocking verses and as much banging and clattering as possible, hence such terms as *charivari*, *Katzenmusik*, rough music, and so on. The censure could take other forms, however, such as barricading windows and doors, dumping a load of manure on the roof, or lining up carts and machinery on the market place.[36] A whole range of bizarre variations have been recorded, pointing to a highly elaborate code which would be understood by the local community. The times of the year when censure was practised were also fixed: for example the twelve nights of merrymaking from Christmas to Epiphany, *Fasching*, *Walpurgisnacht* (the evening before May Day, believed to be a witches' feast), and sometimes *Kermis*.[37] These censure customs were spread right across Europe, from Portugal

---

[33] Shorter, *Die Geburt der modernen Familie*, pp. 250ff.

[34] Cf. the articles gathered in LeGoff and Schmitt (eds), *Charivari*.

[35] Van Gennep, *Manuel de folklore*, p. 202.

[36] Forms from recent times are gathered in E. Burgstaller, *Burschenbrauchtum II – termingebundene Unruhnächte. Kommentar zum Österreichischen Volkskundeatlas*, 3/46 (Vienna, 1968), p. 24.

[37] Ibid., pp. 12ff.

The Civic Quarter Library
www.leedsmet.ac.uk/lis/lss

Borrowed

Customer   Cairns, Tammy Claire Jane

                                Due Date

1 A history of youth   25/10/2010,23:59
1704537229

2 Childhood in quest   25/10/2010,23:59
1702317400

3 The kindness of st   25/10/2010,23:59
1704290848

                    11.10.2010 10:17:34

For renewals telephone (0113) 812 6161
Thank you and see you soon

to Hungary and from central Italy to Norway.[38] The unmarried youth are not always the only perpetrators, for in England in more recent times there were others involved in the 'rough music'.[39] But the general association of these customs with the organized male youth groups is indisputable.

The *charivari* has a particularly long history in Upper Italy and France, where it was opposed by the church as early as the fourteenth and fifteenth centuries. There was no direct connection with the established legal system. The fraternities pursued precisely those offences which could not be prosecuted officially, such as the remarriage of widows, which in terms of church law was perfectly in order. The censure traditions provided a kind of counter-jurisdiction which operated according to local norms and against the centralized norms of the Church and the emerging stage. In this way they sometimes preserved more-archaic concepts of justice against novelties imposed from above, a conservative trait which was typical of rural youth. In one respect, however, the fraternities' system of censure was in harmony with public law: it could only be executed by males. Girls were never active participants. Parallels between male youth fraternities and girls' groups may be relevant in church activities and to some extent at dances, but they break down in this important area. What is surprising is the degree to which traditional rural society allowed its male youth to exercise an independent jurisdiction over the entire local community. It may be tempting to see here an institutionalizing of potential youth protest, but this interpretation misses the mark. The rural fraternities were seldom the source of pressure for social change. Rather, this counter-jurisdiction, restricted as it was to certain festivals, should be seen as a safety valve, just as more generally the upside-down world of the carnival served to support the established order, not to undermine it. So, while the traditions of censure certainly contained the potential for youth protest, it

[38] P. Burke, *Helden, Schurken und Narren. Europäische Volkskultur in der frühen Neuzeit* (Stuttgart, 1981), p. 212; LeGoff and Schmitt (eds), *Charivari*, esp. p. 366; Johannesen, 'Norwegisches Burschenbrauchtum', p. 22. For Italy, see the informative map in C. A. Corsini, 'Why is remarriage a male affair?', in J. Dupâguier et al. (eds), *Marriage and Remarriage in Populations of the Past* (London, 1981), p. 393.

[39] E. P. Thompson, '"Rough music" oder englische Katzenmusik', in E. P. Thompson, *Plebische Kultur und moralische Ökonomie* (Frankfurt, 1980), pp. 131ff.

functioned for the most part as an instrument of social control.[40] The way in which the elements in the repertoire of censure were adapted to suit the individual case showed a great deal of creativity. The theatrical unfolding of the censure provided myriad possibilities for the fantasy of youth. One could say that what had emerged here was a very specific youth culture typified by burlesque, parody and satire. It seems to be these components which were in mind when in 1830 the first French satirical magazine was given the name *Charivari*.

A characteristic feature of the rural fraternities was their eating and drinking culture. Sales to the unmarried *ad bibendum et comedendum* are recorded from the Middle Ages.[41] Both were important for strengthening the group. The enjoyment of beer or wine, like smoking or playing cards, was a hallmark of the communal life of male youth. On the one hand, it marked them off from children, and on the other, from girls. The rituals of joining the rural fraternities frequently involved the drinking of alcohol, or the extending of an invitation to drink. Their specific drinking culture shaped the life of the group. The alcohol itself gave a feeling of community and strength, it created the right atmosphere for all the nonsense which made up the fraternities' 'rites of misrule'. The table regularly reserved for the fraternity at the inn was an important point of reference for the group. Here the fraternity's drinking slate was kept,[42] here hung an oversized penknife or other symbol of the group.[43] Only rarely would the fraternity have its own meeting place. Exceptions were the *Hualevjonkenstuben* in Holstein[44] or the *Äbbehe* in Swabia, where a room was rented for the winter in the farm of one of the boys.[45] Unlike the girls, members of the fraternity seldom met in their parents' homes. When they did have a room set aside, this was a no-go area for the girls, in contrast to the girls' spinning-room, where the boys were received. Nor was the inn a place where girls could meet together.

[40] Cf. M. Scharfe, 'Zum Rügebrauch', *Hessische Blätter für Volkskunde*, 61 (1970), pp. 45ff.

[41] *Schweizerisches idiotikon*, vol. 8 (Frauenfeld, 1936), p. 344.

[42] Petrei, *Die Burschenschaften im Burgenland*, p. 41.

[43] W. Galler, 'Feitelvereine', *Österreichische Zeitschrift für Volkskunde*, 28 (1974), p. 191.

[44] G. F. Meyer, *Brauchtum der Jungmannschaften in Schleswig-Holstein* (Flensburg, 1941), p. 11.

[45] Gestrich, 'Jugend in Ohmenhausen', p. 183.

Eating and drinking at the inn involved expense. However, the peasant-farmers' sons and young farm-hands who together made up the group did not generally have a great deal of money. This explains the role of the 'collecting parades' in the activities of the fraternities. On particular occasions laid down by tradition the lads would go from house to house asking for money. This was not, in fact, begging, but staking claim to an ancient right.[46] Whoever withheld a gift offended against the accepted order and would be justly censured for his meanness. Often the lads would wear masks when demanding money. Both the collection and the censure involved parades, and masks played an important part in both. It is possible that these processions had their roots in cultic traditions. They figure highly in the traditional lore of rural male youth.

The degree to which male youth groups were given a military function was decisive for the group structure, the forms of expression and the role models of the rural fraternities. The mobilization of agricultural workers varied greatly between different regions and periods of history. When it arose, it had a major influence on the life of the fraternity.[47] It is important to make this distinction. The great significance of the military factor lay in its prestige. War, like hunting, was an activity properly belonging to the upper classes. Whenever the rural populations were also involved, they laid great stress on this fact, especially during youth. This phenomenon can be observed right across Europe, from the groups of archers in Bukovina, known as *arcasi*, made up of the entire male youth of a village,[48] to the youth associations in the south of France who publicly paraded their arms in a ceremonial procession known as the *bravade*.[49] The military element was particularly prominent in the Swiss *Knabenschaften*.[50] Groups of unmarried archers and huntsmen are said to have played an important part in the liberation struggle of the early Swiss confederation. Time and again in Swiss history we read of military enterprises by local youth groups leading to skirmishes and revolts. It seems significant that these occurrences frequently coincided

[46] H. Schultze, *Das deutsche Jugendtheater* (Leipzig, 1941), p. 20.

[47] W. Hornstein, *Jugend in ihrer Zeit* (Hamburg, 1966), pp. 119ff.

[48] O. Buhociu, *Die rumänische Volkskultur und ihre Mythologie* (Wiesbaden, 1974), pp. 65, 44.

[49] Van Gennep, *Manuel de folklore*, p. 204.

[50] Kramer, 'Altersklassenverbände', p. 140; H. G. Wackernagel, *Altes Volkstum in der Schweiz* (Basel, 1956), pp. 26ff.; Wolfram, *Österreichischer Volkskundeatlas*, vol. 5, pp. 57ff., 95ff.; Hoffmann-Krayer, 'Knabenschaften', pp. 155ff.

with the traditional 'nights of misrule', and where therefore obviously closely connected with the activities of the fraternities. The important role of the Swiss *Reisläufer* ('travelling' soldier) in the age of mercenary armies led to a diffusion of the structures and mannerisms of the fraternities into European military life. We might mention here the influence of the fraternities' clothing. It often happened that the young people took to the field in their own self-regulated groups, the so-called *Freiharste*. While these would certainly not have been closed groups of local fraternities, it is quite probable that the military formations of the time would have shown structural analogies to those of the youth organization. To the present day, elements derived from the fraternities can still be seen in the recruiting traditions of the Swiss army.[51]

After the French Revolution, the introduction of general national service in various European countries had a great effect on the rural fraternities. In some areas, full membership was made dependent on the completion of military service.[52] In France and also in Rumania year groups formed within the rural youth structures, and these were called up as a unit.[53] There were even parallel girls' groups called *conscrites*. Here we see a similarity to the development of year groups in the young rural population on the basis of Confirmation. Conscription becomes a male rite of initiation.

Like the Swiss *Freiharste*, other forms of voluntary military service also had connections with rural fraternities. In the Thirty Year's War, for example, the *freye holsteinische Knechte* rose up against the Swedish invaders.[54] In Austria, the volunteer corps founded in 1859 adopted the grouse feather from the characteristic garb of the fraternity.[55] In the fraternities, a plume pointing forward was the symbol of an aggressive spirit in the local brawls. It appeared in the First World War as a badge of the Austrian imperial and royal mountain troops, especially the famous *Kaiserjäger*, and

[51] Th. Bühler, 'Knabenschaftliches in Rekrutenbräuchen der Schweiz', *Schweizerisches Archiv für Volkskunde*, 57 (1961), pp. 82ff.

[52] K. Gaal, *Spinnstubenlieder* (Munich, 1966), p. 16; H. Jungwirth, 'Die Zeche des oberen Innviertels', *Zeitschrift für Volkskunde*, 6 (1932), p. 31.

[53] Van Gennep, *Manuel de folklore*, pp. 219ff.; Buhociu, *Die rumänische Volkskultur*, p. 45.

[54] G. F. Meyer, *Brauchtum der Jungmannschaften in Schleswig-Holstein* (Flensburg, 1941), p. 145.

[55] J. Peter, *Gasslbrauch und Gasslspruch in Österreich* (Salzburg, undated), p. 217.

after the war the *Heimwehren*, the civil defence organizations which were put together out of local defensive groups, were sometimes known as the *Hahnenschwänzler* (cocks' tails). The symbol of male aggressiveness here marks a line of development from traditional rural fraternities through military organizations to political groupings in the modern party state. The Austrian *Heimwehren* were widely supported by the fraternities, and the tradition of inn brawling with neighbouring territorial youth groups was carried forward at an inter-regional level into the conflicts of political factions in the inter-war period.

The arming of rural youth groups happened not only when there was compulsory or voluntary military service. In a lesser form it also occurred in situations where the rural population had *de jure* no right to carry arms at all. The most important weapon, in general use in the fraternities, was the knife. It was not only a weapon but also a man's working tool. In the villages of Burgenland it was usual for boys at the age of seven to be given their first knife which they used to cut whistles out of elderwood while looking after the cows.[56] In the alpine regions, even the poorest hill farmer's son possessed his penknife, which has already been mentioned as a symbol of certain fraternities. These were known as *Feitelvereine* (knife bands).[57] The knife was the main weapon used in local inter-fraternity brawls in the inn or at the *Kirmes* festival. Consequently, the prohibition on drawing knives is found in rural legal sources from early times.[58] That it was so often repeated is an indication of the persistence of the tradition of knife fights. For the members of the fraternity it was taken for granted that one carried a knife whenever the group met. In Swabia, Bavaria and Austria, the knife, and other male working-tools which could also be used as weapons, such as the axe and scythe, gave rise to a term which was very widely used and which epitomized all the positive qualities of a young man, namely *Schneid*.[59] The primary meaning of *Schneid* is the cutting power of the knife or similar tool, but it was used figuratively to indicate all the qualities most highly prized in the fraternity which carried the knife: courage,

---

[56] Verdier, *Drei Frauen*, p. 182.

[57] Galler, 'Feitelvereine'; B. Petrei, ' "Feitelvereine" auch im heutigen Burgenland', *Österreichische Zeitschrift für Volkskunde*, 29 (1975), pp. 186ff.

[58] Peter, *Gasslbrauch und Gasslspruch*, pp. 116ff.

[59] Ibid., pp. 122ff.

strength, dexterity, perceptiveness, ability to provide a ready answer, charisma and success with girls. The knife also has a powerful sexual symbolism. In many areas, then, *Schneid* expressed what we today might call masculine sex appeal.

The complex of functions related to arms shows clearly what influence the rural fraternities had in the preservation of traditional gender roles. Wherever the military component dominated the community life of young people there was always a polarization of the role models of males and females, and therefore also of the groups they formed. Only for the young men did arms contribute to social development. But there were defensive elements as well which were not directly linked to the military sphere which influenced the character of rural fraternities. The whole territorial aggressiveness of traditional local youth groups must be seen in this context.

Some of the sporting activities of the fraternities were also connected with their military function, such as shooting, riding, and throwing or slinging stones.[60] The various forms of wrestling and wrangling have their origins not in the defence of the local community but in the conflicts of the local fraternities. They served as a measure of physical strength and demonstrated the great importance of strength in agricultural labour. It is surely no co-incidence that they were commonest in the hill-farming regions where the physical requirements were most demanding. The lifting of heavy stones as an initiation rite in the rural fraternities points to a working context which would have influenced the sporting activities of the fraternities more than the military element. The various stages of development of physical strength in adolescence were important for a young person's rank in working life. They were therefore significant elements in determining status both in the economic community of the household and also in the fraternity. The leader of the fraternity was often chosen on the basis of sporting achievements, for example the *Pfingstkönig* who won the Whitsun horse race.[61] Sporting competitions were not only important for deciding the internal hierarchy of the group; they also shaped its external relationships. From the late Middle Ages onwards we read

[60] W. Schaufelberger, *Der Wettkampf in der alten Eidgenossenschaft* (Bern, 1972), pp. 69ff.

[61] H. P. Fielhauer, 'Alte und neue Pfingstkönige in Niederösterreich', *Österreichisches Volksliedwerk*, vol. 32–3 (1985), pp. 55ff.

of competitions between the male youth of different parishes.[62] The *Kermis* festivals, at which young people from various local groups came together, would have provided a good opportunity. Competitions between the single and married men of a village also have a long history. In traditional rural communities, all sporting activities were dominated by young men. Only very seldom do we find reference to games in which girls and boys compete together.[63]

The educational functions of traditional rural fraternities have a number of quite different aspects. In the first place, the youth group prepared its members in a general way for later participation in the adult male community. The tasks of censure, arms and defending the territorial integrity of the local group are all relevant here. The community of the table at the local inn was surely an introduction to the public life of the men. Beyond this, the fraternities had a specific socializing role which was important for the shaping of adolescence. Learning to relate to the opposite sex was prominent here. Older members of the fraternity introduced newcomers to the techniques of courting. They learned to dance, they learned the often very complicated 'alley rhymes' which were recited under the girls' windows, and eventually they were allowed to take part in the tradition of *Fensterln*.[64] All the traditions of night-time courting involved acquiring skills. And also, more generally, the fraternity was an important framework for introducing young men to the traditional behaviour patterns and characteristics of male gender roles. In this respect it was quite different from other instruments of socialization, such as family and church. Much which would be forbidden there was positively obligatory in the fraternity: excessive drinking, violent encounters, sexual 'conquests' and the like. Numerous activities of the fraternity were illegal and had to be done in secret. The requirement of members to keep silence, which is a very common feature of male youth groups, arose from the contradiction between the norms of the group and the norms of the surrounding society. This contradiction led to a tension which is characteristic of the social integration of young men, a tension which is already present in childhood when boys are rewarded for being naughty. This element of tension was not

---

[62] Davis, 'The reasons of misrule', p. 104.
[63] E.g., Meyer, *Brauchtum der Jungmannschaften*, p. 126.
[64] Peter, *Gasslbrauch und Gasslspruch*, p. 132.

present for girls in traditional rural societies. The social forms of young women did not include patterns equivalent to the counter-norms of the fraternities.

The role of the older members of the fraternity in educating the younger ones indicates a system of rank according to age. So, for example, the *Zechen* of the Innviertel had a rule that an older *Zechbruder* always spoke before a younger one.[65] With the slow development of physical strength in the old rural milieu, being older often meant being stronger, since the peak of physical strength was achieved relatively late. At any rate, physical strength stood alongside age as a second criterion of internal rank. These criteria for social status within the group contradicted the hierarchy of the village community, which ran primarily according to property. In the fraternities wealth played no part:[66] whether farmer's son or farm-hand was unimportant. In industrialized rural communities even workers' sons often remained in the fraternity.[67] A division of farmer's sons and farm-hands into separately organized groupings was unusual and when it occurred it must have been a late de-velopment. Indeed, in traditional fraternities it was often the farm-hands who held the leading position. They frequently married much later and therefore were in the group longer. With respect to social origins, these youth groups were egalitarian. This, how-ever, does not mean that all the members of the fraternity were equal. The sense of rank within the groups could be very marked. It would be wrong to refer to the fraternities as peer groups in the modern sense.

Within the fraternities there occasionally emerged a substruc-ture of age groups.[68] Such year-group camaraderie had a particular solidarity. This was equally true for girls and boys. In Protestant areas these year groups arose principally from shared Confirma-tion, in Catholic areas from First Communion. The influence of conscription on the development of year groups has already been

[65] Jungwirth, 'Die Zeche des oberen Innviertels', p. 32; Meyer, *Brauchtum der Jungmannschaften*, p. 9.
[66] Wikman, *Die Einleitung der Ehe*, p. 371; Petrei, *Burschenschaften*, p. 19; Jungwirth, 'Die Zeche des oberen Innviertels', pp. 31ff.
[67] Gestrich, 'Jugend in Ohmenhausen', p. 177.
[68] Buhociu, *Die rumänische Volkskultur*, p. 45; Petrei, *Burschenschaften*, p. 23; Gestrich, 'Jugend in Ohmenhausen', pp. 177, 288; E. Schulz, 'Konfirmation', *Hessische Blätter für Volks- und Kulturforschung*, 13 (1982), p. 202; Van Gennep, *Manuel de folklore*, pp. 221ff.; Verdier, *Drei Frauen*, p. 72.

mentioned. With the growth of compulsory schooling the influence of the class has had a similar effect. However, this trend to develop single-age groups is quite recent. An older criterion for the internal division of fraternities may have been neighbourhood, especially in sparsely populated areas. This was always a more important factor for girls, since they had a narrower radius of action. Whether the fraternity met in its entirety or in subgroups would depend on the activity in hand.

One expression of the priority of age in the fraternities was the fact that the leader of the group was sometimes simply known as the 'eldest'.[69] More common, however, are terms which point to parallel positions in the spiritual or temporal hierarchies, such as king, prince, judge, *Schultheiß* (mayor), *Landvogt* (governor), *roi*, *évêque*, *abbas* and so on.[70] Allusions like these are to be found in rural groups from Rumania to France. Far less common was for the *roi* to have a corresponding *reine*, or the *Pfingstkönig* a *Pfingstkönigin*.[71] The reason for this lies in the much lower level of communication and organization among the girls. The fraternities did not actually need to have office-bearers, but sometimes this aspect was very strong indeed. The titles of office-bearers sometimes related to the dominant functions of the group, for example barman, dance master, standard-bearer. The appointment of office-bearers was conducted quite differently from group to group. In more recent times voting was usual. But there were also some quite archaic forms, such as lifting up or pulling down the candidate, who was then counted as chosen if he had touched the timbers of the roof with his head.[72] Sporting competitions to decide leadership have already been mentioned. But the simplest system was to have the eldest as leader.

Our knowledge of rural fraternities stems for the most part from surveys conducted in the nineteenth and twentieth centuries. There is a serious risk that such data may give us a static picture of this form of community, without adequate chronological and geographical differentiation. In view of this, it seems sensible to

[69] Petrei, *Burschenschaften*, p. 32.
[70] Kramer, 'Altersklassenverbände', p. 139; Hoffmann-Krayer, 'Knabenschaften', p. 127; Van Gennep, *Manuel de folklore*, p. 205; Buhociu, *Die rumänische Volkskultur*, pp. 54ff.
[71] Van Gennep, *Manuel de folklore*, p. 208.
[72] Buhociu, *Die rumänische Volkskultur*, p. 64.

consider the general social framework, changes in which must have had their effect on the rural youth organizations.

It has already been mentioned that the Reformation and Counter-reformation must have had a sharp effect on the fraternities in religious matters, reducing them in importance. The ecclesiastical brotherhoods in Catholic areas, for example, were not bound to marital status, and this meant that a traditional central distinction for rural youth groups was blurred. This anticipated an effect which the growth of middle-class clubs brought to the rural population in the nineteenth and twentieth centuries. In the Protestant sphere, the consistory took over the fraternity's role as adjudicator of moral behaviour. Right across the board, the Reformation and Counter-reformation led to a deepening of Christian belief as opposed to pre-Christian. As schooling developed, a thorough rationalization took place in the way people viewed the world. The magic practices which had been preserved in the fraternities lost importance. Frequently it can be observed that customs once belonging to adolescence were passed down to childhood. It seems that this has to do with a rationalization of the adult, and hence the adolescent, world by which magic or irrational traditions are seen as more suitable for children. These considerations require to be developed further in the context of the 'emergence of childhood', a historical phenomenon which has resulted in adults and adolescents no longer being able to afford to behave like 'big children'.

The intensification of the influence of the state over the rural population in the age of absolutism must also have had an impact on the character of the fraternities. The traditional customs of censure stood in conflict with public jurisdiction. The state's monopoly on power would not tolerate armed local groups. It is likely that weapons played a far larger part in the earlier phases of the groups' development. When government interfered with the powers of local authorities, this affected the youth groups in that the territorial substratum was often altered.

The processes of industrialization had their greatest influence in the fact that they made populations more mobile, breaking into the exclusiveness of traditional local groups and in particular the endogamous marriage customs on which rural fraternities all over Europe laid such great stress. Of course, it was not only industrialization which could make the rural population more mobile. It is possible that the absence of rural fraternities in Britain is explained by the fact that the mobilization of the agrarian population came particularly early.

The development in the nineteenth century of urban associations, which then established themselves in the country as well, had a decisive impact on the traditional fraternities. This transition to modern clubs began with gatherings which transcended the boundary between single and married. First, there were volunteer fire brigades, then gymnastic and singing clubs. Only in a second phase did youth clubs begin to appear, initially in the form of denominational groups run for boys and girls separately. The new clubs presented the traditional youth groups with strong competition. Often, however, there were direct lines of continuity as traditions of the fraternities were taken over by clubs. Although the new clubs had specific aims, some of them fulfilled a number of functions, so that the multifunctional character of the traditional youth groups was preserved. However, a clear break with the fraternities resulted when there was a polarization between clubs with different ideological positions. It was the gathering of young people into competing inter-regional ideological camps which ultimately spelt the end for traditional fraternities with their loyalty to the local community.

This politicizing of rural youth only began in earnest after the First World War, which was in any case a major turning point for the traditional forms of youth group. Active service in the war caused many young people to break out of their regional perspective. Traditional values began to topple. From many areas it is reported that earlier forms of youth activity could not be picked up again after the war.

The years which followed saw a further erosion of the territorial base which had been so typical of the fraternities. The mass media, in particular radio, created an international youth culture. The opening up of the countryside to traffic, and especially the motorization of young people themselves, made possible processes of social interaction which transcended the local community to an extent never known before. None the less, local solidarity continues to be stronger in rural youth organizations than in urban ones.

Literature on the subject of rural youth groups of the past has often dealt only with groups of young men. Female youth groups are treated as 'subsidiaries', as 'satellite groups', as 'secondary formations'. At parish level this view is indeed correct. However, there were also adolescent group forms in which girls or women formed the basic structure, and the social integration of males took a 'subsidiary' form. These were the so-called 'spinning-rooms' which go back a long way in the history of rural youth, and which had enormous importance in the social life of young people.

The spinning-room was linked to the household, not the local community. However, the social mixing in the spinning-room went far beyond the members of a single household. Female neighbours and friends were invited and boys came to visit them. As a household institution, the spinning-room was not originally an autonomous structure of youth. It fell under the oversight and control of the woman of the house, and therefore, indirectly, of the father. In spite of this, however, the spinning-room did give rise to independent forms of youth culture.[73] Only as an extraordinary development did the spinning-room become a meeting place for young people in a rented room, outside the household community.

Names for the spinning-room are many. In German we find *Kunkelstube*, *Rockenstube* (both meaning distaff-room) and *Spinntrupp*, all emphasizing the work done; and *Lichtstube*, *Lichtkarz*, *Vorsitz*, *Maistube* (May room), *Spielstube* (play room), and so on.[74] The dominant term in French was *veillée*.[75] It simply means an evening spent in company. The German terms alluding to light (*Licht-*) point in the same direction. Spinning, and other textile work done communally in the spinning-room, was usually undertaken in the winter. The spinning season began when it was no longer possible to work in the fields and the farming community had, so to speak, retired to the house. In many areas there was a fixed date for the beginning of the spinning-room gatherings, usually the feast of St Catherine (25 November).[76] She was honoured as the patron saint of young women. The term *Lichtstube* gives us one other clue. The winter work of the women and girls often took place on an inter-household basis, not least in order to save on the costs of lighting. Firewood could also be saved. For

---

[73] H. Medick, 'Spinnstuben auf dem Dorf. Jugendliche Sexualkultur und Feierabendbrauch in der ländlichen Gesellschaft der frühen Neuzeit', in G. Huck (ed.), *Sozialgeschichte der Freizeit* (Wuppertal, 1980), pp. 19ff.

[74] Ibid., p. 22.

[75] Shorter, *Die Geburt der modernen Familie*, pp. 150ff.

[76] Gaal, *Spinnstubenlieder*, p. 25.

this reason the gatherings often took place in barns where animals and steaming dung provided warmth.[77]

The Old High German root *tung*, meaning sunken spinning- and weaving-rooms covered with dung for the sake of warmth, is the origin of a number of words which are widely dispersed, including the Scandinavian *dungja* and Finnish *tunkio*.[78] Underground dung-covered rooms where the women met in the evenings to spin were also found under other names in many parts of Europe, including Burgundy, Champagne and Picardy. They have a particularly long history in the Balkans, where groups of girls would build their work-huts in the autumn and pull them down again in the spring. Both linguistic and archeological evidence suggest that these peculiar forms of communal working-space for women are very old. Their separation from living-space probably had to do with technical aspects of the work. The humidity of these rooms made them especially suitable for the preparation of flax and wool. It was rational that provisional work-huts, which were often only used during the winter months, should have been laid out for several households together.

Another very ancient form of textile work for girls was the early medieval gynaeceum.[79] The Old High German form *geneztunc* provides the link with the sunken work-huts which have already been discussed.[80] The gynaeceum was a work-house for women at the feudal court. It was connected to the *Capitulare de villis*, the legal code which regulated the Frankish manorial system. It was mainly the daughters of subject peasant families employed as maids in the manor, that is to say mostly unmarried women, who were set to do textile work here. It is hard to know whether the gynaeceum was set apart from the other buildings for technical reasons, as early medieval sources suggest, or for moral reasons. The tradition of woman's communal work could have survived the dissolution of the *de villis* capitulary. At any rate, we cannot rule out the possibility that this ancient custom had its roots in manorial law. Certainly, the geographical distribution of the spinning-room extends far beyond the area covered by the

---

[77] Shorter, *Die Geburt der modernen Familie*, p. 152.

[78] B. Gunda, 'Arbeitshütten auf der Balkanhalbinsel', in B. Gunda, *Ethnographica Carpatho-Balcanica* (Budapest, 1979), pp. 282ff.

[79] P. Ketsch, *Frauen im Mittelalter*, vol. I (Dusseldorf, 1983), pp. 83, 88, 102.

[80] Gunda, 'Arbeitshütten', p. 283.

capitulary. It stretches as far as Russia, which had a different manorial tradition, and the Balkans, where no such system was known.

The arrangement of the spinning-room varied greatly between the regions of Europe. For the French *veillées* Shorter has defined a standard model: 'married women sitting with their eligible daughters, and the suitors at the windows'.[81] In Finland, it sometimes happened that the assembled young women and men did not go home after the long winter evening; instead they spent the night together in the house of the host family.[82] In the Balkans, by contrast, the girls' work-huts were strictly taboo for the boys.[83] Differing moral concepts therefore played an important part in group formation. If they were strict, the lads were generally excluded or at the very least an adult would be in attendance. Often these measures were expressly required by the local authorities and were monitored by the police. The Reformation and Counter-reformation periods were often particularly strict.[84] The bishop of Würzburg, for example, attempted in the eighteenth century to impose a complete ban on spinning-rooms, the only exceptions being 'gatherings of close blood relations, where sisters and sisters-in-law, children of sisters and brothers, come together to work in the homes of their father's or mother's brother or sister'.[85] Restricted to the closest family, these meetings could be harmless enough. A basic feature of spinning-room society, and therefore of the social integration of girls in general, is exposed by such rigorous formulations. Contacts outside the home were unproblematic when they were organized through the parents in the framework of the wider network of relations. A similar picture can be seen with young girls going into service. The necessary basis of trust could be established by contacts with neighbours, godparents or friends. The parents required an assurance of honourable and decent behaviour in the house which their daughter was to be permitted to join. Girls' relationships were arranged by parents to a far greater extent than boys'.

In many areas, however, the youthful conviviality of the

---

[81] Shorter, *Die Geburt der modernen Familie*, p. 242.
[82] Ibid., p. 152.
[83] Gunda, 'Arbeitschütten', p. 272.
[84] Medick, 'Spinnstuben', pp. 25ff.
[85] Ibid., p. 31.

spinning-room had substantially or totally broken loose of parental control. The girls' communal work was no longer protected
from the approaches of the boys; on the contrary, it became the
pretext for seeking these contacts. The mixed-age element of the
female working community declined; the adolescent structure of
the youth group became dominant. Of course, the separate roles
of girls and boys were strictly maintained. The girls worked, the
boys entertained them. Only seldom were the males drawn into
the working group.[86] Spinning was woman's work and incompatible with the received male gender role. Young men only spun in
areas where cottage industry specialized in textiles. Then a general balancing of the gender roles took place. The intensifying of
cottage industry affected the significance and character of the
spinning-room. It was no longer restricted to the winter months.
Married women and children were also drawn in.[87]

Wherever the spinning-room became a meeting-place exclusively
for young people, contact with the opposite sex became more
important than work. However, these two functions cannot be
entirely separated. The spinning-room gave the lads an opportunity to observe the girls' abilities at what would be one of their
most important tasks in the household. In a traditional rural society,
such criteria were extremely important for the choice of a partner.
In the spinning-room, dowries were prepared. This was one reason
why it was primarily unmarried girls who went there. Information
about dowries was just as important for the boys.

The developing of acquaintances in the spinning-room took
many forms. When work was completed, the company ate, drank,
played and danced together. It was these activities over and beyond the work itself which led the authorities to view the gatherings
with suspicion. Immoral behaviour was feared. There was also a
concern that daughters and sons, maids and servants might pur-
loin foodstuffs without permission. The problem of resourcing the
adolescent eating and drinking culture has already been touched
upon.

Elements of socializing are to be seen in the spinning-rooms
even when males were excluded. In the work-huts erected for
the winter in the Balkan areas, the communal work of the girls

[86] R. Braun, *Industrialisierung und Volksleben* (Göttingen, 1979), p. 122.
[87] Ibid., pp. 129, 132.

certainly built up a sense of community. Often they sang as they worked. Spinning-room songs developed into a unique form of female youth culture.

Finally, the spinning-rooms also had the function of providing girls with a training. Textile work often required a high level of skill and knowledge which was imparted to the younger girls by the older ones, to the unmarried by the married. In Macedonia, for example, the girls in the winter work-huts were under the leadership of an older girl, known as the *majstor* (master).[88] It would be worth investigating whether there is a connection between the spinning-rooms and the spinning-schools which grew up in the mercantile era.

With the mechanization of spinning, this traditional rural cottage skill disappeared. The spinning-room as a place of social contact continued in many areas, often still under the old names. Other forms of woman's work which had been present in the traditional spinning-room now took centre-stage; sewing, lace-making, knitting and preparing goose feathers. Sometimes, productive work was given up altogether, so that the 'spinning-room' remained just as a meeting place for friends.[89]

The functions of the traditional spinning-room never required an organizational structure. It did not develop into an association with rules and office-bearers like the male fraternities. Unlike the male youth groups, there was no hierarchy or rank. As a little formalized and minimally organized social form, the spinning-room model represents a very ancient type of informal youth group.

II. In the City

In traditional society, urban and rural youth groups had a great deal in common. These similarities are most obvious when contrasted with the social forms of later European history. To begin with, however, we shall look at the differences which were caused by the different residential and working patterns of town and countryside.

One difference which is significant in a number of respects for

---

[88] Gunda, 'Arbeitschütten', p. 272.
[89] H. Hetzer and G. Morgenstern, *Kind und Jugendlicher auf dem Lande* (Lindau, 1952), p. 22.

the character of youth groups is the fact that urban populations are less dependent upon nature. This has a very clear effect on religious life. In the cities, success at work is far less likely to be connected with magic ways of overcoming nature. The forms of pre-Christian fertility cult which played such a major part in the ritual of the rural fraternities were meaningless in the cities. The cycle of annual festivals was also different. The summer and autumn festivals, such as the church fairs which were so important for rural youth, took second place. The winter and spring festivals, especially *Fasching* and May Day, did keep something of their outward form, but lost their original meaning.[90] Consequently, the activities of the youth groups which sustained these customs were also different. Both work and holidays became independent of the rhythm of the seasons. The changing pattern of winter work in turn affected the availability of time for socializing. Communal women's or girls' work which in the country was the basis of the spinning-room was less central in the towns. Certainly the urban milieu did have social forms analogous to the spinning-room but their character was different.[91] And finally, an important difference for the boys' groups lay in the fact that there was not the same necessity for physical strength in city work. Strength and demon-strations of physical power as a criterion of rank do not seem to have been particularly important in the journeymen's associations.

A high degree of division of labour is characteristic of city work. This leads to a differentiation of careers and working milieux. The corporate structure of the traditional urban society was mirrored by a corresponding pattern of youth groups which can be under-stood as subsections of the various parts of society just as the rural fraternities can be understood as subsections of the local community. This was particularly true of the relationship between apprentices or journeymen and the guild. Of course, this corpor-ate structure did not account for the whole of urban society. The lower classes and their young people were not included. The class structure of the city encouraged the formation of milieu-specific groupings of young people.

Unlike the rural villages, the cities were not closed communities when it came to marriage. The principle of professional endogamy

[90] R. Muchembled, 'Des conduites de bruit au spectacle des processions', in LeGoff and Schmitt (eds), *Le Charivari*, p. 233.
[91] Shorter, *Die Geburt der modernen Familie*, p. 151.

replaced that of local endogamy. The urban upper classes, the merchants and, to a great extent also, the artisans frequently chose marriage partners from outside their own cities. Thus the customs of courting, so important in the rural community, lost much of their significance. In so far as they were present at all, they encompassed only a part of the city population. The disappearance of local endogamy also neutralized a factor which was of great importance in the territorial thinking of the rural fraternities.

Because of the greater mobility of the population, cities are less suited than rural communities to the development of youth groups with a territorial base. Moving home is much more common, and there is less expectation that a generation of children will grow up together into adult life. Within the cities a number of different types of territorial unit compete. The city community as a whole is divided into regions. These too need not have a homogeneous character. City parish boundaries do not necessarily correspond to the quarters defined for defensive purposes. Yet both were significant for the development of youth groups. Generally speaking, it may be said that the youth of the upper class was more orientated towards the city as a whole, while in the lower class, territorial groups form around streets, squares and quarters.

An important distinction between urban and rural youth in old European society lay in the distribution of places of origin. In the rural community, unlike in the city, young people had usually all grown up together in the same area, even when there was a strong tradition of moving into domestic service. The urban population traditionally reproduced itself by immigration, principally of young people. In the city trades, for example, the majority of journeymen would have 'journeyed' from other places. It goes without saying that these people had a stronger sense of belonging to their professional group than to their locality. Alongside the journeymen, old European cities had large numbers of other young people who were living away from their place of birth, for example students in the university towns. Usually they banded together in ex-patriot groups. The same is true of young merchants who visited other towns in the course of their training. The great preponderance of young migrants in the cities also explains why initiation ceremonies into the various professional bodies and their juvenile subgroups were given far more weight than in the rural communities.

Group structures which included all the young people of a town were impossible because the size of the community was so much larger than in the country. Fraternities which drew in both journeymen and the sons of middle-class families were only ever found in the smallest towns. In Switzerland, for example, such a group existed in Winterthur; in Bern and Geneva the group covering the whole city was only open to upper-class youngsters; in Zürich there was no such organization.[92] These *sociétés* or *abbayes de jeunesse* or *des enfants de ville*, or whatever term happened to be used locally, could have widely differing functions. In contrast to the rural fraternities, the *Burschenschaften* or 'abbeys', there was usually an element of specialization.[93] The youth group could develop into an urban militia. It demonstrated its military competence with impressively staged processions and parades, mock battles and manoeuvres, and ridings round the surrounding country. The aggressive element occasionally burst out in spontaneous belligerence, sometimes against the will of the city council. The military component of urban youth also emerged when cities had brotherhoods of archers which organized groups of 'young archers' to ensure continuity.[94] Starting in The Netherlands, archery had spread throughout northern France, Burgundy and the Rhineland from the end of the thirteenth century onwards. In peacetime the societies of archers provided a framework for training in sport as well as for social and religious activity. Equally, a specialization of the urban youth groups could be along the lines of the traditional customs of censure or mask-making, though this had a different quality. Many of the group names indicate that they saw themselves a societies of fools, agents of disorder and boisterous merriment. *Fasching*, the Shrovetide carnival, was particularly important for these groups. The *charivari* as a serious attempt at juvenile justice was suppressed in the cities, and it lost its original orientation. As a censure of individuals it was turned less against the remarriage of widowers than against breaches of traditional gender roles. As a general expression of protest, it increasingly took on a political trait. The city tradition of censure tended to take a literary form. It took on comic elements, developed complicated forms of

[92] Lutz, *Jünglings- und Gesellenverbände*; Davis, 'The reasons of misrule', p. 111; Wolfram, *Die Volkstänze*, pp. 193ff.
[93] Wolfram, *Die Volkstänze*, p. 193; Davis, 'The reasons of misrule', pp. 97ff.
[94] T. Reintges, *Ursprung und Wesen der spätmittelalterlichen Schützengilden* (Bonn, 1963), pp. 293ff.; Van Gennep, *Manuel de folklore*, p. 200.

dialogue and was frequently recorded in writing. This specialization could go so far that, in about 1550 the *enfants sans souci*, a
Paris youth 'abbey', formed itself into a semi-professional troop of
actors.[95] The emphasis on the carnival atmosphere in youth groups
also expressed itself in impressive processions in which the burlesque, bizarre and grotesque components of traditional youth
culture were articulated. Another specialization of urban youth
groups was the religious brotherhood. Here too, splendid public
performances had their place, perhaps as part of larger processions.
Various elements of the different specializations were sometimes
brought together, for example when a society of fools attended a
church fair. What the different variations all had in common was
their predilection for communal eating and drinking. The necessary means were seldom gathered in the city by door-to-door
collection; expenses for the activities of the *jeunesse* were frequently standard items in the municipal budget.

However, the payments made by the city fathers to upper-class
youth organizations had their drawbacks. From the sixteenth
century onwards, the authorities made increasing attempts to bring
the societies, brotherhoods and abbeys of the city youth under
their control.[96] Rules were frequently imposed by the city authorities, not drawn up by the groups themselves. Many urban
youth groups became instruments of education, discipline and
control. From the early modern period onwards, they were far less
autonomous than the rural fraternities. The complicated hierarchy
of offices and honours appointed from within the groups should
not be allowed to hide the fact that *de facto* the office-bearers had
very little to decide. Likewise, the tendency which can be observed
in the cities from the late Middle Ages to integrate young people
into organizations which included adults, such as the religious
brotherhoods or the societies of archers, often meant a restriction of adolescent autonomy. Through this development the closed
nature of youth as a status group was lost. The boundary between
single and married people was far less important in the city than
in the rural population. However, the barrier between the sexes
was not broken down in the membership of the urban youth
groups. With the exception of a few of the religious fellowships,

[95] Davis, 'The reasons of misrule', p. 111.
[96] R. Muchembled, *Des jeunes dans la ville Douai au XVIᵉ siècle*, p. 95; 'Des
conduites', pp. 232ff.; Lutz, *Jünglings- und Gesellenverbände*, p. 35.

the groups which had been described were all exclusively male. The development of parallel female groups which is occasionally found in the countryside did not occur in the cities.

Urban youth organizations can be traced much further back than rural fraternities in written sources. In France, the earliest record for the city of Lille stems from 1220.[97] In Italy the trail goes back further still.[98] The principal areas of distribution were Upper Italy, Switzerland, France and The Netherlands. The early modern period saw the beginning of a general decline, although relics survived into the most recent past.

A little later than the societies or 'abbeys' for the resident upper-class youth of the city came the first journeymen's associations.[99] The too reach well back into the Middle Ages. Just as the rural fraternity was built on the existing pattern of the local rural community, so the journeymen's association presupposed the existence of the guild as the corresponding social form for adults. The oldest statutes of an association of this type in the German-speaking world were those of the Regensburg journeyman-bakers of 1341. But as a social form, journeymen's associations would certainly have existed much earlier and have had a far wider distribution than the written records of their statutes indicate. Presumably the journeymen originally felt better able to incorporate themselves into the organization of their particular handicraft as an adolescent subgroup. Their independent organization would have been a secondary development, leaning strongly for its legal base on the model of the ecclesiastical brotherhoods, which were a decisive influence on all new social forms in the late Middle Ages. The formation of co-operative groups would have followed, on the one hand, from the increasing emancipation of the journey-man from the household community of the master's family, and on the other, from the sharpening economic tension with the master. One expression of domestic emancipation was an improved

[97] Davis, 'The reasons of misrule', pp. 102, 299.

[98] For Rome, see G. C. Pola Falletti di Villasfalletto, 'Le associazoni giovanili a Roma e nel Lazio', *Lares*, 16 (1950), pp. 40ff.

[99] On this, see G. Schanz, *Zur Geschichte der deutschen Gesellenverbände* (Leipzig, 1877); E. Coorneart, *Les Compagnonnages en France, du Moyen Âge à nos jours* (Paris, 1966); W. Reininghaus, *Zur Entstehung der Gesellengilden im Spätmittelalter* (Münster, 1980); K. Schulz, 'Die Stellung der Gesellen in der spätmittelalterlichen Stadt', in A. Haverkamp (ed.), *Haus und Familie in der spätmittelalterlichen Stadt* (Cologne, 1984), pp. 304ff.

legal standing; another, in the German language, was the change in nomenclature which took place in the late Middle Ages, as the modern word for journeyman, *Geselle* (fellow), replaced the older, manorial *Knecht* (servant).

Autonomy within the household is an important precondition of any ability to co-operate on a basis which transcends households. A sharpening economic tension was caused in the late Middle Ages by the tightening up of the masters' guilds. A reduction in the number of places for masters, together with preferential treatment for masters' sons, meant that the majority of journeymen had to wait far longer. The attainment of master status was made increasingly difficult by the guilds. Expensive and time-consuming masterpieces were required and set numbers of journeying years became obligatory, all of which sharpened the tension between the generations in the urban handicrafts. In many trades separate journeymen's associations were therefore set up, sometimes spanning several cities. They created their own 'closed shop', their own constitution, their own system of internal discipline, their own seal, their own social fund and their own executive.[100] But even in cases when no separate organizational structure emerged, it may be assumed that the journeymen, as 'grown-up' but not yet married and independent members of the trade, would have had a specific group life of their own.

If we examine the functions of the urban journeymen's associations, we find that they showed similarities to other male youth groups of old European society. A central role was given to eating and drinking. Sometimes the young craftsmen would bring food from the master's house in order to eat in their own group.[101] The tavern was their principle meeting place. Unlike in the rural fraternities, there was always a fixed venue. Besides the tavern which was used throughout the winter, a garden was sometimes rented for the summer.[102] Here again, dancing was a major feature. However, dances were usually organized by the guild as a whole rather than by the youth group. Control of moral behaviour and partner relationships was also left with the guild. The preferred partners were masters' daughters. Local endogamy was replaced

---

[100] R. Sprandel, 'Der handwerkliche Familienbetrieb des Spätmittelalters und seine Probleme', in ibid., p. 333.

[101] Schulz, 'Die Stellung der Gesellen in der spätmittelalterlichen Stadt', p. 314.

[102] Lutz, *Jünglings- und Gesellenverbände*, p. 126.

by professional endogamy.[103] The rules of the guild very much favoured the marriage of journeymen to masters' daughters. Correspondingly, the groups' sense of identity related to the craft and not to the locality. With this proviso, however, it may be said that group solidarity was just as pronounced as in other forms of youth group, with the same clear demarcation of the group from the outside world.

Brawls with journeymen of other trades, or indeed with any other group, were just as common as rural skirmishes between fraternities of neighbouring villages. In both cases there was the same provocative behaviour, the same display of strength, the same exaggerated sense of honour which was offended by trivialities. Much of the tradition of the rural fraternities was carried on by the urban journeymen:[104] masked processions, *Fasching* activities and, to some extent also, the tradition of censure. Rites of initiation were stronger in the journeymen's associations than in the rural fraternities.[105] Among the characteristic motifs of *Gesellenmachen* were: crude tortures, often connected thematically with the craft in question, such as the 'planing' of young joiners; lectures on the behaviour of guildsmen; changing of clothes; bestowing of new names; and vows of secrecy. The ceremony often carried overtones of a baptismal ritual. Even though we are dealing here with a parody,[106] the renewal of baptism on taking holy orders which had been introduced by the monastic movements of the late Middle Ages can still be regarded as a model for these rites, for adolescent counter-culture always takes on something of the culture which it mimics. Elements taken directly from the brotherhoods may have been brought to bear through the participation of the journeymen's associations in major church festivals. The military element was stronger among the journeymen than in most of the rural fraternities. Often young craftsmen formed their own societies of archers. The civil defence duties allocated to the guilds were often delegated to the corresponding body of adolescents.

However, the journeymen's associations had a number of

---

[103] Sprandel, 'Der handwerkliche Familientrieb', p. 335.
[104] H. Möller, *Die Klienbürgerliche Familie im 18. Jahrhundert* (Berlin, 1965), pp. 168ff.
[105] K. S. Kramer, 'Hänseln', in *Handwörterbuch der deutschen Rechtsgeschichte*, vol. I, pp. 2003ff.; O. Schade, *Über Jünglingsweihen* (Hanover, 1857), pp. 298ff.
[106] Davis, 'The reason of misrule', p. 100.

functions which went far beyond those of the rural fraternities. In the first place, they were involved in social work, made necessary by the deterioration of the social conditions of many journeymen in the late Middle Ages. They provided financial assistance from a relief fund for members who had got into difficulties; they offered support in case of sickness; they met the funeral costs of a member who died; all responsibilities which in earlier times had rested with the head of the household, but which master-craftsmen no longer acknowledged. They provided help in finding work, increasingly a problem in the crafts. They ran their own hostels in which journeymen who had newly arrived in town might be fed and quartered. These hostels became inter-regional meeting places and information centres as compulsory migration forced the associations to look beyond their own cities. These wider perspectives were particularly important in view of their role in labour disputes. Conflicts between masters and journeymen about rates of pay and working hours can be traced back in France and Germany to the mid-fourteenth century. The most common weapon was to 'denounce' either an individual master or the whole craft in a city. The 'denounced' masters would then be unable to find either journeymen or apprentices. Strikes were also used successfully by the associations in the late Middle Ages. Such measures required both a high degree of solidarity and a great deal of resilience. The need to maintain this hardiness was one reason why journeymen absolutely refused to marry before being accepted as masters. In the Middle Ages, married journeymen may have been more common in some places.

The revolutionary role of the journeymen's associations in labour disputes was one of the reasons why they were opposed and oppressed by municipal and national authorities alike from the early modern period onwards, but especially in the age of absolutism. In France, journeymen's associations were banned in the first half of the sixteenth century. In Germany, the first imperial measures were taken around 1570. A general ban followed in 1731, and in a number of territories this was imposed with draconian ferocity. At this point the German associations went underground, just as in France the *compagnonnages* had survived as a secret society. The ancient tradition of secrecy in male youth groups now stood them in good stead. With these traditions, of course, the whole brimborion of their quaint, antiquated formalism was also continued. The tendency to preserve received forms is always strongest among oppressed groups. Consequently, the journeymen's associations were not suitable forms of organization to meet the needs of employees when in the industrial period new kinds of conflict broke out under quite different circumstances. None the less, it must not be forgotten that in the early period of the labour movement there were strong lines of continuity leading back to the social forms of the young craftsmen.

Among the traditional journeymen's associations, the various building and construction trades have always had a special position. Early development of paid labour brought about by the scale on which work was organized, a high degree of regional mobility allowing wide-ranging contacts, and a particular emphasis on secrecy because of the specialist technical knowledge of the church masons' guilds, all meant that unique social forms emerged here. In the present context they are important because they served as models for the masonic lodges.[107] Freemasonry was not exclusively a youth organization, but in its beginnings and in its years of ascendency young people were its driving force. Because of its role in spreading the ideas of the enlightenment, freemasonry was a movement of social renewal in the eighteenth and nineteenth centuries. In its group structure and in its form, however, it kept firmly to the historical traditions. Among the specific expressions of adolescent life to which it gave rise, a distinctive mysticism is particularly striking. In keeping with its recruitment pattern (freemasons were recruited principally from the middle and upper classes) and with its political, social and moral aims, it developed stronger ties with the student fraternities than with the trade organizations on which it was formally modelled. These academic fraternities were the third main type of male youth group in the traditional urban milieu.

From its inception in the high Middle Ages, the university had a decisive influence on adolescent group formation.[108] In respect

[107] Gillis, *Geschichte der Jugend*, pp. 87ff.

[108] H. Feilzer, *Jugend in der mittelalterlichen Ständegesellschaft* (Vienna, 1971), pp. 98ff., 221ff.; H. Denifle, *Die Universitäten des Mittelalters bis 1400*, vol. I (Berlin, 1885); G. Kaufmann, *Die Geschichte der deutschen Universitäten*, vols I and II (Stuttgart, 1888); F. Paulsen, *Geschichte des gelehrten Unterrichts auf den deutschen Schulen und Universitäten vom Anfang des Mittelalters bis zur Gegenwart*, vol. I (Leipzig, 1914); H. G. Good, *A History of Western Education* (New York, 1947).

of the adult world to which it related, the student body was not
limited by a territorial principle or restricted to a professional field
as were other youth groups in old European society. Its point of
reference was, in the first place, the Church, on account of the
university's religious origins, but later also the emerging state and
its leading classes, as state universities began to spring up and
study abroad went into decline. So when young academics discussed problems, made social critiques or mounted protest movements, they did so in a far wider framework than rural fraternities
or journeymen's associations. For this reason, students in history
were always in the vanguard of youth protest or renewal movements; indeed, in the early stages they were the sole proponents.

Student social forms initially modelled themselves on the religious household. The college and the hostel survived longer in
some European education systems than in others. The college had
a lasting influence in Britain; not so in Germany. Alongside it there
developed other forms of gathering, of which the brotherhoods
and ex-patriot groups were of great importance.[109] The student
brotherhoods were bodies with a strongly religious character. Like
the associations of young craftsmen they stood under the patronage
of a saint. Like them, they took responsibility for all arrangements
on the death of a colleague. The emphasis on ritual and ceremony
was another point of similarity. Feasting and carousing played the
same important role. Particularly striking are the highly developed
initiation rites which, as in the trades, have continued into modern
times: humiliating chicanery to which the novice was subjected,
symbolic acts purporting to show that he was becoming a new
person, solemn vows to betray nothing of the life of the organization to those outside, and so forth. Various forms of this so-
called 'deposition' were known in Italy, Spain, France, Germany,
Britain and Scandinavia. In the early modern period the authorities
in many areas attempted to stamp it out, but it survived none the
less.[110]

Certain forms of censure had a distinctive role in student tradition.
In Britain, the tradition of 'misrule' was cherished in the universities
and upper schools. Festivals of fools and masked processions long
survived in the academic milieu. Traditional customs and distinctive

---

[109] Ariès, *Geschichte der Kindheit*, pp. 349ff.
[110] Schade, *Über Jünglingsweihen*, pp. 315ff.

rituals were very important for group solidarity. We find the same exaggerated sense of honour and the same feeling of superiority among student groups as we encountered with the journeymen. Here again, it frequently led to disputes and brawls. Indeed, the journeymen were frequently the opposition. The aggressive rejection of those outside became sharper when students began to carry arms. Conflicts were now restricted to those capable of giving 'satisfaction' but were the more dangerous for that.

In the question of relationships with the opposite sex, students were in a very different position from craftsmen. The journeyman courted the master's daughter; there was no counterpart for the student. Besides, the original status of students as half-clerics and their orientation towards a spiritual career ruled this whole question out *de jure*. Even as the religious nature of the university began to fade, academia remained a male preserve. A ritualized pattern of courting like those of the rural fraternities or the journeymen's associations never evolved among students. For centuries, the question of relationships with girls remained particularly problematic.

The most important basis for the organization of scholars in the Middle Ages was a common place of origin. As early as the first half of the twelfth century, the French cathedral schools had a division of students along these lines.[111] In Bologna, the two great societies around which the whole university structure was built, the *citramontani* and the *ultramontani*, were originally ex-patriot groups of students.[112] Similarly, in the city grammar schools there is evidence that pupils from outside the town sometimes grouped together according to their homeland. In the Middle Ages this was the usual form of self-help when abroad. The same pattern was found among merchants. Only by acting collectively was it possible for foreigners in the medieval town to enjoy legal protection. And for students this protection was particularly important.

The colleges and hostels must have contributed significantly to the inner cohesion of the ex-patriot communities, as teachers and scholars from a particular country were often accommodated together. It sometimes happened that the founder of a hostel would

[111] P. Classen, 'Die hohen Schulen und die Gesellschaft im 12. Jahrhundert', *Archiv für Kulturgeschichte*, 48 (1966), p. 173.
[112] Kaufmann, *Geschichte der deutschen Universitäten*, p. 190; Classen, 'Die hohen Schulen', p. 174.

specify that places had to be kept free for his own relatives.[113] Influential members of a university often brought with them a whole group of relatives, friends and acquaintances from their own home. Such clientele had an important place in the life of the medieval university.[114] Many students already knew one another before leaving home. Sometimes they actually travelled together to a distant university. As the entries in the university matriculation registers show, scholars frequently turned up not individually, but in small groups. These could be groups of social equals but could as easily include people from different social classes. Similarly, in terms of age such groups were frequently mixed, the younger ones sometimes being in service to the older.[115] Relationships of these kinds were important for the internal structure of the ex-patriot groups, and for the formation of peripheral groupings.

The heyday of the ex-patriot student groups or *Landsmann-schaften* was the seventeenth century. In the age of absolutism they were frequently suppressed by governments, but survived as secret societies. In the last third of the eighteenth century they provided the setting in which the student orders emerged. These were more rigidly organized and saw themselves as sodalities of eternal friendship. In their moral and philanthropic aims they had clear connections with freemasonry. Influenced by these, two new movements emerged out of the ex-patriot groups about the beginning of the nineteenth century: the duelling corps and the student fraternity (*Burschenschaft*, the same word which we have used for the rural fraternities). The experience of the wars of liberation against Napoleon had a particular impact on the student fraternities. The duelling corps and student fraternities became the models for the multitude of societies which developed in the German-speaking universities in the nineteenth and twentieth centuries. Differences between these groups centred on ideological orientation, attitudes to duelling, and the wearing of heraldic colours in the form of the traditional student garb. The social forms of German students preserved many elements of the old European youth groups: ancient initiation rites were preserved in enrolment ceremonies known as *Rezeption* or *Burschung*;

[113] K. Schrauf, *Die Universität, Geschichte der Stadt Wien*, vol. II/2 (Vienna, 1905), p. 996.
[114] P. Moraw, 'Zur Sozialgeschichte der deutschen Universität im späten Mittelalter', *Gießener Universitätsblätter*, 2 (1975), pp. 50ff.
[115] Ariès, *Geschichte der Kindheit*, pp. 356ff.

name-changing in *Couleurname*, archaic drinking rituals in the organized bout known as the *Kneipe* or *Kommers* with its strictly regulated *Komment* or code of conduct. In the 'town and gown' atmosphere of many of the smaller universities in Germany, such as Heidelberg, Tübingen, Marburg, Göttingen or Jena, it was possible for these historical structures and customs to survive in an unbroken tradition until very recent times. Because of the geographic distribution the societies in the different university locations were very decentralized. In Britain, too, the isolation of the student body in the smaller university towns had a conservative effect. In France, on the other hand, university life was concentrated on Paris and the students were much more integrated into the life of the capital. The atmosphere of the *Quartier latin* stood in sharp contrast to the romance of Old Heidelberg. In Paris, the student societies had a long tradition of free association without binding group commitments.

The student society extended right into the era of the middle-class club, a last relic, albeit thoroughly overhauled, of the older tradition of youth community. As one of the few forms of auto-nomous adolescent group life in the age of the youth club, it influenced the evolution of other independent group forms. This is seen, for example, in the attempts of secondary-school pupils to imitate the social forms of students. In spite of their archaic traditions, student societies were major factors in the spread of liberal-democratic structures. However, they could also provoke a counter-reaction. The determination with which the school pupils and students in the German *Jugendbewegung*, the Free Youth Movement, struggled to create radical new forms of community was in no small part a rejection of those customs and practices which at that time still dominated the community life of German students.

The fourth type of traditional urban youth group is particularly difficult to define. This difficulty begins with the question of ter-minology. If we speak of 'street-gangs' we are using the language of middle-class condescension. It even smacks of criminality. The German words *Meuten* (packs) and *Rudel* (herds) allude to animal communities, suggesting something primitive, wild and danger-ous.[116] There are no names for these urban territorial groups of

---

[116] R. Lindner, 'Straße–Straßenjunge–Straßenbande. Ein zivilisations-theoretischer Streifzug', *Zeitschrift für Volkskunde*, 79 (1983), p. 198.

working-class youngsters which do not contain a value judge-
ment. Our knowledge of them is also small. Anthropological studies have paid far less attention to them than to the rural fraternities.
The same is true of social history. Moreover, what information we
do have is not of a kind which would allow any generalizations
which might be valid for a longer period of time. The situation
which could be observed earlier in the twentieth century was
shaped by the industrial revolution. It is not possible to extrapolate
back to earlier periods. A further problem is that these groups
are often most easily observed in exceptional circumstances. The
wilde Cliquen in Berlin, for example, were in their ascendency
at a time of high unemployment.[117] It is difficult to say how much
could be explained by that immediate situation, and how much
was a reflection of the longer-term structures of this adolescent
social form. Street-gangs had, by their nature, a shorter life than
rural fraternities. Unlike the rural groups, they did not have a fixed
place in the structures of the adult world. We should therefore not
expect the same element of continuity down the years.

Despite this lack of continuity, however, there do seem to have
been a number of basic patterns which historically are relatively
old, and which crop up repeatedly in the large cities of Europe.
Youth groups belonging to particular quarters of the city with
strong bonds of solidarity existed in Florence in the fourteenth
century.[118] At carnival time, these street youths would be involved
in fighting under the bridges along the Arno. About 1380–90 two
gangs under the names *Berta* and *Magroni* battled it out every night
for 50 days. In sixteenth-century Lyons there were about 20 youth
'abbeys', most of which were organized according to their quarters.[119] Legal documents from about the same time speak of gang
warfare in Douai which ended in deaths. The protagonists were
the *fils à marier*, aged about 18 to 22. Once again, territorial loyalty
played the decisive role in the formation of adolescent groups.[120]

---

[117] H. Lessing and M. Liebel, *Wilde Cliquen* (Bernsheim, 1981); D. Peukert,
'Die "wilden Cliquen" in den zwanziger Jahren', in W. Breyvogel (ed.), *Zur Theorie
und Geschichte des Jugendprotestes* (Essen, 1983), p. 71. For England, see S.
Humphries, *Hooligans or Rebels: An Oral History of Working-Class Childhood
and Youth, 1889–1939* (Oxford, 1981), p. 187.
[118] R. C. Trexler, 'De la ville à la Cour. La déraison à Florence durant la
République et le Grand Duché', in LeGoff and Schmitt (eds), *Le Charivari*, pp.
169, 166.
[119] Davis, 'The reason of misrule', p. 110.
[120] Muchembled, *Des jeunes*, pp. 89ff.

The historical continuity of local gangs of young workers in Paris can be clearly traced. Elements which could still be seen in the 1960s can here be traced back as far as the eighteenth century.[121] In nineteenth century Manchester this group life was known as 'scuttling'. Here we have a special term for the determination to protect one's own district from the youth group of the neighbouring part of town.[122] Similarly in London in the nineteenth century there were bands of youths with a fierce animosity towards strangers, especially rivals, and a tradition of courting the favours of the girls.[123]

A city official from Aachen wrote in his chronicle in 1757 of frequent 'boys' wars' which became particularly dangerous when the 'big boys' became involved.[124] A connection between gangs of young boys and gangs of youths is to be expected. In the town, as in the country, a sense of territorial belonging would begin in childhood. This connection was addressed in a report from Cologne, describing the situation in 1810. It states: 'Even youths, for whom conscription with all its bitterness of heart knocked at the door, were not ashamed to play in the public streets', and then continues:

Often we saw on the city squares how the youth fought heated battles; for the various squares, such as the Cathedral Court, the Old Market, the Hay Market and the Augustinian Square, and also the various schools, regarded each other with hostility, and this hatred broke out right often among the boys in wild encounters in which windows and street lanterns were not spared and which frequently required the intervention of the police. An eternal and irreconcilable state of war existed between the scholars of the secondary school – formerly the Jesuit grammar school – the Boosch as the Cologne people say, and the pupils of the surrounding parish schools, a hatred which can be traced back to the days of the imperial free city, when moreover the so-called students of the three grammar schools which at that time existed were constantly at loggerheads and with the greatest of obstinacy used against one another the tails of their coats in which even stones had been tied. These boys' brawls which took place repeatedly in the summer had

---

[121] H. Lafont, 'Jugendbanden', in P. Ariès et al., *Die Masken des Begehrens und die Metamorphosen der Sinnlichkeit* (Frankfurt, 1982), pp. 209ff.

[122] Gillis, *Geschichte der Jugend*, p. 74.

[123] Ibid.

[124] J. Schlumbohm (ed.), *Kinderstuben. Wie Kinder zu Bauern, Bürgern, Aristokraten wurden 1700–1850* (Munich, 1983), p. 222.

the result that a boy could not go unaccompanied from his own district into another, for which reason the remainder of Cologne apart from our neighbourhood, the parish, was a veritable *terra incognita*.[125]

This report is significant in several respects. It clearly shows how even pre-adolescent groups were shaped by a sense of belonging to a 'patch'. The conditions described are pre-industrial. Obviously, the parish was the standard geographical substratum of community feeling at that time, as indeed it was in the country. It had a direct influence on young people's thinking in two ways, first, through the schools which had a parish base, and secondly, through the church squares which were the gathering points for children and later for youths. Industrialization altered these aspects of the city's infrastructure. None the less, central institutions, whether old or new, continued to be the points of crystallization for the structuring of local urban youth communities.

Territorial groups of working-class youngsters were most likely to develop where workers' districts had developed out of older pre-industrial units. In Floridsdorf, a workers' district in Vienna, it is recorded that as late as the 1960s a gang of 'bikers' demanded that one of 'their' girls should break off a relationship with an 'outsider' unless he was prepared to 'buy himself in' by paying for a round of drinks. The two areas of the two involved were both former villages which had been incorporated into the working-class suburb.[126] Likewise in urbanized industrial regions like the Ruhr valley, older territorial structures were preserved. This report comes from about 1930:

From childhood on, brawls between lads in the neighbourhood and feuds between militant street-gangs belonged to the everyday experience of miners' sons. The lad who came out the victor in numerous street fights became a gang leader and was given the greatest social prestige. The gangs in an area would in turn join forces against the gangs in a neighbouring district. A *fremder Hahn* would not be tolerated in the gang's domain . . . Anyone from Karnap who tried to flirt with a girl from Ebel would be in trouble. The

---

[125] Ibid., p. 243.
[126] Petrei, *Burschenschaften*, p. 10.

same applied the other way round . . . He would be pursued with flying stones until he had disappeared over the Emscher bridge. That was the boundary between Karnap and Ebel.[127]

In more densely populated residential areas, fairgrounds were important territorial points of focus.[128] In Germany this area was sometimes called the *Kirmes*, reflecting the life of the older rural fraternities. Parks too were favourite meeting places. But often a group would include only the lads of a particular street. In Britain the street-gangs were often named after streets or parts of the town.[129] The same thing was occasionally found in Germany. At any rate, the geographical situation was the principle factor shaping the sense of group identity.

The identity of the adolescent street-gangs was at its clearest when expressed in terms of the opponents whom they met in bloody conflict. In extreme cases the degree of violence was fearsome, as can be seen from the choice of weapons: knuckle-dusters, sharpened bicycle-chains, knives, cudgels, pistols.[130] Traditionally these clashes were focused primarily against gangs from the next district. The situation could be exacerbated when foreign ethnic groups arrived, for example Polish and Russian Jews in Manchester and Tottenham before the First World War, bringing additional competition for scarce jobs and resources.[131] Ethnic strangeness added to the image of the enemy. In late phases of development, however, alliances of territorial groups could arise. In Berlin from 1927, the gangs of the North, South, East and West Rings united to form the *wilde Cliquen*.[132] Their principal opponents here were political youth groups, especially the National Socialists but also Christian groups.[133] Relationships with members of the various youth clubs and organizations which were particularly strong at that period were generally very bad. This included the young workers'

---

[127] M. Zimmermann, 'Ausbruchshoffnungen. Junge Bergleute in den dreißiger Jahren', in L. Niethammer (ed.), *'Die Jahre weiß man nicht, wo man die heute hinsetzen soll'* (Berlin, 1983), p. 124.
[128] Peukert, 'Die "Wilden Cliquen"', p. 72.
[129] Humphries, *Hooligans or Rebels*, pp. 174ff.
[130] Ibid., p. 192.
[131] Ibid., pp. 196ff.
[132] Lessing and Liebel, *Wilde Cliquen*, p. 19.
[133] Ibid., pp. 80ff.

movement.[134] Tensions between gangs and youth clubs therefore cannot be understood simply on the basis of class differences. Class was a major factor, though as can be seen in Paris. Opposition to the middle-class *minets* at the beginning of the nineteenth century developed into clashes around 1830–40 between, on the one side, the 'apaches' and the 'lions' or young rowdies, and on the other side, 'dandies' and students.[135] But alongside this there were also the usual clashes between youngsters of different areas or blocks. Class-related conflicts and territorial conflicts long existed side by side. Only the latter corresponds to the ancient pattern.

A great deal can be deduced about the sense of identity of the street-gangs from the names they chose for themselves. Often these were provocative, signalling hardness, courage, violence and masculinity. Among the English gangs, typical names of this type were Bengal Tigers, Black Hand Gang, Redskins, Cowboys, Hell Hounds, and Bell and Pistol Club.[136] The *wilde Cliquen* of Berlin included such groups as the *Ostpiraten, Zigeunerblut* (gipsy blood), *Tartarenblut, Wildsau, Waldbanditen, Apachenblut, Seeräuber* (pirates), *Galgenvogel* (gallows bird), *Wolfsblut, Sturmfest* (steadfast), *Tarzan, Santa Fee, Nachtschwärmer* (night owls), *Sing Sing, Blutiger Knochen* (bloody bones), *Todesverächter* (death scorners), and so on.[137] It is easy to see how these chosen identification symbols smack of trivial literature, of adventure novels and 'dirty' books, and also of films, which have had a similar influence on the fantasies of youth.

In addition to these characteristic names, the traditional urban youth gangs had other ways in which they expressed symbolically the binding nature of the group. The *wilde Cliquen* in Berlin often even had their own flags,[138] a mark of community which would usually only have been found among well-organized, long-term groups. A common feature was uniformity of clothing, which signalled the values which united the group: masculinity, aggressiveness, independence and freedom. Among the *wilde Cliquen* of the inter-war period and the *Edelweißpiraten* who played a

---

[134] Peukert, 'Die "Wilde Cliquen"', pp. 69ff.
[135] Lafont, 'Jugendbanden', p. 221.
[136] Humphries, *Hooligans or Rebels*, pp. 174, 189.
[137] Lessing and Liebel, *Wilde Cliquen*, p. 79.
[138] Ibid., pp. 20ff.

certain part in the opposition to the Hilter youth,[139] the wearing of edelweiss in hats and clothes as a symbol of freedom was common. Plumes and coloured ribbons were also to be found in the elaborate costumes of the *wilde Cliquen*. Other group symbols included conspicuous ear-rings and tattoos, which were also a feature observed in Paris.[140] A tattoo was an indelible mark of belonging, and is therefore a seal of a vow of loyalty. It is characteristically male, both because its execution, usually in ceremonial form, is a test of courage, and because it is an adornment for the muscles, drawing attention to physical strength. It is hard to miss the parallel with naval and foreign legion traditions in which tattooing is also very common. The same is true of the ear-ring, which symbolizes the freedom of the person who has left his place of origin. It hints at the free spirit of the gipsy or the privateer, both frequent motifs in the symbolism of the street-gangs. These signals indicted on the one hand the strong solidarity of the group and on the other a clear break with the family. For these young people, most of whom lived in depressing conditions, the group did in a sense provide an emotional substitute. The powerful compulsion to express group identity through outward signs was a characteristic feature of this social form.

The solidarity of the traditional street-gang was limited to male youth. Only males could form a gang. Girls certainly joined in on certain group activities, but they were clearly in a subordinate position, far more so than in the rural fraternities. The rural girls' group which stood, at least in some respects, as a unit parallel to the fraternity had no counterpart here. Far more isolated, the girls only gained access to group life by having relationships with boys. The German slang sums it up: the girls were *Cliquenkühe*; the gang leader was the *Cliquenbulle*.[141] The social climate of the street-gang was marked by a strong sense of machismo.[142] The girls were principally seen as sexual objects.[143]

The masculinity myth of the street-gangs also found expression in a culture of physicality. All forms of measuring strength had

---

[139] A. Klönne, *Jugend im Dritten Reich. Die Hitlerjugend und ihre Gegner* (Cologne, 1984), p. 256.
[140] Lafont, 'Jugendbanden', pp. 223ff.
[141] Lessing and Liebel, *Wilde Cliquen*, p. 62.
[142] Peukert, 'Die "Wilden Cliquen"', p. 68; Lafont, 'Jugendbanden', p. 218.
[143] Lessing and Liebel, *Wilde Cliquen*, p. 81.

their place. Boxing and wrestling dominated sporting preferences.[144] Physical strength was the criterion for the internal hierarchy of the group. The idea that 'might is right' was unquestioned as the principle of leadership. Courage and agility were also highly prized. Whoever failed in these matters could be excluded. Frequently these qualities were tested prior to admission to the group.[145] Occasionally there were initiation rites, tailored to these criteria. There might even be a change of name, the use of the new name being binding on the group.[146]

In all these matters, entry, leadership, decisions about group activity and the formal structure of group life, the traditional urban territorial gangs were entirely autonomous. This applies also to the regulations governing behaviour, which were frequently developed into a stylized code of honour according to the value-system of the group. The degree of self-determination seems to have been greater than in the rural communities because the street-gangs were not part of a larger community which placed limits on them.

This uncontrolled independent life with its values and behaviour patterns deviating from middle-class norms was one of the reasons why the youth welfare work of the late nineteenth and early twentieth century addressed itself in a special way to the world of the street-gangs.[147] In England the settlement movement began in the 1880s, and Germany followed suit around 1910. These attempts to 'domesticate' the youth gang involved adopting certain structural elements from the groups themselves. The newly founded youth clubs were localized in particular districts, and the element of territorial solidarity was taken into account. The new groups were not led by adults but by older youths. The size of the groups also followed the model of the gangs. Even the names of the clubs sounded like 'soft' variants on the 'hard' gang names, for example, Arrows and Bear Pack. The 'bad' gangs were to be transformed into 'good' youth clubs.

[144] Peukert, 'Die "Wilden Cliquen"', p. 68; Lessing and Liebel, *Wilde Cliquen*, p. 23; Humphries, *Hooligans or Rebels*, p. 179.

[145] Lessing and Liebel, *Wilde Cliquen*, p. 25.

[146] Lafont, 'Jugendbanden', pp. 212ff., 224; Klönne, *Jugend im Dritten Reich*, p. 248.

[147] Gillis, *Geschichte der Jugend*, p. 146; R. Lindner, 'Bandenwesen und Klubwesen im wilhelminischen Reich und in der Weimarer Republik', *Geschichte und Gesellschaft*, 10 (1984), pp. 352ff.

Remnants of the urban gangs have survived to the present day. The report *Jugend '81* states: 'Established rockers are engaged in a struggle to keep wild rockers out of their district. The wild rockers are endangering the rockers' group by chaotic organization, unregulated street fights and the theft of cultic symbols.' Such groups, however, are part of an international network of bikers' groups which share names, emblems and forms of expression.[148] The old style of gang seems to have died out as a form of adolescent community. Many things have contributed to this: the 'loss of the street' as the meeting place particularly of lower class youngsters as a result of increasing motorization in the course of the twentieth century; the decline in importance of territorial social forms in general because of increased regional mobility; the breaking down of gender stereotypes among young people[149] which is incompatible with the macho tradition of the street-gangs; and the overall decline in youth communities with highly formalized and ritualized group lives. What little remains of the traditional urban street-gang must today be classed under the heading of informal youth groups.

III. Clubs and Young Society

The community life of young people departed only reluctantly from the social forms of the old world. The middle-class club, which marked a watershed in the social history of these forms,[150] worked its way very hesitantly into adolescent life; at any rate, as a free association with a claim on autonomy from the adult world it was slow to come. This seems paradoxical, since the young contributed so much to the development of the club in its early years. One thinks of their role in the masonic lodges, in the secret societies and friendly societies of the eighteenth century.[151] The fact that the autonomous youth club did not develop simultaneously with clubs in general has to do with its specific character.

[148] *Jugend '81* (Opladen, 1982), p. 483.
[149] Lafont, 'Jugendbanden', p. 221.
[150] T. Nipperdey, 'Verein als soziale Struktur in Deutschland im späten 18. und frühen 19. Jahrhundert', in *Gesellschaft, Kultur, Theorie* (Göttingen, 1976), pp. 174ff.
[151] Gillis, *Geschichte der Jugend*, pp. 87ff.

The middle-class association or club, as it emerged in the German-speaking world mainly in the second half of the eighteenth century, broke through the boundaries of traditional society. It broke through, for example, the barrier between married and unmarried, which had been so important in old European society. In this, it was continuing a development which had already begun in the cities, for example in the religious brotherhoods, the societies of archers, and also in the Pietistic conventicles, which must be seen as an important precursor of the free association. As the distinction between married and unmarried lost its edge, the old equation of youth and singleness also began to blur. This was of great importance for the development of our modern concept of youth. Older 'youths' could belong to clubs which allowed them to maintain their traditional groupings, for example among students or journeymen. However, the middle-class club was usually dominated by married adults. At any rate, it was from their organizations that the club emerged. Even clubs in which young people were particularly active, gymnastics clubs, for example, were not on that basis to be regarded as youth clubs. These only emerged when junior sections were required in order to cater for those who were too young to join the club itself, and they were therefore to be classed as targeted youth work which led to the founding of a club. German law placed a lower age limit of 21 on membership of political clubs. In 1908 this was reduced to 18.[152]

Another characteristic feature of the middle-class club is its principle of voluntary membership. Here, too, it had predecessors in older urban societies and brotherhoods. This principle stood in opposition to the rigidity of the territorial or professional organization of older society. It had a decisive influence on the group life of young people. Whereas the traditional patterns of rural fraternities, journeymen's associations, student ex-patriot groups and urban street-groups all comprised groups of young people of the same class, origin, profession and so on, without any element of personal choice in the matter, the youth club had to be formally joined. In this way groups formed within groups. Adolescent clubs formed within the group of young people of the parish, university clubs within the ex-patriot group or even

---

[152] T. Nipperdey, 'Jugend und Politik um 1900', in *Gesellschaft, Kultur, Theorie*, p. 351.

transcending it, denominational or ideological groups within the body of young tradesmen which crossed traditional boundaries between trades. Membership of a youth community was no longer dependent only on status. Through new connections on the basis of choice, young people's social forms became freer than in the past.

A third characteristic of the club is its specialized aim. People gathered together to read, to discuss, to sing, to do gymnastics, to deepen themselves spiritually or engage themselves politically. The old multi-functional social forms which touched on all aspects of life were in this respect abandoned. Certainly, older clubs have sometimes preserved some of this traditional variety, especially in small towns and rural areas. For example, an organization might be called a singing club, but its members could share together in any number of other leisure activities too. This traditional multi-functionality was particularly strong in youth clubs. Often they attempted to cover as completely as possible the whole life of the young person. Here, too, we can observe a delayed effect. Gradually, however, the trend is in the direction of a separation out of different spheres of activity, leading inevitably to a less-complete integration of the person as an individual.

A significant fact for the social life of young people in the age of the club is that originally the middle-class club was purely a male organization. For a long time women were excluded, longer *de jure* than *de facto*. Therefore, the first youth clubs were clubs for young men. However, the concepts of social equality which were implicit in the club inevitably came in the long run to apply to gender differences too. After the usual time-lag, youth clubs also accepted this idea. At this point, the principle common to all the old-style youth organizations that girls were secondary attachments to male groups was abandoned. As soon as girls were allowed to join clubs, they were allowed to become full members. None the less, the incorporation of females into clubs was a late development.

Youth clubs were most successful at developing into autonomous groups when they built on traditional groupings of students or journeymen. Among the student societies of the nineteenth century, a wide variety developed, reflecting diverse ideological standpoints and attitudes to student tradition. Reading societies, literary clubs and religious groupings also emerged. From the turn of the century, the student reform movement placed more emphasis on sporting and artistic activity, training in good citizenship and assisting in social problems.[153] The student body provided a vivid reflection of the colourful variety which was to be found in the specialized clubs of the educated middle class. The same thing was happening in the upper school. Occasionally in the early nineteenth century, and increasingly throughout the century, school pupils were meeting for literary, academic and lyrical workshops.[154] They produced pupils' magazines and practiced Latin and vernacular oratory. Even football clubs were founded at that time. Above all, they were keen to follow the students' lead. Pupils' clubs were to be found in almost all secondary schools, whether tolerated, suppressed, or disdained.[155] School administrations were generally unhappy about pupils' organizations which went beyond simple singing or gymnastics clubs. But reading, music and shorthand clubs were all established, usually under the patronage of a teacher.[156] This was more a form of youth work run by adults than any autonomous activity of young people. This same tendency towards adult involvement can be seen in many journeymen's associations. In the case of denominational youth fellowships, there was always an appointed adult in the background. Meetings often had less to do with 'fellowship' of young people than with a continuation of religious education from above. Boundaries between club and extra-mural schooling can be quite vague.

Of the plethora of clubs with specialized aims, singing and gymnastics clubs were the most popular with young people. Sporting and musical activities already had a long tradition in the youth groups of older society. Besides, sport is naturally an activity of youth because of its physiological requirements. Gymnastics and singing clubs really took off in Germany in the 1840s.[157] By the beginning of the 1860s the German Gymnastic Association (*Deutsche Turnerschaft*) had a significant number of youth divisions where youngsters between 13 and 17 who had left school could practise the sport under the supervision of a qualified adult.

[153] *Handbuch für Jugendpflege*, p. 52.

[154] F. Blättner, *Das Gymnasium* (Heidelberg, 1960), p. 168; R. S. Elkar, *Junges Deutschland im polemischen Zeitalter* (Düsseldorf, 1979), pp. 229ff.

[155] H. Pross, *Jugend, Eros, Politik. Die Geschichte der deutschen Jugendverbände* (Bern, 1964), p. 44.

[156] *Handbuch für Jugendpflege*, pp. 431ff.

[157] Nipperdey, *Gesellschaft, Kultur, Theorie*, p. 187.

The number of members in this age bracket rose from 30,000 in 1884 to 184,000 in 1912. In addition, there were 62,000 school-boys and 25,000 schoolgirls: a very considerable number of girls in view of the male domination of clubs in general at that time.[158] In the German Workers' Gymnastic Federation (*Deutscher Arbeiterturnerbund*) the number of members under the age of 18 rose to more than 100,000, more than half the total membership, despite harassment from the authorities. The young members had a vote from the age of 14 and were eligible for appointment to important positions.[159] Such broad democratic participation, how-ever, was not to be found in other clubs of the same period. The socialist and nationalist gymnastics clubs had a strong political orientation, as did the Christian ones set up in opposition.[160] These organizations were by no means restricted to sporting activities. The German Gymnastic Association, for example, also had social gatherings, evenings of entertainment, instrumental performances, patriotic commemorative services, and Christmas and Founder's Day celebrations.[161] Female and juvenile members were often present at these diverse events. The gymnastics clubs took over many different social functions which went far beyond the basic stated aim of the organization, especially in the country and in small towns. Like the singing clubs, they multiplied among the rural populations. Their political alignment often led to an ideo-logical polarization which contributed to the disintegration of tra-ditional comprehensive youth groups.[162] The mixing of married and unmarried was also a factor here. This was a principle also found among the voluntary fire brigades which grew up about the middle of the nineteenth century, frequently under the influence of the gymnastics clubs.[163] Because of their strong political leaning, gymnastics clubs could effectively take on the function of the youth section of a particular party. This was frequently the case with the German Workers' Gymnastic Federation. Independent youth sec-tions of political parties only began around the turn of the century.

Autonomous clubs which were made up exclusively of young

---

[158] *Handbuch für Jugendpflege*, pp. 416ff.

[159] G. Herre, 'Arbeitersport, Arbeiterjugend und Obrigkeitsstaat 1893–1914', in Huck (ed.), *Sozialgeschichte der Freizeit*, pp. 196ff.

[160] Nipperdey, *Gesellschaft, Kultur, Theorie*, pp. 200ff.

[161] *Handbuch für Jugendpflege*, pp. 416ff.

[162] Gestrich, 'Jugend in Ohmenhausen', p. 208, on the example of Ohmenhausen.

[163] Nipperday, *Gesellschaft, Kultur, Theorie*, p. 445, n. 81.

people and which catered for their specific needs were few and far between in Germany in the nineteenth century. The overwhelming majority of youth clubs existing at that time were set up by adults. They were the products of efforts which since the end of that century have been known generally as 'youth welfare work'. The early forms of this work can be traced a long way back and are ultimately to be found in the Church, where they amounted to a specialist ministry.

Within the Catholic Church, the Jesuits were the first to develop a ministry devoted specifically to youth. On this were founded the Marian congregations, made up of young people, the first in Rome in 1563.[164] Special Christian education classes for young people who had left school provided another possible starting point for the development of youth groups.[165] When in 1770 this so-called *Christenlehre* was made compulsory in Austria – at about the same time, incidentally, as Austria made its first steps towards compulsory schooling – one of the main arguments for it was that it would prevent young people from spending their free time at the inn. This was an argument which was to be taken over fairly directly by the state-run youth welfare work a hundred years later.

In their conception, Catholic youth clubs were intended to be entirely religious. Social problems only really came to the fore in the Catholic Journeymen's Association, founded by Adolf Kolping in 1849.[166] In the second half of the nineteenth century, the idea of spending leisure time engaged in communal religious activity dominated the many youth clubs which had their origins in church-based initiatives. In the urban clubs they had sections for theatre, music, gymnastics and sport, for saving and for publishing.[167] In the country they had their monthly gathering, their festivals, often also their own bands of musicians. Together they made pilgrimages, and this led to interregional connections.[168] The spiritual supervisor had a dominant position in these clubs. He embodied the authority of the Church, even in secular matters.

[164] G. Schultes, *Der Reichsbund der katholischen deutschen Jugend Österreichs* (Vienna, 1967), p. 25.

[165] Ibid., p. 26.

[166] H. Giesecke, *Vom Wandervogel bis zur Hitlerjugend* (Munich, 1981), p. 60.

[167] G. Schultes, *Der Reichsbund der katholischen deutschen Jugend Österreichs* (Vienna, 1967), p. 46.

[168] Ibid., p. 35.

In the Protestant lands, at first youth clubs with a purely religious orientation were prominent. As early as 1768, the *Missionsjünglingsverein* was founded in Basel,[169] with a strongly Pietistic approach. The first Protestant youth clubs in Germany were founded in the 1820s.[170] In 1834 a youth club was set up in Bremen which placed its emphasis on leisure and conviviality. The new groups modelled on this pattern which sprang up over the next few years soon began to combine. The *Rheinisch-westfälische Bund* was established in 1848, the *Ostdeutsche Jünglingsbund* in 1856, and the *Nationalvereinigung evangelischer Jünglingsbünde* in 1900. International connections were fostered through the YMCA movement, founded in London in 1844 (YWCA in 1855), which spread to America in the 1850s and to Germany in the 1880s.[171] At the beginning of the twentieth century, church-based 'welfare' organizations were by far the strongest youth clubs. Girls were also well represented.

Both denominational and non-denominational youth work in Germany in the nineteenth century was carried out exclusively by private organizations. Only with the beginning of the twentieth century was youth welfare work placed on the agenda of the state. In 1901 an edict was sent out to the chairmen of the regional councils. Three more followed in 1905, 1908 and 1911. The last of these, which pledged a million Marks to a subvention fund for youth organizations, had a particularly powerful impact,[172] resulting in a veritable foundation mania.[173] Major institutions called for urgent support of this 'national' work: the army, the churches, the 'Inner Mission', the Prussian Soldiers' Federation, the Federation against Social Democracy, the Welfare Bureau and the Trade and Industry Convention.[174] The list of supporting groups clearly shows the real thrust. In bringing up the younger generation to 'community spirit and fear of God, love of home and fatherland', a principle aim was to combat the internal enemy, socialism. State welfare

---

[169] Pross, *Jugend, Eros, Politik*, p. 22.
[170] H. Giesecke, *Vom Wandervogel bis zur Hitlerjugend. Jugendarbeit zwischen Politik und Pädagogik* (Munich, 1981), pp. 60ff.
[171] Pross, *Jugend, Eros, Politik*, pp. 24ff.
[172] Giesecke, *Vom Wandervogel*, pp. 62ff.
[173] L. Roth, *Die Erfindung des Jugendlichen* (Munich, 1983), p. 125.
[174] K. Saul, 'Der Kampf um die Jugend zwischen Volksschule und Kaserne. Ein Beitrag zur "Jugendpflege" im wilhelminischen Reiche 1890–1914', *Militärgeschichtliche Mitteilungen*, 9 (1971), p. 114.

work was one of the main instruments in the militarization of society, a process which was working in a very similar way in France at the same time.[175] 'Welfare' organizations aimed at raising the number of potential men-at-arms were a major group among the organizations receiving state support. After teachers, the largest group of youth leaders were officers, who were supposed to bridge the gap between school and military service. With compulsory primary education, on the one hand, and compulsory national service, on the other, the state had two important anchors for social control, at least as far as male youth was concerned. Youth welfare work was used to secure the link between school and barracks. This implicitly meant a redefinition of youth, which now had identifiable age thresholds.

The purposes for which money could be granted to youth clubs from the subvention fund were: preparing meeting rooms; setting up hostels; establishing youth publishing houses; holding evenings of music, singing, reading or speaking; reading plays; visiting museums and exhibitions; encouraging swimming and skating; and spreading the habit of physical exercise.[176] From this catalogue we can see clearly what had changed between the youth organizations of traditional times and the group life of young people in the early twentieth century. In rural areas at this time, traditional groups were sometimes still intact.

A central gathering-place for young club members is the community centre or youth club building. In the country, young men used to gather on the street or at the inn, young women within the framework of the home. The street and the inn were two of the main opponents of state-sponsored youth welfare work and the clubs associated with it. Both underwent a radical change in quality as a result of the processes of urbanization and industrialization. The city pub was not the centre of a strictly ritualized and therefore controlled adolescent drinking culture. Rather, it was the refuge of young people for whom there was all-too-little space in the overcrowded residential areas where they lived or lodged. Young people were now at particular risk of falling victim to alcoholism. The commercialized pattern of socializing in the public

[175] G. Murdock and R. McCron, 'Klassenbewußtsein und Generationsbewußtsein', in J. Clarke et al. (eds), *Jugendkultur als Widerstand* (Frankfurt, 1981), p. 17; *Bericht über die französische Jugend* (Munich, 1968), pp. 225ff.
[176] Giesecke, *Vom Wandervogel*, p. 66.

houses of the big cities and industrial belts had a very different character from the traditional ways of village life. Male–female relationships also slipped out of the control of the received order. Dealing with the uncontrolled sexuality of youngsters in the metropolises was one of the main objectives of the new youth welfare work. When youth workers stylized 'the street' as the epitome of all they saw as negative in young people's social behaviour, this must be seen in terms of their efforts to counter genuine neglect. One of their principle aims was to give youth clubs their own premises, as a way of taking account of the changes in group life in the urban milieu.

The setting-up of youth libraries reflected a fundamental new requirement. Urban young people read books, in itself an individual activity but one which had a great impact on adolescent community life. The names of the city street-gangs with their air of adventure offer a glimpse of the dream-world from which their symbols of identity were drawn. The libraries under the auspices of welfare work were an attempt to raise the quality of reading above the level of 'trash' literature. Literary evenings and play-reading sessions were also intended to offer better alternatives. The attempt to offer young people a broad cultural experience was an innovation. In traditional youth groups, cultural activities stood in quite a different context. The traditional censure customs, for example, contained many elements of youth theatre,[177] but these were firmly rooted in a wider social function of the group. Theatre was not performed for its own sake. Youth music was closely linked to dance, and was tied up with the business of courting. In the youth clubs, music was completely separate from these activities. There was no room for dancing or courting.

The special emphasis on sport in the welfare tradition of clubs also reflects a new set of needs. Youth welfare work took off at a time which had been preceded by a phase of intensive urban growth. Life in the big cities involved a different balance of physical pressures, especially in the growth period of adolescence. This was obviously true in the new sphere of office work and in school, but also in the factories where the physical burden, though real, was of a different kind from on the land. Gymnastics and sport

---

[177] Schultze, *Das deutsche Jugendtheater*, pp. 13ff.

were partly encouraged in the interests of military potential. The routine medical examinations given to new conscripts had clearly shown how working and living conditions in the big cities were damaging the health of young men. The result had been a sharp rise in the numbers being declared unfit for service. By encouraging sport and gymnastics, it was hoped to counter this effect. After all, at that time physical activity was regarded as the panacea for all the diagnosed ills of youth, especially the abuse of alcohol and nicotine and pre-marital sexuality.

Sporting activity could not be carried by the clubs alone. Facilities such as swimming pools, gymnasia and skating rinks had to be provided by local government.[178] From the beginning these facilities were centres for adolescent community life far beyond the limits of the clubs. In comparison with the sporting activities of traditional rural youth groups, young people in the big cities were far more dependent on an infrastructure. The same is true of other facilities. To some extent this infrastructure was provided by the market. Bars, dance halls, cinemas and fairgrounds were among the commercial possibilities. State welfare youth workers had other ideas of the 'right' sort of adolescent community life and attempted to build an alternative infrastructure. Here we see a dilemma which became sharper as the processes of modernization continued. Groups of young people were by themselves less and less in a position to provide the material basis for their collective activity. More and more they were becoming dependent either on the market or on the public purse. In the face of these powers, it was increasingly difficult to maintain independence.

The struggle for an independent community life was a feature of a movement which ran parallel to the state-sponsored welfare movement. The German *Jugendbewegung*, the Free Youth Movement, began with the founding in 1896 at the Berlin Steglitz school of a hiking group called the *Wandervogel* (bird of passage).[179] The Free Youth Movement sharply rejected the institutionalized authority of adults. In place of leadership by teachers, officers and clergymen it advocated leaders appointed by young people from among their own number. It dismissed all thoughts of regimentation from

[178] *Handbuch für Jugendpflege*, p. 265.
[179] Literature on the German *Jugendbewegung* is gathered together in U. Herrmann et al., *Bibliographie zur Geschichte der Kindheit, Jugend und Familie* (Munich, 1980), pp. 96ff.

without and placed great emphasis on the idea of autonomy. Youth groups should not arise out of initiatives from above but from the free decision of a circle of friends. Free Youth objected to all attempts on the part of bureaucracy to make young people's decisions for them. This was how it saw the national associations of youth organizations, and even more so the state welfare programme. Against these, it promoted the free development of group life according to the needs of the young people themselves. With the principles of free association on the basis of individual choice, self-determination of the group, and autonomy with respect to outside influences, the Free Youth Movement was taking the basic thinking of the liberal clubs and applying it to young people. For those in the early years of youth, mainly school pupils but also apprentices, these structural principles of community life were new. For the older ones, students and journeymen, autonomous groups had long existed. In terms of the idea of autonomy, then, the Free Youth Movement was extending what already existed to younger age groups, to adolescents in the modern, more limited, sense of the word.

The new idea of leadership from within the group does not, however, mean democracy by election. What emerged in Free Youth was more along the lines of the charismatic leader.[180] The historical model of the royal entourage had a powerful influence. The leader of the group had continually to legitimize his position by achieving particular objectives set by the group, and if he failed in these he could be removed. To begin with, it was the planner or expert who stood in the foreground.[181] The best hiker, cook or camper should lead the group. As the movement developed, this element of specialization faded. Total identification with the leader became more important; the leadership role was endowed with an element of mysticism. In place of older adolescents, adults were increasingly involved. As the concept of leadership changed, authoritarian components began to appear.

It was not only in group structure that the Free Youth Movement brought radical innovations. The activities of the groups were also re-examined. Hiking was already a perfectly common youth activity when the *Wandervogel* first took to the road, but the

---

[180] S. N. Eisenstadt, *Von Generation zu Generation* (Munich, 1966), pp. 328ff.
[181] Giesecke, *Vom Wandervogel*, p. 97.

importance which hiking now took on for the development of an independent group culture was new. The forms of community life and the expressions of culture, such as clothes, language and songs, all bore the stamp of the wanderers. Hiking brought new geographical foci for group life, the camp, for example, or the accommodation which had been rigged up somewhere in a remote cabin or an abandoned workshop.[182] The idea was to leave behind the urban milieu and create one's own counter-world elsewhere. This meant young people distancing themselves from adults to a degree scarcely known before. No historical youth group of earlier periods had ever consciously withdrawn from the world of their parents' generation in such a way. This radical geographical distancing also contributed to the autonomy of the youth community. It also concealed elements of escapism which had implications for the political behaviour of these young people.

The rough travelling style of the *Wandervogel*, with its consciously exaggerated physical demands, led to the creation within the Free Youth Movement of a new masculinity myth which did nothing to encourage female participation. The hiking movement did include young women. Groups of young girls undertook romantic journeys on foot, leaving behind their home milieu just as the boys did.[183] However, the formation of a full female organization, or indeed of mixed groups, was not pursued very far. Mixed hikes were rejected on the grounds that 'the boys will grow soft, and the girls will become tomboys'.[184] Despite all the readiness in principle to break with tradition, received gender stereotypes were perpetuated. The concept of the 'Free' Youth Movement was one of freedom of association for males.

The idea of the autonomous youth group, which the *Wandervogel* was so decidedly successful in developing, corresponded to a general trend at the turn of the century. It was strongest among secondary school pupils, who were suffering under a highly authoritarian school system. As early as 1883, a number of pupils from Elberfeld had organized a retreat to the country for shared Bible study. This initiative led to the establishment of pupils' Bible

[182] Pross, *Jugend, Eros, Politik*, p. 113.
[183] Ibid., p. 121.
[184] Hans Breuer, cited in K. Seidelmann, *Gruppe – soziale Grundform der Jugend*, vol. II (Berlin, 1971), p. 58.

study groups.[185] A German Hikers' Federation, parallel to the
Wandervogel, grew out of a pupils' club in Hamburg, and had
more-comprehensive aims. There were workshops for chamber
music, singing, photography, theatre, creative writing and so on.
The community experience of the group was not given the same
prominence as in the *Wandervogel*. The approach was more
objective, less romantic.[186] What both had in common was a sharp
opposition to the student organizations with their coloured ribbons and caps, which at that time were also widespread among
school pupils. In rejecting the traditional student drinking culture
they stood alongside other reforming groups within Free Youth
which promulgated the idea of abstinence.[187]

Shortly after the first autonomous groups of pupils and students
came the beginnings of the young workers' movement. The
Federation of Apprentices and Young Workers was founded in
Berlin in 1904.[188] Here again, the driving force came not from adults
but from the young people themselves. In terms of aims, the pro-
letarian youth movement was quite different from that of the middle
class. Most important for the young workers was the development
of solidarity as a basis for pressing for political objectives. Their
most urgent demands were laws to protect young people in the
workplace, and better educational opportunities. The free time in
which middle-class youth engaged in group activities had for the
most part still to be won. All in all, the young workers' movement
was orientated far more towards immediate, concrete questions,
was less romantic, more rationalistic. Unlike the middle-class
Jugendbewegung, it accepted girls from the start.[189]

The groups under the umbrella of the Free Youth Movement
included only a very small percentage of young Germans, but
their ideas, their style, their outward forms, their new activities
and group structures all sent out ripples which had an enormous
impact on the group life of young people in much wider circles.
Many traditional youth groups borrowed particular features. The
concept of autonomy spread far and wide. However, the principle
of young people being led by their peers also received a strong

---

[185] Pross, *Jugend, Eros, Politik*, p. 54.
[186] Ibid., pp. 90ff.
[187] Ibid., pp. 139ff.
[188] Ibid., pp. 87ff.; Giesecke, *Vom Wandervogel*, pp. 39ff.
[189] Pross, *Jugend, Eros, Politik*, p. 88.

stimulus from other models, in particular from the Boy Scouts. The Scout Association was founded in 1908 by Sir Robert Baden-Powell and soon spread far beyond Britain.[190] Although it had strong overtones of youth welfare work, Scouting was strongly orientated towards young people's own needs. In the youth clubs which it influenced, it certainly had the effect of encouraging a more strongly self-determined youth culture.

The First World War meant a major break in continuity for the youth organizations. In the years which followed, the ideas of Free Youth and those of the welfare tradition were picked up and carried forward. The changed political and social situation, however, meant a whole series of new emphases. In 1932 a contemporary observer gave a vivid description of youth organizations in the time between the wars:

> Marching, uniformed troops of boys in closed, disciplined ranks. They march in step, the flag at the head, sometimes the red flag of the coming socialist state, sometimes the swastika of the coming third Reich, sometimes again the cross of the young Catholics or Protestants, or the black flag of resistance to the Treaty of Versailles. Standing and marching in rank and file is for all of them an expression of their most powerful sense of vitality, for all it is an elementary experience, to all it is intoxicating.[191]

Many important components of the changed situation of youth groups in this time touch on this point: the tendency to form political camps, the building of mass organizations, the power of big events with their mass ritual, militarization, discipline, male domination, and the important role of public appearances for the group experience of young people.

The tendency for young people organized in clubs to form into camps was a logical consequence of the application of the club principle to their generation. After all, the club originally evolved as a way of articulating new political interests. Although it was forbidden for young people to join political clubs before the age of 21, reduced in 1908 to 18, the politicization of youth clubs goes

[190] On the situation in England, see Gillis, *Geschichte der Jugend*, pp. 149ff. On Germany, see Pross, *Jugend, Eros, Politik*, pp. 103ff.

[191] J. Fischer, in *Das junge Deutschland 1932*, pp. 39ff., cited in Giesecke, *Vom Wandervogel*, p. 176.

well back into the nineteenth century. A major reason for the foundation of church-based youth groups was to immunize young people against supposed dangerous ideas. And even the state-run welfare work, though nominally apolitical, had a significant political element. Even before the First World War political parties began to found their own youth sections, although these remained quantitatively a clear minority among the many youth organizations on the political battlefield. The years between the wars saw both an increasing affiliation of youth organizations to party political camps and a powerful consolidation of youth groups directly integrated into political parties. This was especially true for the Social Democrats who in the nineteenth century had regarded the foundation of an organization for the youth of the party as of little importance.

The intensified polarization of young club members into camps brought a new kind of group consciousness and new ties of loyalty. The individual local group lost importance and adherence to an inter-regional community of conscience took its place. Older ties to territorial and social units were broken. Ideologically orientated youth organizations pushed their way into communities where they had previously had no place, especially in the rural population. The changed group consciousness was particularly obvious in the conflicts of the young men. The traditional pattern of brawls between the lads of the neighbouring villages disappeared. It found its continuation in a far bloodier pattern of clashes between youth groups of differing ideological persuasions.

The tendency to form camps corresponds to the trend towards mass organizations. Here, too, the beginnings go back well before the war. There were two main developments which led to the growth of wide federations of youth: the alignment of local groups with shared aims into inter-regional organizations, and the setting up by a central institution of new local groups on a standardized model. Both are phenomena which only began in the age of the youth club. Inter-regional affiliation, which involved the suppression of the local element in the self-awareness of the group, was *ex definitione* quite foreign to the older pattern of territorially minded youth groups. By the beginning of the twentieth century, the development of large inter-regional federations of youth groups was already well advanced. The advance of nationalism as a philosophy did much to encourage the organization of young people at national level. State-sponsored welfare work also fostered this. The Free Youth Movement had the opposite emphasis. Its demand for autonomy was not conducive to the growth of federations which required a large bureaucracy. In the period after the First World War, even Free Youth showed a tendency towards larger forms. The growth of ideologically and party-politically orientated youth federations heightened the trend towards mass organizations. One of the many factors in the background which encouraged these developments was the improvement of the systems of communication. This facilitated not only more-intensive personal contacts between local youth groups, but also a more-intensive exchange of ideas through indirect media. For example, locally produced magazines played an important part in the inter-regional processes of integration.

The trend toward polarized camps and mass organizations also brought a widening of the age range of the young people involved. Whereas before the First World War the main targets for the youth federations were school-leavers who were not yet of an age to begin national service, there was now an increasing interest in winning school pupils. Ten- to fourteen-year-olds were now cultivated. This meant that the concept of youth, in so far as it was defined by membership of youth organizations, was extended downwards. This broadening out made an internal division into age bands necessary. The first mass youth organization to introduce an age structure was the Scout Association. From there, the idea quickly spread to the socialist youth organizations.[192] The principle of age-based subgroups which had long been established in the schools now became normative for youth organizations.

The mass nature of the youth organization became especially evident at big events, which were at the time a major element in adolescent self-esteem. Torchlight processions, running in relay and shouting in unison were all new forms of expression in this period. Mass demonstrations of sporting prowess were integrated into the ritual of the big event. Formation marching was particularly important as a demonstration of strength. Marching had a long tradition among male youth, particularly among youth groups with military responsibilities. There were also thematic links with older forms of parade in rural society, the money collection, the masked

---

[192] Giesecke, *Vom Wandervogel*, p. 121.

procession and the censure tradition, but between the wars the military component was certainly the most important. It corresponds to the widespread wearing of uniform among youth groups.

A military influence could also be detected in youth groups at points which were not designed to be in the public eye. Camping and wide-games were increasingly popular. The wide-game was already known in the First World War as a kind of pre-military field exercise, especially in those youth organizations which made the grooming of military personnel a priority. The camp picked up on the hiking tradition of the Free Youth Movement, but in the course of the inter-war period it changed its character considerably. In the place of the loosely organized camp of Free Youth there now emerged the large camp with military-style discipline, duty rotas and marching practice.[193] Youth groups were no longer wandering hordes; they were marching columns.

The military component also influenced the underlying thinking of the youth organizations in the inter-war period. The role model for male youth was front-line soldier. Military virtues like bravery, hardiness, camaraderie and readiness for action dominated their value system. The group ideal was the male cohort. There was little room for emancipation. Equal participation rights for girls were closest in the socialist youth organizations, but here too a lower-middle-class climate clouded the relations between the sexes.[194] The proportion of female members of youth groups in the inter-war years lagged well behind that for males. In 1927, 56 per cent of young men belonged to an organization, but only 26 per cent of young women.[195]

Overall, about 40 per cent of German young people were members of youth organizations at this time. The era of organized youth had reached its climax. After 1945 the figures may only have been a little lower, but the power of this kind of youth group to hold its membership had certainly declined.

The fact that this golden age of organized youth clubs, the Weimar Republic, was followed by a period of state control had, of course, nothing to do with the internal dynamics of youth groups. This was primarily a result of a change in the nature of the state.

[193] Klönne, *Jugend im Dritten Reich*, p. 57.
[194] Giesecke, *Vom Wandervogel*, p. 129.
[195] Ibid., p. 140.

None the less, it is important to realize that there was not a completely abrupt break but certain lines of continuity did extend into
the Hitler period and beyond. It is significant that leading members of the resistance made plans to maintain the state youth
organization under the leadership of specially trained officers after
the fall of Hitler.[196] As late as 1953–4 almost a quarter of all young
West Germans were in favour of a unified state youth structure.[197]
It is, after all, not a phenomenon restricted to Nazi Germany. It
was found at the same time in other Fascist states, especially in
Italy, in Hungary and in the Corporate State of Austria. Likewise,
it could be seen in the Soviet Union, and after 1945 it was adopted
by the new communist countries.

Two trends which hint at the development of the structures of
a state youth movement can be seen even before the founding of
the Third Reich. The first was the emergence of centralized, controlled, unified, large organizations associated with ideological
camps. A typical example of this was the attempt of the Catholic
Church to suppress the colourful variety of Catholic clubs, and
in particular, Catholic youth clubs. According to the grand plan of
Pope Pius XI, the stratified structure of Catholic Action should
include a unified Catholic Youth Movement which, like other
sectional organizations, would be under strict leadership through
the hierarchy. It would be worth researching whether this concept was in any way influenced by the developments taking place
in Fascist Italy. At any rate, there was clearly an attempt made
to replace the club structures with their autonomous or semi-
autonomous small units by a centralized and authoritarian unified
organization. Obviously, this tendency was not restricted to Fascist
groups. The second trend can be seen in the fact that, long before
the foundation of the Third Reich, the growth of state welfare
work had provided an instrument which could be used to aid the
transition of the existing youth organizations into a state movement.
Certainly, the state youth programmes of the Wilhelminian and
Weimar periods were designed to promote the welfare of youth
people indirectly, through other agencies, but at the same time it
created a basis through which the state could take control of their
social life outside the school.

[196] Klönne, *Jugend im Dritten Reich*, p. 283.
[197] Seidelmann, *Gruppe – soziale Grundform*, p. 25.

Elements of continuity between the youth groups of the Weimar Republic and the state youth movement of the Nazi period can also be seen in internal structures, activities and community forms. National-Socialist youth work took over a great deal from the tradition of Free Youth:[198] hiking and camping, wide-games and social evenings, the repertoire of songs, many organizational terms, and even the principle that young people should be led by young people. Most of the leaders in the Hitler Youth (HJ, *Hitlerjugend*) and its girls' section, the *Bund Deutscher Mädel* (BDM), were only a few years older than the youngsters in their groups. The continuity is clearest when we take account of the developments of Free Youth after the First World War. However, if we compare the structures of the Hitler Youth with those of the early stages of the Free Youth Movement we also find striking contrasts: here, elitist small groups striving for intimacy, there, mass operations; here, camaraderie based on personal relations, there, solidarity on the basis of state control; here, autonomous group decisions, there, an authoritarian structure of command.

As it developed, the Hitler Youth achieved very high rates of membership. At the end of 1933 less than one-third of 10–18-year-olds were members, but by the beginning of 1939 this had apparently risen to 98 per cent.[199] If we consider that in 1927 only about 40 per cent of young Germans had belonged to clubs, it is easy to see how many youngsters had their first experience of an organized youth group through the HJ. This proportion was particularly high among girls and in the rural populations.

When, at the end of the Nazi period, membership of organized youth groups again became voluntary, the proportion of young people involved sank even lower than it had been in the Weimar years. In 1953 only 35 per cent of youngsters between the ages of 14 and 21 declared themselves to be members of a youth organization.[200] In the decade which followed, the figures seem to have remained steady, possibly rising slightly. Then came a new drop: in 1970 the proportion of 10–25-year-olds in youth organizations was estimated at around 25 per cent. Since then, this downward trend has apparently continued.

[198] Giesecke, *Vom Wandervogel*, p. 204; Klönne, *Jugend im Dritten Reich*, p. 103.

[199] Klönne, *Jugend im Dritten Reich*, p. 34.

[200] Seidelmann, *Gruppe – soziale Grundform*, pp. 21ff.

In the period since the Second World War, interesting changes have taken place in the structures of organized youth. A clear growth can only be seen in sport clubs. In the 14 years from 1953 to 1967, the proportion of youngsters involved in this type of organization rose from 15 per cent to 23 per cent.[201] In the same period, the proportion attending church-based groups declined from 12 per cent to 7 per cent. For political clubs and youth sections of trades unions the drop was from 4 per cent to 2 per cent. These trends have continued since then.[202] Sport clubs belong to the category of youth organization where people gather for a stated purpose. Denominational and political associations, on the other hand, make more-comprehensive demands which young people are increasingly reluctant to accept. They are no longer prepared to be bound to other people on the whole spectrum of issues involved in group life. With specialist clubs which primarily offer a particular service, such strong bonds are not required. Relationships here are objectivized and purpose-orientated. The growth of these clubs, and the simultaneous decline of more-comprehensive ones, indicates a significant change in the place of the club in the social life of young people. In their parents' and grandparents' generations a youngster was a Scout, a young worker or a *Wandervogel* 'with heart and soul'.[203] Even clubs with specific aims had far-wider social involvement. This willingness of young people to be totally integrated has been declining since the 1950s. Limited integration on the basis of stated objectives has taken its place. Under these conditions it is perfectly possible to be a member of several clubs at once. Often club membership means little more than paying a subscription which entitles the member to use a facility as often or as seldom as desired. A comparison of club membership figures today with those prior to the Second World War must be seen in the context of these changes in the levels of commitment involved.

An analysis of the membership figures of youth organizations reveals that they are increasingly accepting children as members. In 1980 the sports clubs, which had experienced such a sharp growth in numbers, had their largest female contingent in the age

---

[201] Ibid., p. 20.
[202] S. Bartjes and F. Kroll, 'Sportvereine', *Demokratische Erziehung*, 6 (1982), p. 56; B. Schäfers, *Soziologie des Jugendalters* (Opladen, 1982), p. 178.
[203] Wurzbacher, *Gesellungsformen*, p. 60.

group 7–14.[204] In this age group we are certainly not dealing with autonomous youth activities which compete with the parental home. None the less, the extension of club membership to children should be taken as an indication that opportunities for voluntary social contacts outside the family are coming at an increasingly early age.

Another change in the composition of organized youth groups in recent times has been a dramatic increase in the number of girls involved. Whereas in the early days of youth clubs the male organizations were clearly dominant, the situation is now much more balanced. However, when we consider diverse types of youth associations, clear gender differences can still be observed. Church-based organizations are overwhelmingly female: sport and hobby groups mainly male.[205] Within the sports clubs, areas of specialization vary according to gender. For the girls, gymnastics clubs are most popular; for boys, football clubs head the list.[206] However, there is much evidence to suggest that, as youth associations have developed, even these differences have levelled out.

Significant changes have taken place since the Second World War in the forms of group life. Often several historical layers exist side by side within the same organization. So for example, in the CVJM (*Christlicher Verein junger Männer*), the German YMCA, which has a wealth of traditions, it was noticed in 1967 that simplified, three basic forms could be identified.[207] In the 'ministry' model, the minister or an adult appointed by him stood at the centre and provided for the young people from the age of Confirmation onwards. In the 'free youth' model, the traditions of the German Youth Movement took priority. The 'informal group' model, which was most common in the big cities, followed American precedents; from a centre of action with an 'open door' a wide range of hobbies, activities and themes are offered. This analysis of organized youth activity allows us to make a generalization. Here we see reflected the three most important stages of development in the history of youth clubs, which can now exist together in a variety of hybrids.

[204] Schäfers, *Soziologie des Jugendalters*, p. 178.
[205] *Jugend '81*, p. 702; *Bericht über die französische Jugend*, p. 203; 'Jugend zu Beginn der achtziger Jahre', in *Österreichischer Jugendbericht*, I (Vienna, 1981), p. 201; Seidelmann, *Gruppe – soziale Grundform*, p. 271.
[206] Schäfers, *Soziologie des Jugendalters*, p. 178.
[207] Seidelmann, *Gruppe – soziale Grundform*, p. 63.

The most important development in young people's group life since the Second World War has been the development of a new kind of club.[208] It is characterized by unforced social interaction created principally by the sharing of space. Formal membership plays a subordinate role in this organizational model. The club is open to all. Friends can be brought along. A loose network of informal contacts forms around a nucleus. There are many possible activities: dancing, games, discussions, or simply sitting around without any pressure. A person can fall in with this or that activity as the mood dictates. Many traditional youth organizations have gone over to this looser form of community life,[209] their youth work becoming more like the modern youth centre. Since the late 1950s, this kind of club has also developed specialist varieties. There are dancing clubs, jazz clubs, film clubs, record clubs, fan clubs, political clubs, all combining specialist content with a loose form of social structure. This development is in some respects an intermediate form between the traditional youth club and the informal group.

The development of youth centres epitomizes the trends in the community life of young people since 1945. They provide a gathering point for youngsters who are not part of an organization, and are therefore an expression of the decline of the traditional forms of youth club. Their roots go back well before the last war, and in Britain back to the end of the nineteenth century.[210] In Germany the youth welfare work at the beginning of the twentieth century experimented with open forms in an attempt to gain access to the lower-class youth of the big cities. However the 'open door' idea only made a real impact after 1945. The initiative for this form of youth work now came not only from the churches and the youth associations but increasingly also from municipal authorities, an indication of the growing need for the public purse to support the infrastructure of adolescent group life. To begin with, youth centres were shaped by adult ideas of what was 'appropriate' for youth. The programme included readings, discussions, charades, impromptu plays and amateur dramatics, singing and music-making, energetic games, parlour games, sport, gymnastics, handicrafts, hiking, camping, expeditions, sightseeing tours and general

[208] Wurzbacher, *Gesellungsformen*, p. 62; Seidelmann, *Gruppel – soziale Grundform*, pp. 286ff.
[209] Seidelmann, *Gruppe – soziale Grundform*, pp. 21, 215ff.
[210] Wurzbacher, *Gesellungsformen*, p. 68.

educational work groups; not, however, modern social dancing or films.[211] Youth work which sought to meet actual needs had to address changing leisure interests if it was to reach those young people not already in organizations. Questions of programming and social control were the principal sources of conflict in the youth centres in the years which followed. The users of the youth centres became more and more alienated from the organizing bodies. The conflict between authoritarian concepts of youth work and young people's desire for autonomy virtually became an institution.

Youth centres stand historically in the tradition of the youth clubs, which find here a setting for their new, more open style. But they also serve as a focus for informal youth groups, offering them an alternative to such commercially run venues as the pub, coffee shop, cinema or disco. Rendering these uncontrolled forms controllable was one of the original aims of youth welfare work. The same is true of the street as a centre of juvenile community life. The street had been very important as a setting for shared activity, particularly for boys from the lower classes. The dramatic increase in traffic in the decades since the Second World War led to what has been described, from the young folk's point of view, as the 'loss of the street'. The youth contacts which used to be centred on the street were now also in part transferred to the youth centre. In every respect it was becoming the point of crystallization for the informal group life of young people.

IV. Individuality and Community

The emergence of the informal gathering of friends as the most important form of adolescent community in the present day should be seen in terms of the interaction of a number of general tendencies which need to be described. The first of these can be labelled the de-institutionalization or de-ritualizing of adolescent community life. A basic feature of informal groups is that they do not have formalized structures. In this they differ substantially from youth clubs, but also from the older forms of territorial

[211] U. Lohmar, 'Die arbeitende Jugend im Spannungsfeld der Organisation in Gesellschaft und Staat', in H. Schelsky (ed.), *Arbeiterjugend gestern und heute* (Heidelberg, 1955), p. 220.

and professional youth groups. Not even group membership is institutionalized. There is neither the social pressure to participate which was seen in the rural fraternities and the journeymen's associations, nor the voluntary short- or long-term commitment of the youth organizations. The intensity and duration of group membership are left entirely to the individual to decide. The informal youth group has no fixed events at which attendance is expected. In the traditional local groups, meetings were to a great extend dictated by the Church year or other points on the calender; the youth club has its programme of events tailored to suit its own purposes; the informal youth group meets spontaneously, or gathers in the context of a larger event, perhaps at a youth centre. For this reason it needs no office-bearers or leaders. In keeping with its informal structure, the necessary minimum of organization is done by team-work. There is no club house and no kitty. Public houses or private flats often serve as meeting places. The increasing availability to young people of private space is an important prerequisite for the informal group. To a certain extent, shared norms do still develop, but these are neither set down in writing nor elaborately expounded, as would have been the case in the statutes of an older fraternity.

Ritual forms of behaviour had an important role in traditional youth groups. They were part of the institutional framework which gave the group its identity and solidarity. In rural youth lore especially, most common activities were linked with ritual. Ritualism began to disappear with the growth of the youth clubs, although the oldest clubs still had many ritual features. We may think of the highly developed ritual laid down in the codes of conduct of some student societies. Some of the more-recent youth groupings also have their rituals, for example the *Wandervogel* and the Scouts. However, this seldom happens in single-purpose clubs. The informal youth groups are generally de-ritualized. There is no rite of entry with vows of allegiance or a formal commitment for a given period of life. There are no ritual celebrations, like the anniversary of the foundation of a club, or the *Kermis* festival in the rural fraternity. There are no rituals of eating and drinking, courting and dancing. Indeed, modern dancing strikingly reflects the rejection of formal ties and the development of personal freedom of expression. This has gone so far that at parties, which provided an institutional context for private dancing, the formal element has been so completely lost that it is no longer necessary to dance at all. Certainly, new rites of youth have developed. But these are not regimented patterns for the meetings of informal groups so much as formalized modes of expression at big events, rock concerts, football matches and the like. As components of international youth styles, they belong in a much wider context.

One purpose of ritual is to give outward expression to the sense of community within a group. The conviviality which binds the informal group has no need of this. Other group symbols can also be dispensed with, such as the flags, pennants and coats of arms which were and are widely used in youth organizations. In historical youth groups, identity of clothing was important for the identity of the group. In old European society, traditional costumes expressed locality and distinguished the married from the unmarried. Youth organizations were frequently uniformed, especially those which were attached to ideological camps. Particular symbols identified subgroups within the organization. Informal youth groups usually lay no value on uniformity of clothing and do not display their identity to the outside world. In so far as similarity of clothing does exist, it is an expression of community which goes far beyond the small group. Clothing certainly has not lost its function of declaring attitudes and values. The fact that informal groupings do tend to consist of young people who share a particular outlook means that, notwithstanding the radical decline of ideologically orientated youth organizations, there is a line of continuity to be drawn from youth groups of the past.

Similarities in clothing, and also to a great extent in hairstyles, have in the last decades increasingly become an expression of internal uniformity within the international youth culture. From the teddy boys, *Halbstarke* and *blousons noirs* of the 1950s to the punks of the late 1970s, identity-consciousness in adolescent subcultures has to varying degrees been expressed in outward appearance. A principal function of these fashions is to create a social demarcation[212] which can then be directed against other groups. It marks them off from other adolescent subcultures, especially those connected with a different social milieu, as can be seen in the clashes between mods and rockers or between skinheads and hippies. Equally, there can be a demarcation against

[212] J. Clarke, 'Stil', in Clarke et al. (eds), *Jugendkultur*, p. 141.

the adult world, which is radically rejected. In this respect they have common ground with many historical youth protest movements. In their original milieu, mostly in particular districts of English big cities, such youth styles may have begun as a demarcation against other territorial youth groups. As the various elements of style spread to other regions, this element dropped into the background. Consequently, the structure of the individual group which feels identified with such expressive fashions varies considerably. Many of these groups have an informal character. Generally speaking, social networks are more intense among young people who are influenced by such youth styles than among those who are not. Involvement with outward group styles seems to vary according to the age, gender and social origin of young people. It is stronger at the beginning of youth than in the later years, stronger with boys than with girls, and stronger in the lower class than in the middle and upper classes.[213]

The name of a youth group is an expression of its institutional character and a symbol of its internal solidarity. The name relates to the specifics of group identity, the aims of the group, its values, often also the ideals of its dream-world. In traditional rural groups, identity was entirely determined by territorial factors. With later urban territorial groups, on the other hand, we have encountered names which relate to fantasy-world ideas of the character and qualities of group members. Youth clubs and organizations are distinguished by titles they have chosen themselves. With informal youth groups, on the other hand, with their relatively de-institutionalized and temporary character, there are no specific names. There are, however, terminologies for the wider contexts of youth styles, and these include names originating within the groups as well as names applied by others. These often relate to the outward appearance, which is obviously given great weight.

A general tendency which has encouraged the growth of informal groupings has been the dropping or separating of functions. Older historical youth groups encompassed a wide range of areas of life which were important for the individual. They were comprehensive and multi-functional. Many of these traditional functions have been passed to other institutions or social forms, many more have been divided up between a number of different groupings,

[213] *Jugend '81*, pp. 551ff.

and some appear no longer to be observed by groups at all, but rather have been individualized.

One of the most important functions of youth groups in traditional rural societies was, as we have seen, the regulating of contacts between the sexes. Organizing dances was therefore an important task. Some youth groups, student societies for example, kept this function in the era of the club. It is still a task in some informal groupings. However, there are also social milieux in which the organization of dances has been taken over by the family, a phenomenon typical of the upper classes. More importantly, a strong tradition of commercially organized dances has grown up, culminating in the modern disco. Public dance-floors in cafés and bars have taken this responsibility away from the youth group. It can, if it wishes, continue to organize its own dances, but there is no longer any necessity since there are alternatives on offer.

In so far as it was possible to speak of sporting activities in the life of traditional rural youth, these were carried out entirely by the youth groups themselves. On this basis, the development of modern youth sports would have been impossible. These require facilities and equipment which are often very expensive. From the archery ranges of the Middle Ages to modern indoor swimming pools, countless facilities have been provided by the local community. Others were financed by clubs, and others again were erected on a commercial basis. Shared sporting activities are today focused on these, as it is no longer possible for a group of friends in an urban setting to meet for a game of football without having a field where the game is permitted.

A major part of the function of the traditional youth group was connected with preparing to enter the adult world. This is to be seen most clearly in the rural fraternities. The tradition of censure, for example, served to encourage a constant awareness of the central norms and rules of society, while at the same time giving an introduction to the more serious judicial functions which were expected of adult men. In modern times, youth groups are certainly not in existence to provide training for adulthood in any comparable way. Processes of social conditioning have been taken over by the school. Rather, youth groups have become places where this conditioning may be called into question.

These few examples serve to illustrate how, on quite different levels, functions belonging to youth groups have in the course of history been given over to other institutions. Both national and local government have been involved, as well as commercial enterprise. These institutions have in turn given rise to new social forms which are made up exclusively or predominantly of young people, but which are not youth groups in the strictest sense. In this context, Wurzbacher speaks of the 'multitude in concord'.[214] He is thinking, for example, of young cinema-goers, of audiences at sporting or cultural events, of youngsters at public dances or in jazz clubs, on the ski slopes or by the seaside. Such examples of the 'multitude in concord' are, of course, not restricted to youth, but many of them cater specifically for young people or are dominated by them. These provide a framework for the social interaction of young people, sometimes as couples or in groups of friends, but also as individuals. Certainly, similar social contexts did exist in old European society, but their importance for the group life of young people has expanded greatly in recent times.

The large number of facilities available to young people has led to a greater flexibility in groupings. In comparison with earlier times, in particular with old rural society, the spectrum of possible group activities has increased enormously. Furthermore, there is a large number of possible partners. Consequently, the composition of the group can change according to the activity in hand. It is possible for young people to be involved in the most varied group combinations. Freedom of choice extends both to what they do and whom they do it with. This too is an important characteristic of the informal youth group.

The principle of more and more freedom of choice has led to significant changes in the relationship of the individual to the group. This forces us to question how far traditional groups like the rural fraternities allowed the development of personal identity in our modern sense at all. The pressure to conform seems to have been very great. Not even group membership was a result of personal choice in the way that it was with the later youth club. It was an automatic consequence of residence in a local community. The high degree of ritualization in all areas of life left little room for individual expression. Participation in every group activity was in principle expected; if the group ran a dance, one had to dance. There was also very little room for manoeuvre in the realm of

[214] 'Die gleichgestimmte Menge', see Wurzbacher, Gesellungsformen, pp. 44ff.

ideology and values. Whenever ideological or political polarity appeared, it led to an erosion of the group. No doubt the over-whelming desire for social conformity and the relative intolerance of strangers are also reasons why there was so frequently an aggressive reaction even against the youth of the neighbouring village. Youth groups with less pressure for conformity do show such an intense vilification of outsiders.

The informal youth group stands at the other extreme. The choice of partners is for the most part free, the only external influence being that institutionalized activities may already have produced ready-made circles of social interaction. For example, many informal groups are built on school contacts. Within this larger context, however, choices are made on the basis of personal empathy. Emotional criteria figure far more largely in informal groupings than in historical youth groups. Personal friendship is the most important element in their constitution. All the functions which made membership of historical groups obligatory had to disappear before friendship could become the major factor in the shaping of adolescent group life.

In the circle of friends who make up the informal group there is no need whatsoever to share every activity. Group composition can vary according to interest, for individual interests are the main factors drawing the group together. Freedom of choice extends beyond the choice of partners to the more fundamental choice of whether to be in a group at all or to act alone. Among the favourite leisure activities of young people there are many towards the top of the list which do not involve groups at all but are done on an individual basis.[215] Reading is the most obvious. Listening to music is also frequently done alone. As the number of young people with their own rooms has increased, so has the popularity of isolated leisure activity. The new-found possibilities of individu-alization make it perfectly possible to decide against any kind of group involvement at all. The process of individualization which has led to the overthrow of all obligatory forms of community life for young people therefore seems to be ambivalent in its result: it offers them the possibility to shape their time alone or with friends according to their own personal preferences and ideals, but it also brings a danger of loneliness and isolation.

Looking back over history it can be seen that youth is the phase

[215] W. Strzelewicz, *Jugend in ihrer freien Zeit* (Munich, 1965), p. 22.

of life in which gender differences are brought into strong relief. This is clearly expressed in the social structures of young people, which have always had great importance for the development of sexual identity. As these groups developed towards the modern era it is possible to observe a general trend of growing equality between the sexes. Groups with clearly formulated gender roles went into decline, as did those where the sexes were organized separately. Mixed groups of youngsters of the same age became the primary form. The participation of girls in what had been male peer groups increased until a balance was achieved.

This general movement from a gender-specific youth culture to one where differences were less accentuated can be seen particularly clearly in the development from the traditional rural patterns to the modern informal group. In the older rural territorial groups, the roles of the two sexes were defined in quite different ways. Many activities, for example the entire tradition of censure, were exclusively male. Even when girls were brought into the activities of the fraternity it was on a basis of total inequality. The boys always organized and invited. They had the active role. Activities initiated by the girls were exceptional. An even-greater polarity can be observed in the urban territorial groups. This was a decidedly machoistic youth culture. The role of a girl in the group was as the 'bride' of a male member of the gang. It is hard to find an analogy for this macho culture in the various forms of clubs and associations. Instead, the sexes tended to be organized separately. To begin with, youth clubs were only for boys anyway. When girls' organizations were introduced, their group life was based on entirely different activities. The stereotypes at work here were particularly obvious in the Nazi youth organizations, the HJ and the BDM.[216] On the other hand, obligatory participation in state youth organizations did mean that girls had a better opportunity than ever before to take part in group life with other girls of their age. In some rural areas this had hitherto been completely unknown. The new kind of club which developed after 1945 brought the greatest gender mixing and gender equality so far. However, it was in the informal gathering of friends, and not in organized groups, that a group culture with no sexual discrimination finally developed.

[216] Klönne, *Jugend im Dritten Reich*, pp. 77ff.

The tendency to balance out historically received sexual differences in adolescent community life can be seen in the way that the venues of group culture have changed. Traditionally, interaction between adolescent females and males lay in an area of tension between house and street. Typically, girls met within the home, on the spinning-room pattern, while boys met outside the home, either on the street itself or in the pub, the tavern, the inn, the café. When the old fraternities rented a room in a house this was still outside the parental home. A line of development can be traced from here to the first youth clubs with their own premises. These were initially male youth clubs. One of the new trends in more-recent developments has been for groups of boys or mixed groups to gather within the home. The party culture is an expression of this. At the same time, female group culture has been moving out into the public domain. Its geographical radius of action has expanded. Girls can now meet one another in a pub. It is possible for them to go out alone. This is particularly obvious in youth tourism, in which girls participate on a completely equal footing.

A tendency to eliminate gender differences can also be seen in the international youth style. Whereas in the 1950s the teddy boys, *Halbstarke* and *blousons noir* represented a culture with strong elements of demonstrative masculinity,[217] this is not so obviously the case with more-recent group styles. Certainly, there have been times when youth styles with differing role concepts existed side by side. The rockers criticized the 'effeminate' mod style, and the skinheads saw the blurring of gender-specific contours among the hippies as direct provocation.[218] Class-related differences may have played a part here. However, despite the continued presence of macho elements in group styles which had a membership recruited mainly from the working class, a radical thrust against gender differences runs through all the subsequent movements in youth fashion. This is also reflected in popular dancing. Although the rock 'n' roll of the 1950s stood in opposition to received styles of dancing, it still had a number of conventional features: the man

---

[217] M. Fischer-Kowalski, 'Halbstarke 1958, Studenten 1968: Eine Generation und zwei Rebellionen', in U. Preuss et al. (eds). *Kriegskinder–Konsumkinder–Krisenkinder* (Weinheim, 1983), p. 65; *Bericht über die französische Jugend*, p. 96.

[218] Clarke et al. (eds), *Jugendkultur*, pp. 142ff.

asks the woman to dance, he leads in the dance movements, he takes the weight in the somersaults, lifts and pull-throughs.[219] More recent developments have seen increasingly balanced forms, in which there is no active or passive partner. Both can turn their mood into movement in exactly the same way. Indeed, partners are not actually needed at all. Dance is becoming individualized. Fixed roles are thus rendered obsolete.

However, in spite of these equalizing trends, it must be stressed that gender-specific differences are still clearly to be seen in the preferred choices of leisure activities, and therefore in the content of group life. Motorbike groups and football supporters' clubs are overwhelmingly male-dominated.[220] Sport in general seems still to have a strongly gender-specific influence on adolescent group culture, both in terms of active participation and of the social importance for spectators. This is less obviously the case with youth music. But the important thing is that the proportion of female youth involved in peer groups has risen sharply and is now comparable with that for males.[221] This is a clear break with the traditions of the past which placed girls primarily in the mixed-age community of the domestic group. The single-age group, which originated as a male bastion, has now become a social form which is equally accessible for young women.

---

[219] P. Zimmermann, 'Aufwachen mit Rockmusik – Rockgeschichte und Sozialisation', in Preúss et al. (eds), *Kriegskinder–Konsumkinder–Krisenkinder*, pp. 110ff.
[220] *Jugend '81*, p. 494.
[221] Ibid., pp. 494, 531.

5

The Youth Generation?

Among the general trends which can be observed in the historical development of youth groups, that which has brought about the most far-reaching changes has been deregionalization. Territorial groups have lost importance, wider geographical contexts have increasingly become part of the picture. Social relationships are possible which extend far beyond the primary unit of the youth group. This ever-widening social network draws in more and more young people who experience their youth together.

Sociology offers us the world 'generation' as a term for comprehensive social units of young people. A generation is defined as 'the totality of individuals within a larger social block, such as a country, who are linked to one another and clearly distinguished from an older and/or a younger generation by shared values, experiences, attitudes etc.'[1], or as 'the sum of all people of roughly the same age within a cultural circle who share similar attitudes, motives, orientations and values as a result of their common socio-historical situation.'[2] A distinction is made between a generation and a cohort: 'Youth is to be thought of as a cohort when common contemporary historical conditions and experiences lie behind it, as a generation when it gives rise to common activities of historical importance.'[3] Using the word in the sense indicated by these definitions, sociologists have described youth generations of various moulds. Helmut Schelsky's 'sceptical generation' is well

[1] B. Schäfers, *Soziologie des Jugendalters* (Opladen, 1982), p. 13.
[2] H. M. Griese, *Sozialwissenschaftliche Jugendtheorien*, 2nd edn (Weinheim, 1982), p. 73.
[3] K. R. Allerbeck and L. Rosenmayr, *Einführung in die Jugendsoziologie* (Heidelberg, 1976), p. 26. Cf. also L. Rosenmayr, 'Jugend', in R. König (ed.), *Handbuch der empirischen Sozialforschung*, vol. 6 (Stuttgart, 1976), pp. 197ff.

known, and in imitation various other labels have been applied, such as the 'uninhibited generation' or the 'unpredictable generation'.[4]

Generations in the sense of comprehensive units of young people as understood by the above definitions did not exist in old European society because of the prevailing patterns of social interaction. The structure of this society was particularistic, that is, it was comprised of a multitude of regional, local or work-related social units between which there was relatively little communication in comparison with modern times. For the young people who lived in these many sub-units of society, shared formative experiences were minimal. Even more remote was the possibility of developing shared attitudes and values, particularly ones which might distinguish them from an older generation. In the homogeneous world-view of this society there were few alternative forms of ideological orientation, and the communication structure of the time ensured that what little alternative was possible was available only to a minority of young people. In the Middle Ages this group was limited to students and clerics. They had personal contacts beyond the local area, and their knowledge of reading and writing made them also recipients of indirect communication. Perhaps the youngsters who were in the forefront of the movement of the mendicant orders can be seen as one such wider grouping with a new set of values. Much the same could be said of the Reformation which was led primarily by young people. As in the Middle Ages, all the early youth movements of the modern era were limited for the most part to students and other educated young people. This is true of the *Sturm und Drang* movement of the late eighteenth century and the student fraternities of the nineteenth. Looking at complete cohorts, however, all these youth movements affected only a tiny proportion of contemporary young people. The entire rural youth and the majority of urban youth stood in the wings. They were left untouched by the aims of the young academics, and besides, they had quite different problems. It is questionable whether such alternative-thinking minorities can be classed as generations in terms of the sociological definitions of the word.

[4] H. Schelsky, *Die skeptische Generation. Eine Soziologie der deutschen Jugend* (Düsseldorf, 1957); V. von Blücher, *Die Generation der Unbefangenen* (Düsseldorf, 1966); E. Gehmacher, *Jugend in Österreich. Die unberechenbare Generation* (Vienna, 1981).

For the rise of such generations several key requirements were missing in the particularistic world of old European society.

The Free Youth Movement of the early twentieth century stood at a point of transition. This, too, was mainly a movement of school pupils and students. Its alternative values were for the most part directed against the educated middle class from which these young people stemmed. But at the same time there was the parallel phenomenon of a young workers' movement. While this had completely different points of conflict with the adult world from those of middle-class youth, and while there was no organizational link, the fact remains that what could be seen here was a pattern of adolescent behaviour which for the first time crossed the boundaries of class. However, the numbers of young people who sought to distance themselves from the older generation were still quite small.

If we compare the opposing youth styles of the present and the recent past with older historical trends to reject adult society, the degree of change which the twentieth century has brought to the social patterns of youth becomes clear. Such a comparison is perfectly proper. Even youth styles which appear to be restricted to outward features like clothing or hairstyles have a strong political content and are an expression of specific attitudes.[5] These youth styles of the last decades have an increasingly international character. Both in outward forms and in value systems there exists a high degree of uniformity among young people of many European countries. Unlike their historical predecessors, these youth styles are mass phenomena. Wide circles of young people can identify with them, far beyond the leading nuclei.[6]

The basic requirements for the rise of popular youth styles are a general equality among young people and the development of inter-regional mass communications. We have already noted the convergence of different milieu-related historical family forms. This has meant that the potential points of conflict for young people within the family have become more similar. Young people have been drawn more deeply into areas of conflict in wider society. The growth of schooling in recent decades has meant that that part of the adolescent population which traditionally involved itself

---

[5] *Jugend '81* (Opladen, 1982), p. 499.
[6] Ibid., pp. 494ff.

most intensively with social questions has expanded greatly. Schools and colleges present young people with a relatively standardized lifestyle, and consequently with a relatively standardized range of problems. Greater differences exist for youngsters at work. In comparison with the historical gap between urban and rural conditions, however, working life in the modern, predominantly urban and industrial world has lost many of the old distinctions. The most serious differences in the situation of young people today are therefore surely between those in education and those in employment. Many of the distinctions in trends of youth styles break down along precisely these lines.[7]

The communications revolution has facilitated great similarities between youngsters of different areas. We are thinking here both of direct communication through increased personal mobility and indirect communication through the mass media. At an earlier stage the railway and the bicycle were certainly factors in breaking down the traditional rural group identity, firmly based as it was on the local community. However, the deregionalization of the last few decades has opened up completely new dimensions. Youth tourism has become a mass phenomenon. More leisure time and a higher standard of living have revealed totally new possibilities. Young unmarried people have far greater opportunities for travel than adults. In this area of youth travel a whole subculture of tourism has developed. The pilgrim shrines of modern youth culture, such as London, Amsterdam, Copenhagen and Berlin, have all come within easy reach. Increased mobility also allows direct participation in big youth meetings, political demonstrations and peace marches, or cultural events such as open air concerts.

For the growth of international youth styles, indirect communications are even more important than direct. Inter-regional group culture would be unthinkable without the modern mass media. The influence of cinema, wireless and gramophone in the first half of the twentieth century was really quite modest compared to the intensity of media influence on youth since the 1950s. The most obvious new elements have been television, transistor radios, cassette decks and videos. But the printed media have also contributed to the growth of youth culture, especially in the form of magazines designed for teenagers.

[7] Ibid., p. 494.

These two factors, greater equality among young people and the development of mass communications, created the environment in which it became possible for the particularistic world of old European youth to give way to the opposite experience of youth as a generation. And yet in view of the multitude of different youth styles in the present and recent past, it is questionable whether there has ever really been the similarity of attitudes, motives, orientations and value systems which the strict sociological definition of the word 'generation' implies. The various youth styles represent quite different value systems, and it is by no means possible to say that all of these have been in conflict with the values of the adult world. There are public group styles which lean towards political protest, but others represent a retreat into conservatism.[8] Only the former fulfil the terms of the generation concept.

Adolescent group styles engaged in active protest display vividly a phenomenon which may be described as 'juvenocentric'.[9] The principle characteristic of this is a black and white, 'friend or foe' mentality. While identifying with others of the same age-group and defending their norms and behaviour, one rejects both adults in general and particular adults in functional roles, such as police officers, teachers, parents and so on, perceiving their norms, expectations and behaviour as illegitimate and hostile encroachments into adolescent life.[10] The concept of the 'juvenocentricity' was developed by analogy with that of the 'ethnocentricity', which refers to a rigid attachment of the individual to everything which seems to him to be culturally fundamentally proper and in accordance with his own position, combined with an equally unyielding rejection of anything strange. It was ethnocentric behaviour which was at work when the traditional youth groups reacted against other groups from neighbouring localities. In the political youth organizations of the inter-war years this 'friend or foe' mentality expressed itself in aggressively entrenched camps. If in the present day this has been transferred to the relationship between adolescents and adults, it represents an important new dimension in adolescent group identity.

In view of the widening gap between youth and adulthood the

[8] Ibid., pp. 498ff.
[9] Ibid., p. 654.
[10] Ibid., p. 620.

question we must ask is whether these developments are leading to a polarization of the generations. It would be quite wrong to attempt to answer this question by an extrapolation into the future of the historical processes which have led up to the present. More constructive would be to seek the reasons for these developments and to ask whether there are any ways to change them. The growing contrast between the values and behaviour of young people and adults is certainly connected with the speed of social change. It is much harder for adults to change their views to meet fresh circumstances than it is for adolescents. This is a logical consequence of the traditional concept of adulthood which defines an adult as a person whose personality has already fully developed. The adult is the finished product. His views and attitudes are not supposed to be subject to significant further change. In the light of the accelerated pace of social change, the unavoidable question is whether this static view of adult roles can still be maintained. It could be replaced with a new concept, that of the lifelong learner who is prepared to accept changes encountered in his environment and work them into his personal development. Learning in the traditional sense is a facet of youth. Such a redefinition of adulthood would blur the boundary between the two phases of life, but it would go a long way towards bridging the 'generation gap'.

Subject Index

adolescence, 6
  crises, 10–11
  cross-cultural comparisons, 11–12
  definition, 17
  historical non-existence, 13–14,
    15–16
  modern perceptions, 30–1
adulthood
  admission to public life, 51
  and identity, 27
  as static state, 31, 240
  concept, 1
  evidencing personal maturity, 43–4
  rejection, 228, 237, 239
  roles, in defining adolescence, 18
  social interaction, 89
  transition from childhood, 13
age of consent, 59, 61
agrarian societies
  age at marriage, 80–1
  carrying arms, 56, 57, 57n
  children remaining at home, 91
  farms passed to sons, 19, 91
  gender-specific farm tasks, 68–9
  inheritance, 112
  need for physical strength, 4, 50
Anabaptists, 25, 26, 52, 53
ancestor cults
  and initiation rites, 64
  emphasis on fertility, 49
Anglo-Saxons, age for bearing arms,
  55
apprentices and apprenticeships, 91,
  124, 183
  and admission to youth groups, 66

after Confirmation, 54
  duration, 69
  for girls, 71–2
  living with parents, 93, 93n
  working relations, 132
arms
  associated ceremonies, 57
  carrying, in agrarian societies, 56,
    57, 57n
  eligibility to bear, 45, 46, 87:
    age, 55; connected to civil
    rights, 62; dependent on
    physical strength, 50;
    importance as rite, 55
  training in use, 56
  warrior class, 56
  see also military service
authority, 15
  and going out alone, 44
  and youth centres, 225
  and youth clubs, 212
  European marriage pattern, 21
  in agricultural family economies,
    111
  or *magister*, 135
  of parents and teachers, 142
  of workplace, 116–17
autobiographies, evidencing
  self-reflectiveness, 27

baptism, 52–3
  adult, 25–6, 49, 52
  analogous Hungarian rite, 64
bar-mitzvah, 47–8
bat-mitzvah, 47

Name Index